FIGHT, DIG AND LIVE

*This book is dedicated
to all those Sappers
who gave their lives
in the Korean War*

FIGHT, DIG AND LIVE

The Story of the Royal Engineers in the Korean War

by

George Cooper

Pen & Sword
MILITARY

Copyright © George Cooper 2011

ISBN 978-1-84884-684-5

A CIP catalogue record for this book is available from the British Library

Typeset in 10.5/12.5pt Palatino by Concept, Huddersfield, West Yorkshire

Printed and bound in England by CPI

Pen & Sword Books Ltd incorporates the Imprints of Pen & Sword Aviation, Pen & Sword Family History, Pen & Sword Maritime, Pen & Sword Military, Pen & Sword Discovery, Wharncliffe Local History, Wharncliffe True Crime, Wharncliffe Transport, Pen & Sword Select, Pen & Sword Military Classics, Leo Cooper, The Praetorian Press, Remember When, Seaforth Publishing and Frontline Publishing

For a complete list of Pen & Sword titles please contact
PEN & SWORD BOOKS LIMITED
47 Church Street, Barnsley, South Yorkshire, S70 2AS, England
E-mail: enquiries@pen-and-sword.co.uk
Website: www.pen-and-sword.co.uk

Contents

Maps

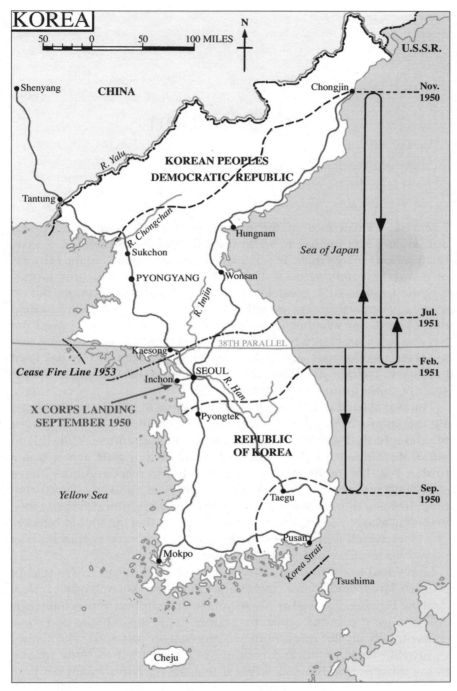

Map 1. Korea, 1950

vii

Introduction

I played a small part in the Korean War as a Troop Commander but when I was invited to write the 'Story of the Sappers in Korea', I had serious misgivings. To write the Story, as opposed to the History, of a war that took place well over fifty years ago and now largely forgotten, relies to a great extent on personal reminiscences but so many of the participants are either dead or beyond the ability to help that I wondered whether I would have sufficient material. I need not have worried and have been delighted that so many people have sent me their recollections despite my initial misgivings. It has not been possible to include all of them, but they have helped to bring to life the story of those tumultuous days.

The War started in 1950 and though the actual fighting ended with the signing of an Armistice after three years of conflict, there was always the thought that war might break out again at any time. With this in mind, the United Nations forces remained on full alert and it was a further year before they felt they could begin to relax and thus I have continued my story to include the activities of the Corps until that time. It was a thoroughly unpleasant war, perhaps more so than most, involving a large number of troops, under the aegis of the United Nations. The story which follows gives an insight into the very significant part played by the Corps of Royal Engineers.

I have had to confine my story to our own Corps but it was part of a much larger endeavour, involving Canadian, Australian and New Zealand Engineers as well as American. Their contribution was immense.

There are numerous books that cover the historical side so I have concentrated on the more human aspects with just sufficient history to provide background and continuity. I have tried to write mainly in the third person but was advised that the narrative might be more readable if I used the first person when quoting personal involvement. This is only too apparent when relating incidents concerning the Hook where I was personally involved for some weeks. 'Self glorification' is not intended!

Sadly many of those who fought in Korea have since died and there are inevitably gaps in the narrative. All of those who are left are 'elderly', if not 'old', but I hope I have done justice to what was a great endeavour, one of which the Corps of Royal Engineers can be justly proud.

George Cooper
2011

Acknowledgements

I have quoted liberally from Brigadier Barclay's *First Commonwealth Division* and the *History of the Royal Engineers*, and other publications in the Royal Engineers Library at Chatham, all of which have provided much background information. Major General Tony Younger's *Blowing Our Bridges* and Colonel Dan Raschen's *Send Port and Pyjamas* give an insight into what life was like in Korea in those days. Though the latter is a light-hearted autobiography, the undertones are serious and he was in Korea as a Regimental officer for half the period of fighting. I have quoted (and hopefully not misquoted too often) from numerous accounts to produce what I hope is a coherent story and am most grateful to everyone who has helped.

Among the many people who supplied personal reminiscences are, in no particular order or rank: Peter Chitty, Larry Lamble, Ian Bruce, Bill Moncur, Peter Leslie, John Page, Alan O'Hagan, Spencer Hannay, Oliver Keef, Ross Mason, Ian Thomson, John Wilks, Stanley Ireland, Jeffery Lewins, John Elderkin, John Cormack, Ted Sharp, Tony Kendall, Alex Freer, Ronald Overd, David Brotherton, Mike Bruges, Sam Sowton, Terry Hawton and Reuben Holroyd.

I have also consulted a number of books, details of which are included in the Bibliography.

My grateful thanks also go to the Staff of the Institution of Royal Engineers, especially Lieutenant Colonel David Hamilton and Mrs Jacqui Thorndick whose help was invaluable. Finally, I would like to thank Gerald Napier for all his suggestions and comments – without his encouragement this story might never have seen the light of day.

Foreword

By General Sir Peter Wall KCB CBE
Chief Royal Engineer

This is the 'Story' – and what a story it is – of the part played by Sappers in the Korean War. It is a war that is largely forgotten by the general public, yet it was the first war to be fought under the auspices of the United Nations, it lasted three years and the human cost was immense. Over a hundred thousand soldiers of the UN forces, including those of the Republic of Korea, were killed and three hundred thousand wounded. Civilians suffered heavily as well, with thousands killed and hundreds of thousands made homeless. The Chinese, a brave and resourceful enemy, suffered grievously too.

The Korean campaign was unique in the quantity and variety of engineer work, firstly because of the extremes of climate and secondly because of the undeveloped nature of the country. Rivers would freeze to a depth of a foot or more in the winter, yet become raging torrents in summer. The River Imjin, a thousand feet wide, would rise from a fordable three feet to over forty feet in little more than a day. At the height of the floods even the most substantially built steel bridges were liable to be carried away and sometimes large areas would be isolated by the floods.

Initially there were few roads in Korea, and those few that did exist were mostly tracks, and very often mountain tracks at that. Ground that could be bulldozed for roads during the spring and summer would freeze to a depth of three feet and to a consistency of rock during the winter months; every inch of the way had to be blasted before even the heaviest bulldozer could work.

Sappers laying mines on a winter night in front of our forward positions would be unable to perform the intricate task of arming with detonators for more than a few minutes at a time because fingers would freeze and be liable to frostbite.

During the early summer, unbelievably heavy and choking clouds of dust had to be reduced on roads near the front line, mainly by spraying with water, and roads in forward areas often had to be camouflaged if in view of the Chinese. Water also had to be supplied to the troops from waterpoints throughout the year, whether rivers were a mass of ice or raging torrents.

In the famous Imjin battle in 1951, Sappers took part in the defence of the Brigade area and fought gallantly as infantry during a critical stage of the battle. Other Sappers were called to act as infantry in subsequent operations, either on patrols or holding portions of battalion positions. This included 12 Field Squadron, who were called upon to occupy defensive positions for over a week when the Chinese recaptured Hill 317 in the autumn of 1951. Sappers joined the infantry in close-quarter fighting during the Hook battles in the later stages of the war.

In short, the Sappers of the Commonwealth Division did a fine job under difficult conditions, which often called for unusual methods and improvisation because of the extremes of climate and terrain. There is no doubt that their achievements materially affected the course of the war to a considerable extent and made possible many operations which otherwise could never have been undertaken. Their gallantry was recognized by numerous awards, including a CBE, an OBE and eight MBEs, two DSOs, thirteen MCs, eight MMs and perhaps the most prestigous of all, a Distinguished Conduct Medal (to Sergeant Orton), often called the Live Man's Victoria Cross. There were grievous casualties amongst the Sappers too, including forty-two killed and several hundred wounded.

In writing this book, George Cooper (later General Sir George Cooper GCB MC DL) who was himself decorated in Korea as a Troop Commander, has filled a great gap in the annals of the Corps. With many personal anecdotes from those who took part, he has brought to life the various aspects of the immense contribution made by the Sappers in this unique and extremely exacting campaign. We are greatly indebted to him for compiling such a polished and entertaining account.

Peter Wall
2011

Prologue

The Background to Conflict

Korea had been a country keeping little contact with the outside world, and placing considerable emphasis on self reliance. From 1259 the country was ruled by the Mongols, after that the Chosen Dynasty, which lasted until 1910. At the end of the nineteenth century there was conflict with China and Japan and, in 1904, the Japanese moved a strong army into Korea, annexing the country as a colony in 1910 to be run for Japan's benefit. So little was generally known about the country, though, that it was often referred to as 'The Hermit Kingdom'.

In the 1939–45 War the USSR was not initially at war with Japan, but the United States was concerned at the high casualties that they had incurred in the Pacific and expected major casualties in any landing on Japan, so at the Potsdam Conference in July 1945, the USA encouraged the USSR to enter the war. Among the agreements made was one that Korea would be independent.

The timetable of the USSR's participation was very short. On 9 August 1945 they invaded Manchuria, then occupied by Japan, and advanced into Korea. The atomic bombs were dropped on Hiroshima on 6 August, and then on Nagasaki on 9 August. The peace terms with Japan were set out on 11 August and VJ Day was 14 August, so the USSR's war against Japan lasted six days! Although the USA had not intended to occupy Korea, on 10 August the Americans decided to do so, and agreed in haste with the USSR that Korea would be divided on the 38th Parallel. It was not until 8 September that the first US troops landed, but the Russians, who had been there a month already, honoured their agreement and had stopped at the agreed dividing line. The arrival of the US forces was almost Gilbertian. When the convoy was twenty miles away from the port of Inchon they were met by a small boat, whose occupants, immaculately dressed, presented themselves to the US general as the representatives of the Korean Government. The US advance party of fourteen moved on to Seoul from Inchon and was surprised to find a city of horse-drawn carts with the occasional charcoal-powered motor vehicle. They saw three Europeans in a shop, and hastened to greet them, only to find that they were part of a small Turkish community, who spoke no English. They met White Russians, refugees in Korea since 1920, who spoke to them in German. It was a time warp for the Americans.

What became a major difficulty was that no Korean they met appeared to speak English, and there was only one Korean speaker on the staff whose ability was insufficient to conduct negotiations. The stabilizing influence that they had to rely on was Japan: Japanese colonial officials were confirmed in their posts, Japanese soldiers and police were responsible for law and order. Japanese was the principal language of communication. The Americans misunderstood the hatred between the Koreans and their former masters but eventually General MacArthur ordered the removal of all Japanese and in the next four months 70,000 Japanese colonial civil servants and 600,000 soldiers were sent back to Japan. This is an interesting figure as to the numbers required to run the country and control the population. When the Japanese left, the vacuum was filled, as agents of the American Military Government, by many who had been longstanding collaborators and who were equally hated by their fellow countrymen. The police force had been 20,000 strong, of which 12,000 were Japanese; when they went, others were promoted, the police expanded, and it was from this force, armed by the USA, that the South Korean Army was formed. Meanwhile there was jockeying for position between the embryo political parties, among which were some strong communist cells, and there were also politicians who had been in exile for as much as twenty years who did not have much of a following. Then there was the arrival from Chungking of the self proclaimed Korean Provisional Government, but the man whom the Americans favoured was Dr Syngman Rhee, then aged seventy, who had been imprisoned in Korea between 1899 and 1904 for political activities. He had then gone to the USA where he had remained for the next thirty-five years and had pushed the Korean cause, but by being absent had not fallen out with other aspiring politicians.

The Americans installed a military governor in October 1945, with an eleven-man Korean Advisory Council. The military government continued until elections were held in 1948. Out of a population of 20 million in South Korea, 95 per cent of the 7.8 million registered voters went to the polls. On 14 August 1948, the third anniversary of VJ Day, the US flag was lowered over the Capitol in Seoul and the flag of the Korean Republic raised. It had taken three years to form a government, its leader Syngman Rhee.

By June 1949, all US troops had been withdrawn, except for a 500-man Military Assistance Group, and the USSR had withdrawn all their forces from North Korea. The United Nations Commission was still charged with preparing for the unification of the country, but its work was increasingly involved in monitoring.

The US policy in Korea was clumsy and ill-conceived. They did not understand the country, and saw it, as they did with China and Vietnam, as a brick in the wall to contain the spread of Communism. Furthermore, the imposition of US political institutions and bureaucracy did not fit in with the Korean people's way of life. The Americans began to back off, denying South Korea arms while the Russians supplied the North with a large arsenal of tanks, artillery and military aircraft. In the early summer of 1950 there were indicators that there would be an invasion from North Korea, and there was continuous guerrilla warfare, as there was in Malaya. Communist threats appeared on the occupation boundaries of Europe, in Trieste, among the oilfields of the Middle East, in Greece, and in Yugoslavia. Korea was well down the list and in any case a long way away, but there was a conflict waiting to happen.

At dawn on 25 June 1950, North Korean armed forces crossed the 38th Parallel and began advancing into South Korea, thus starting the Korean War. Britain was among the forty-three countries sending forces as part of the United Nations response to the invasion. Formed units went to Korea direct via the port of Pusan but most people went via Japan and their first glimpse of the country came from the deck of a troopship as it steamed into the Japanese Inland Sea, entering the fifteen-mile sound between Kyushu and Shikoku, passing a fleet of little fishing boats, some of them fishing with cormorants, a scene straight out of a Japanese print. Threading its way between innumerable small islands, passengers had their first glimpse of pink cherry blossom and the bright fresh green of rice paddies as their ship slipped in to the harbour of Kure in Japan, which is separated from Korea by the Korean Straits, only 120 miles wide, thus providing a ready base for operations.

The Japanese Base
After the surrender of Japan in 1945 Kure had been allotted to the British and when the Korea War started it had been the natural place to become the British Commonwealth base. It had been an important port during the Second World War with large shipyards which had been bombed heavily by the Allies, but the Japanese were already restoring the rusty cranes and the yards were now busy building large tankers. The town was overshadowed by the shipyards which provided employment for hundreds of workers, hammering, riveting and welding as the new ships took shape, rising like a phoenix from the ashes of wartime

3

devastation. The people looked reasonably prosperous, and there were numerous small workshops with men beavering away on lathes and other machinery, but it was the small children that drew one's attention, all colourfully dressed and smiling.

Kure was the home of a Royal Australian Engineers unit, part of the post-war Occupation Forces, and soon after the outbreak of the Korean War it became the BRITCOM Engineer Regiment. The CO became CRE British Commonwealth Forces, Kure (BCFK), more commonly known as 'BUKFUK'. The Regiment, which acquired a small British establishment, was responsible for all engineer stores and works outside the divisional area. It also had works detachments across the sea dividing Japan from Korea, in Seoul and Pusan, and it provided stores, machinery and workshop facilities to the divisional engineers once they were in theatre. Most sapper drafts and individuals, both to and from Korea, passed through the Joint Reinforcement Base Depot at Kure (JRBD) and were helped by the BRITCOM Engineer Regiment who also handled postings, reinforcements, wounded and, occasionally, individuals on leave. Its hospitality was renowned.

The administrative backing for British forces in Korea was considerable and, in the early stages, most of the requirements were met from American sources. It was easy to take for granted the routine process of delivering daily large quantities of supplies, such as food and mail, and arranging for fluctuating requirements in petrol and ammunition, as well as the movement of reinforcements, not to mention arrangements for R&R, the repair of equipment and provision of spare parts, but it required a complex administrative system, all of which relied on the Japanese Base. The evacuation of the sick and wounded from Korea and their efficient treatment was particularly important and the Commonwealth Division was well served by its Field Ambulances, the best known being 60th (Para) Indian Field Ambulance which served throughout the war. Tall, bearded Sikhs with their maroon headgear were a familiar sight driving through the divisional area, and were much photographed by visiting Americans. Seriously wounded were usually taken direct to the Norwegian MASH by helicopter and were subsequently flown to the British Military Hospital in Kure, which had a high reputation and could not be faulted

While convalescent, patients welcomed a change of scenery at a Rest Camp which was established nearby on the island of Miyajima. The island first became known during the Second World War when Kamikaze pilots spent their last few days there before taking off on their solitary suicide missions. Commonwealth soldiers arrived on the ferry from the mainland at the colourful harbour to find that they had been transported back a hundred years in time. This peaceful island and its tranquil atmosphere provided a total contrast from Korea and

4

the war. Exploration revealed a charming village of little shops, temples and parks, around which friendly sacred deer roamed. Along a path lined with stone lanterns and carved lions – the lions were always in pairs, one smiling and the other growling – was a shrine where visitors who wished to pray first clapped their hands loudly to attract the attention of the gods before going about their devotions. Behind the village was a steep hill with the inevitable temple at its crest, but careful reconnaissance to the foot of the hill revealed some two thousand steps from the formal entrance to the summit. Recuperating patients usually found that discretion was the better part of valour and settled for a boat trip round the island instead.

There was a small Bomb Disposal Section forming part of the Regiment and, amongst other things, they dealt with a number of unexploded bombs, including three 'influence' activated sea mines. There was also a Works Section, a BRITCOM Movement Control Group and a Transportation Squadron, dealing with docks and water transport.

One of the most important contributions the Royal Engineers could make was through the Base Post Office in Japan and the Commonwealth Division Postal Unit in Korea. They provided a most welcome and efficient service. Letters, parcels, magazines and newspapers arrived regularly, even during the big withdrawal from North Korea in the winter of 1950. It was always important to keep everyone abreast of what was going on, not just in the Korean theatre of war, but also in the world outside. Sunday papers, on a scale of one per five men per week, were flown out from the UK, together with a number of magazines and books on a generous scale, which came by sea, but this was not really sufficient and later on 29 Brigade produced their own paper on a weekly basis. This was the *Circle News*, the title being based on the Brigade 'flash' and affectionately referred to as the 'Frozen A***hole'. On the formation of the Commonwealth Division in July 1951, this was absorbed into a Divisional daily newspaper and on 8 October the first edition of *Crown News* was launched. It contained a crossword and various competitions, but perhaps more importantly it reported the football results. In that first edition, it recorded Manchester United 2, Derby County 1, and Charlton 2, Liverpool 0. Arsenal lost to Preston North End (who?) 0–2.

Crown News gradually expanded to include news from Australia, Canada and New Zealand and provided an ideal means of sending special messages to all ranks on occasions such the Coronation and the Queen's Birthday. It also contained Special Orders of the Day and even published the menu for Christmas lunch.

Other papers published in the Theatre included *The Korean Base Gazette* and *Japan News*, a Forces Edition of which was produced by the Japanese in Tokyo and issued free to the Forces. During the Armistice,

5

HQRE produced *The Kansas Tract, Journal of the Royal Imjineers*, complete with photographs, crossword and comic strip.

Kure thus provided the setting for the war and was the base for all Sapper operations across the Straits. This is their story.

Chapter 1

Early Days

War Breaks Out

The Communist attack started at 4.00am, local time, on 25 June 1950. It was Saturday afternoon in Washington, and achieved complete surprise. North Korea was able to deploy 135,000 men, in ten divisions and an armoured brigade of Russian-made T-34 tanks, with ample supporting artillery and 200 fighter and bomber aircraft. They were well provided with Russian equipment and had trained under Russian supervision since 1945. The South Korean Army, on the other hand, had only been formed in 1948 and was a little over 50,000 strong with one third deployed along the frontier with North Korea. They were under pre-pared, under-trained, had only six days' stock of ammunition and few spare parts. Their staffwork was elementary and they were in effect little more than an internal security force.

It soon became clear that this was no mere border raid. In the Republic of Korea (ROK) Army, many men were away on weekend leave, and in Washington on a Saturday night they too had shut up shop for the weekend. Early on Sunday morning the US State Department met with the Korean ambassador, who asked for military aid. The US saw the attack as a major threat, and that it should be referred to the United Nations. The Security Council met on the Sunday afternoon. On 13 January 1950 the Soviet delegate had walked out of the Security Council, in protest that the Chinese seat should not go to the Communist Chinese, and he was still absent so there was no veto. At 6.00pm that same evening, a UN resolution was passed by 9–0 condemning the North Korean attack and calling for their forces to withdraw behind the 38th Parallel. From subsequent UN resolutions concerning conflict it is interesting to note that the resolution was not for a peacekeeping force, but came down on the side of one of the combatants.

The immediate orders from Washington were to evacuate all American civilians from Korea, to send equipment and ammunition to the ROK

Army and to deploy the US 7th Fleet to segregate the Korea Peninsula. On Tuesday 27 June a further resolution was passed by the Security Council, this time 7–1, calling on member nations to assist the Republic of Korea to repel the armed attack and to restore peace and security. It is of note that there were only fifty-eight members of the UN at that time and thirty of them immediately contributed forces in some form or other.

In London at the Tuesday Cabinet meeting the topics for discussion included: the French and German coal industries, white fish, grants for marginal hill land, and lastly support for the UN in Korea. The Cabinet decision was to order the Far East Fleet to join the Americans in Korean waters. Where could the Army find units? The immediate response was to increase the period of National Service to two years, and to recall reservists. The Royal Marines raised 41 Independent Commando, which was flown by BOAC to Japan, and after three weeks training they were committed to operations on the east coast of Korea. On 20 August, 27 Infantry Brigade sailed from Hong Kong with two under-strength battalions: the Middlesex Regiment and the Argyll and Sutherland Highlanders. They were joined at the end of September by the 3rd Royal Australian Regiment, and so came into being 27 Commonwealth Brigade. Would they be in time to influence events?

The only army formations close at hand were four under-strength American divisions in Japan: the 1st Cavalry Division and the 7th, 24th and 25th Divisions. They were employed on occupational duties, were not trained for active operations and were certainly not ready for a campaign on foot, over rugged hills and in an inhospitable climate. They also had serious equipment shortages. On 2 July the first American ground troops arrived in Korea, only eight days after the invasion by North Korea.

In the meantime, the North Korean forces quickly swept south and, by the evening of 27 June, tanks were nosing into the northern suburbs of Seoul, the capital of South Korea, which was captured on 29 June. Thousands of citizens fled south, towards the Han river, a kilometre-wide, crossed by four bridges which were blown by ROK army engineers in the early hours of that last day while the iron spans were still crowded with refugees. Hundreds perished.

Advanced elements of 24th US Division participated in the fighting near Suwon, which was captured on 5 July, but by the third week in July the 1st Cavalry Division and the 25th American Division had landed in South Korea. Totally unprepared, the UN forces were put under great pressure and by August had been forced back into a perimeter, based on the Naktong River, about fifty miles from the port of Pusan. Things became very desperate and there was a good chance that the UN forces would be thrown into the sea.

8

British Forces Arrive

British naval forces had been in Korean waters since the first week in July, but the nearest British troops were based in Hong Kong, nearly 1,500 miles away, and Headquarters 27 Infantry Brigade and its two infantry battalions were unable to reach Pusan until 28 August. They were in action a week later, with the Argyll and Sutherland Highlanders on the left and the Middlesex on the right. There were no British supporting arms at this time and the Brigade had to rely on the Americans for artillery and armoured support, as well as engineer. For the next fortnight they carried out numerous patrols and maintained contact with North Korean forces. By the end of the first week in September the invaders had shot their bolt and United Nations forces were able to undertake operations which, by the end of the month, were to bring about a dramatic change in the Korean scene.

On 16 September American troops counter-attacked in strength, forcing the North Korean army back. The British Brigade crossed the Naktong and, after heavy fighting with severe casualties, advanced north. This was the prelude to one of the most dramatic moments of the war.

General MacArthur, seventy years old and effective emperor of Japan as well as Supreme Commander, had decided in July that there should be an amphibious landing at Inchon. This landing was fraught with difficulty due to the tidal conditions, the limited harbour facilities and the likely difficulties of maintaining the troops ashore. The landing went ahead on 15 September and a force of 70,000 men was soon ashore. It took until 25 September to advance the eighteen miles to Seoul, as there were 20,000 men defending the city who put up a strong resistance. A formal ceremony was held on 29 September to welcome back the ROK Government and MacArthur flew home from the ceremony convinced that the Korean War had been won. It was to continue for another two years and ten months.

The UN advanced almost to the border with China, before the Chinese entered the conflict, passing off their Army as volunteers. On the night of 25 November, bugle-blowing Chinese troops swept down from the mountains upon Americans celebrating what had seemed an easy victory.

The Land of Morning Calm

Korea is often referred to as the 'Land of Morning Calm', not that many of those who served there would agree. The United Nations' forces soon realized that the country was stuck in a time warp, an undeveloped country of extremes which had to be experienced to be believed. To Sappers it provided an exceptional, perhaps unique, varied and interesting challenge, but the country could hardly have been called a Sappers' paradise. In paradise one would not need to eat salt pills in summer to avoid heat exhaustion. On roads through paradise one should not have been travelling through thick clouds of finely powdered dust on one summer's day and churning through deep mud on the next. In late summer one should not have expected such torrential rain, with flood waters on the main rivers breaking up one's bridges; nor in winter almost unbearable cold, unless adequately clothed; followed in spring by a thaw with broken ice up to ten inches thick coming downstream liable to pierce and sink the pontoons of floating bridges.

The Korean countryside follows a similar pattern of extremes. In winter it is a monotonous and barren looking brown, except when covered by snow. In spring, though, it can suddenly become incredibly beautiful with colourful outcrops of tiny purple iris and other wild flowers and, in the higher valleys, occasional wild fruit trees bearing blossoms of delicate pastel shades, intermingled with bright yellow forsythia. Beyond the coastal plains in the vicinity of the 38th Parallel there were steep rugged hills covered with scrub, azaleas and occasional pines, and with marshy paddy fields on the lower ground.

Those who have never campaigned in really cold weather, such as confronted everyone during the first winter, can hardly comprehend the difficulties, especially when the arrangements have been hastily made and there is a lack of proper winter clothing and equipment designed for a cold climate. Apart from the discomforts and hardships, the most irksome and difficult measures were necessary for the preparation of food and to maintain equipment in serviceable condition. The first winter was exceptionally cold and the British forces were not adequately equipped to meet the arctic conditions. String vests, 'long-johns' and wind-cheaters were the only extra items to normal clothing and much hard bargaining went on with American troops for some of their kit. The only item that was better than the American was the UK double thick sleeping bag which was so good that it could be put down straight onto ice or snow. Fortunately, all this was to change for the second winter, but that was still a long way off.

The dress of the Korean peasant showed a remarkable uniformity throughout the land: the men wore white jackets and baggy white trousers, heavily padded as a protection against the biting cold, while the women wore voluminous skirts fastened under the armpit, with a padded jacket. Sleeves were long enough to make gloves unnecessary and they had fur hats which could be pulled down over the ears when it was really cold. Older men's headgear was most unusual and consisted of a small round top-hat-shaped creation made of horsehair, which was perched on top of the head, while women wore conical hats made of bamboo in summer.

The Korean people themselves were cheerful, tough and resilient, living in simple thatched houses, in pretty primitive conditions but were quick to help us whenever possible. The countryside was sparsely populated and the few roads were designed for bullock carts but those that did exist were incapable of handling heavy military traffic and being flanked with paddy it was difficult to deploy off the roads, except in the dry season or when the ground was frozen solid. Rainfall could be extremely heavy, up to twenty inches in a week, and rivers such as the Imjin could rise thirty to forty feet in as many hours, becoming a raging torrent 1,000 feet wide flowing at over eight knots, causing tremendous hazards for bridges and ferries, particularly when compounded by floating debris. The winter was extremely severe, with temperatures falling as low as minus 30° C. Weapons had to be kept dry for lack of suitable oil, and the firing pins of automatic weapons broke after a few rounds, due to the intense cold, necessitating a rapid air-lift from UK with special cold-weather pins. Digging in frozen ground was usually impracticable and necessitated the use of explosives before earthmoving plant could be effective, vehicles had to be parked on straw and hot water poured into radiators froze almost immediately as there was a shortage of anti-freeze. At night all vehicles and tanks had to be started up and moved every hour. There was a danger of frostbite and the cold placed a great strain on troops working in the open, particularly on minelaying and mine clearance tasks where manual dexterity was so essential. Gloves were available but could not be worn if one needed one's fingers to insert or extract safety pins, or do other fiddly work. It was standard practice for every sapper to have a handful of pins in his pocket for this work. Some people were lucky enough to have mittens with fingers which could be folded back when necessary. Frostbite took many sappers back to the Military Hospital in Kure, which had already become the British Base in Japan. The cold, followed by the spring thaw, caused disintegration of roads which had to be seen to be believed.

The so-called Land of Morning Calm didn't really live up to its name.

Chapter 2

55 Field Squadron goes to Korea

At the end of July 1950, 55 Field Squadron was stationed at Perham Down, on Salisbury Plain, when it was ordered to go to Korea with 29 Infantry Brigade. Tony Younger was appointed OC and started the complex task of reorganizing the squadron. The whole establishment had to be changed from that of a 'normal' squadron in a regiment to that of an 'independent' squadron with a larger headquarters, more transport, two officers in each Troop and a Park Troop to hold engineer equipment. Many of the NCOs and men, and all the Troop officers, had to leave, as they were coming to the end of their National Service and were not eligible for what might be a long overseas tour, but luckily some of the senior NCOs stayed on, including Squadron Sergeant Major Brown, who turned out to be a tower of strength.

In common with most of the units that formed 29 Brigade, 55 Squadron was grossly under strength, in what was still a post-war rundown period, and held about 150 men all told. It had to be made up to a little over 350, but a decree had been issued from Whitehall recalling Class A reservists to the colours for the duration of the Korean crisis, so men of experience were anticipated. When a large 3-ton truck arrived and the tail-board was dropped, out jumped a policeman with a tidy row of medals and a letter from his station commander requesting his immediate return when the undoubted error of his recall could be sorted out. A second man alighted who explained that his wife had just given birth to twins and had nowhere to live, and in any case he was a refrigeration mechanic which he felt was a skill that would not be needed in Korea. The third, and last, man had only one leg.

Luckily things soon started to improve and the screening process for reservists developed into a smooth routine and out of about some 450, 150 were retained. Nearly all were married, with young children, and were facing rent or mortgage problems attuned to their civilian pay scale, which was often up to three times what the Army would give them. Nevertheless, when things became really tough in Korea they proved their worth in no uncertain manner. Many were hard-drinking and were quick to womanize when they had the chance, but the more awful the conditions, the more unshakeably reliable they became. The final 100 required to complete the squadron came as volunteers from other units.

The position regarding officers was rather better. The first to come was Desmond Holmes, a Canadian who had seen service in North Africa, Italy and North West Europe, who went to command 1 Troop; the next Captain to arrive was Bertie Bayton-Evans who had won an MC in Europe and was a strong personality with a streak of genuine originality and a good grasp of wartime engineering problems. He was posted as 3 Troop Commander, while 2 Troop Commander was John Page (later Major General J. H. Page CB OBE MC) who was to prove to be admirably relaxed when under fire and was the sort of leader who completes his task, however difficult or dangerous, without comment or complaint. Keith Bean was the last Captain to arrive, taking over as Second-in-Command. All four had a nice sense of humour and were experienced and professional. They made a good team.

New subalterns also arrived: Keith Eastgate, who had the build and stamina of the heavyweight boxing enthusiast that he was, and who had to be called Big Keith to avoid confusion with Little Keith Bean; Danny Cadoux-Hudson, Larry Lamble, Peter Chitty and Brian Swinbanks. The latter was the most experienced and was put in command of the new Park Troop. Lastly, a very young Second Lieutenant Robinson was posted in as a Battle Casualty Replacement (BCR), scheduled to wait in Japan with a dozen men until such time as they would be needed. Sadly, they would all be needed.

The six weeks allotted for preparations passed all too quickly and was mostly taken up with administration, but a full training programme was devised for the voyage ahead in order to keep physically fit and improve technical skills wherever possible.

The squadron set sail, together with 1st Battalion, the Gloucestershire Regiment, in mid-September 1950 on board the *Empire Windrush* for the six-week voyage to Korea. They kept themselves fit and, with plenty of ammunition on board, one of the most popular training sessions was that of rifle shooting over the stern of the ship and gradually the standard of shooting improved, something that would bear fruit at their destination. At Port Said a ten-mile route march and a swim was followed by a rather unfortunate incident. A couple of Sappers went on shore and tried to buy a souvenir from one of the stalls. The Sapper who was buying was short-changed, so he tipped up the table whereupon the stall owner became furious and started shouting. A crowd quickly gathered and some police arrived and started to lay into the Sappers with their lathis, hitting the Sappers quite badly. Luckily a group of Glosters came along and sorted it out and got the Sappers back to the ship. One of them, Sapper Breen (though not the one who tipped over the table), had a rather unpleasant split spleen and had to go into the ship's sick bay where he was operated on.

After leaving Port Said and going down the Red Sea, the ship's Captain gave orders that no more shooting would take place over the stern of the ship as one of the men had shot a dolphin. This was considered to be most unlucky and would mean that there would be a death on board. Nothing would make him change his mind, and by the time they were off Aden the Sapper who had been hurt in Port Said had died ...

A short run-around at Colombo and Singapore had to suffice until, on 10 November, the engines were cut and the troopship inched slowly into the run-down harbour of Pusan at the southern tip of the Korean peninsular, where they were greeted by a US Army Band playing 'When the Saints Come Marching In'. They had arrived in the Land of Morning Calm, at a squadron strength of ten officers, a warrant officer, ten sergeants and 273 other ranks.

Transportation
Whilst Kure, in Japan, was the base for British Forces, Pusan was the main port of entry into Korea. It was the Headquarters of the US Army's No. 7 Transportation Military Port and hosted a small Royal Engineers Transportation unit. Approximately once a month a troopship arrived from the United Kingdom, its gleaming white paintwork standing out against the uniform grey American shipping. The unit's main job though was to discharge maintenance vessels on a bread-and-butter, twenty-four run from Kure, mainly by two smallish vessels called the *E Sang* and the *Wo Sang* which had been employed on work in the China Seas and had their bridge and accommodation protected by anti-piracy grills. These ships had been converted to carry nearly 400 troops and had two holds for cargo. Other vessels included some Landing Craft Tanks (LCTs) operated by civilian crews and which often carried ammunition as well as their normal complement of vehicles. This was the first military port to work with pallets, but there were never enough and the Quay Foreman, WO2 Jones, used to get hold of the civilian fork-lift driver when it was dark and say to him 'Forkee: fetchee pallets'. By next morning there would be a working stock of (American – surely not?) pallets.

The unloading of ships was checked meticulously by a Sapper Sergeant, backed up by an equally efficient NAAFI Sergeant (personnel held military rank on Active Service as part of the Expeditionary Forces Institute (EFI) of NAAFI). The most valuable single item was not whisky, as one might expect, but razor blades, each case worth thousands of dollars. On their return journeys they carried thousands of empty 25-pounder shell cases for their scrap value.

Captain Ross Mason, already due to attend the Long Transportation Course back in UK, spent some time with the unit while waiting a boat home and became the main Embarkation Staff Officer responsible not only for the embarkation of troops leaving Korea but also for troops moving up to the Division by train. There were inevitably security problems, but the biggest concerned the transport of Asahi beer which came over from Japan in crates in consignments of about 10,000 twice a week. The sight of a stack of beer waiting overnight to be loaded onto a train next day was just too much for some and the pilferage rate was high. With the connivance of the NAAFI sergeant, the solution was to get the Transit Camp to send down a homeward bound soldier to guard the stack overnight with his loaded rifle. The sentry was invited to count the stack and was told it would be counted again the next morning. If the numbers tallied he would be given a crate of beer and assurance of a berth on the next boat home. The pilfering rate dropped dramatically.

To and Fro

Winter 1950–1951

55 Squadron's transport arrived on a separate ship and when the two had married together they drove north some 300 miles to Suwon, just south of Seoul, the capital city, where they settled in for a couple of weeks. Tony Younger went with them, to get a feel for the country, while the rest of the squadron travelled by rail. There was not much to look at on this trip: hills covered by low scrub and small stunted trees, everything a dull brown colour. Houses all had thatched roofs, the thatch often a yard thick, going right down to the ground on the north side, so there were no doors or windows there, with all activity taking place on the warmer southern side.

By this time the war in Korea was going well for the United Nations forces and American troops were up to the very north of North Korea, near the Yalu River. Well aware of his lack of knowledge, Tony Younger managed to arrange a trip north to discover what conditions were really like there. He took Desmond Holmes, who had flown out as the Advance Party officer in October and had already achieved a great reputation with some of the American units, and hitched a lift up to Pyongyang on a US transport plane. From a Sapper point of view, he wanted to know what the country was like, were the hills steeper, how wooded was it, were the roads any better or worse than in the south, was stone and gravel available, how wide were the rivers, what were the bridges like, and so on.

The northern capital was desperately damaged by bombing, but they managed to borrow a Jeep with a Korean driver and drove slowly north along roads jammed with American transport until they reached the River Chonghon, crossing by a military floating bridge near the ruined town of Anju. In the foothills just north of the river they reached the headquarters of 27 Brigade. The Brigade was deployed tactically round a perimeter of hills so that battalions could support each other in the event of an attack. The whole set-up looked sensible and professional. Though it was not readily evident from local maps, they were blocking the route from China that the Mongols had taken in the early thirteenth century and the Manchus in the seventeenth century. They little knew that their professionalism would be most severely tested by yet another Chinese mass invasion very soon.

Some idea of the difficulties that had been faced on their advance north to the River Yalu was described by Ian Kaye, a soldier in the Argyll and Sutherland Highlanders, in a poem entitled 'Korea':

> *Where the mighty ragged mountains*
> *Rip the guts out of the sky,*
> *And the desolation chills you*
> *To the marrow of your bones,*
> *Where the blinding drifting blizzards*
> *Sear the unprotected eye,*
> *And the biting bitter wind*
> *Across the Yalu River moans.*
> *A wild and savage landscape,*
> *With its valleys grim and dreary ...*
> *Crag on wolfish crag, piled up, and*
> *Glittering with the snows.*
> *A harsh and brutal kingdom,*
> *That would make an angel weary ...*
> *But your Scottish Soldier fought there,*
> *And he knows ... my God, he knows!*

Having seen what conditions were like, Tony and Desmond moved on to the American 1st Cavalry Division, but they had not gone far when it became obvious that something was seriously wrong with their Jeep. Their Korean driver looked under the bonnet and then announced, 'We frozen'. After collecting bits of wood from a damaged house, he lit a fire under the front of the bonnet, and after a quarter of an hour he suddenly announced, 'OK, now,' and started the engine.

They were met with great friendliness but were told how cold they looked in their totally inadequate British Army uniform. This was soon put right and they were re-clothed with a proper American hat with padded earflaps, and a long-sleeved khaki jacket lined with nylon fur. Calf-length winter boots completed their outfit, together with well-padded sleeping bags with a waterproof canvas outer bag.

During this reconnaissance, Desmond Holmes earned himself newspaper headlines by taking forward orders to an isolated American force whose radio had been destroyed. He then rallied them to retake ground they had lost. 'The bravest man I know', the local commanding officer told reporters that night. Whilst this was going on, news filtered through of a massive Chinese attack on 25 November. Their intervention found the American forces over-extended after their rapid advance, and in ten days the broken American units were driven back 120 miles, losing most of their weapons and equipment. The foray to the north was mostly remembered for the intense cold and the disappointment. Nothing appeared to have been achieved and millions of dollars worth of valuable equipment was destroyed without a shot being fired or any effort being made to evacuate it. No contact had been made with the enemy for several days, yet no attempt had been made to make a stand. Seldom has a more demoralizing picture been witnessed than the abandonment of the American forward base before an unknown threat from Chinese soldiers who, as it transpired, were still inadequately armed and on their feet. Though 27 Brigade held their positions brilliantly, the Brigade was forced to take part in the general withdrawal, passing through the newly arrived 29 Independent Infantry Brigade Group which had been ordered to send a force up to Pyongyang to act as a rearguard. This included 55 Field Squadron, the first Sapper unit to enter the war and Tony Younger immediately ordered 3 Troop under Bertie Bayton-Evans, with Larry Lamble as his Troop Officer, to carry out any demolitions that might delay the Chinese advance. North Korean forces were not in evidence and in all the subsequent fighting over the following years it was the Chinese army that faced the Americans and British.

The situation had changed dramatically with the intervention of the Chinese and resulted in what the Americans euphemistically called 'a redeployment of forces' southwards. To 29 Brigade, it appeared to be more of a rout, in that they were often ordered to 'redeploy' so fast that the Chinese found it hard to keep up. At Pyongyang Larry was sent to blow up as much as possible of the railway marshalling yards, which had been built up by the US Army as a major administrative centre. The base was full of wagons crammed full of rations, clothing, POL* etc and he had to use hundredweight bags of sugar to help extricate his Bren-gun Carrier when it became bogged down. In addition to destroying as much as possible in the short time available they found time to acquire enough American raincoats for the whole Troop, which was most welcome in that winter weather.

* POL – Petrol, Oil and Lubricants

Larry was next ordered to be the 'Close Bridge Garrison' to a US Engineer Firing Party over one of the bridges on the withdrawal route. In the lull whilst waiting the order to fire, the West Point Lieutenant and Larry were able to compare the differences between his Academy, West Point, and Sandhurst. In the course of conversation, the Lieutenant said, 'Have you guys got anything to compare with our Bailey Bridge?' With commendable restraint, Larry replied, 'I was talking to Sir Donald Bailey at his Bridging Establishment only a few weeks ago' (untrue!) in order to convince him of its UK origin. It also transpired that the US forces only taught three phases of war and did not include the Withdrawal. In the weeks and months that followed it became evident that the US, and their protégés the Republic of Korea (ROK) Forces, had no idea of conducting a withdrawal, either in or out of contact with the enemy.

The Sapper tasks during this phase were mostly demolitions of bridges and route denial and, of course, the constant need to set up Water Points for the Brigade. As regards demolitions, they were given a pretty free hand since it was accepted that the United Nations Forces were never going to reoccupy North Korea. Everything from railway trains to factory chimneys – a Sapper's delight!

All too soon Bertie and Larry were back with the Squadron, but the former was not a man to miss a chance and on his way south he spotted a slightly damaged D8 bulldozer, abandoned by its American owners. Rather than leave it for the Chinese, and knowing how valuable it could be to the squadron, which was only equipped with the much smaller D4s, he hoisted it on to a low-loader and delivered it to the Park Troop who soon had it in running order. Somehow the squadron forgot to report the find to its American owners and it proved to be a most valuable asset.

Returning from the far north, the Squadron was tasked to build a floating bridge over the River Han just upstream from Seoul. The four-day task, with American equipment, provided an excellent opportunity to weld the squadron together after their sketchy training on Salisbury Plain and the long sea voyage. Tony Younger commented later that he thought the American Corps Engineer had given them this task to find out how good they were. The Han was an enormous river and there always seemed to be one of his staff officers watching while they built the bridge. Luckily it was built in slightly less than the standard text-book time and from being looked on as 'helpless strangers' by the US Army Engineers, the Sappers were suddenly accepted as equals.

The bridge became a key element in the American withdrawal route and the Squadron retained responsibility for its maintenance and immediate approaches. One dark night when the American withdrawal was still in full flow, the junction before the bridge became a veritable bedlam as vehicles converged on it from several directions and pushed and shuffled to get onto the bridge. Some drivers were so impatient that they must have imagined that they had the whole Chinese Army sitting on their tail. Out of this shambles a well-spaced column of British vehicles emerged and drove gently down to the bridge. Standing calmly in the midst of the maelstrom, wearing his red cap and impeccably pressed old fashioned greatcoat, was the Regimental Sergeant Major of the Brigade Provost Company. With his white luminous gauntlets he was in complete command of the situation and stood no nonsense from any drivers or officers, regardless of race, rank or colour. It was a most impressive performance.

In the meanwhile, Captain John Hackford, who had been posted as a Staff Officer to HQ British Element Korean Base, embarked at Southampton, some six weeks after 55 Squadron, on the SS *Charlton Star* with about 750 others, including a mixture of All Arms and some nursing sisters. The ship was Greek-owned with a largely Scottish crew and their departure was held up for two or three days as the standard of accommodation and catering did not pass a Board of Trade inspection. John was appointed ship's Adjutant.

They had quite an eventful passage to Singapore. The ship's crew had a secret cache of Red Hackle whisky and they, and some of the soldiers, over-indulged at night and tended to run riot. John had to give the Master-at-Arms an escort of RMP* to enforce 'Lights Out'.

When they reached Aden, the ship was 'arrested for steaming straight up to the quay to tie up without making use of a pilot'. It took a lot of urgent signals to and from London before the ship was released. Then they couldn't sail because the ship's stewards had mutinied and picketed the ship's capstans and other areas to stop the deck crew from casting off, because the Chief Officer had knocked a drunken steward off the gangplank into the sea! John had once again to use the RMP to 'persuade' the stewards to go below. Guards then had to be placed on the nursing sisters' cabins, and the next excitement took place in the Indian Ocean when the ship turned back on its course for two or three hours as an officer had failed to appear at morning muster and could not be found after a ship's search. It was thought he had fallen overboard, but he was later discovered sleeping things off on top of some deck awning!

On arrival in Singapore on 5 December 1950, some of the passengers were immediately transferred to HMS *Unicorn* for passage to Japan and John Hackford was appointed OC Troops and given a cabin on

* Royal Military Police

the quarterdeck with a Royal Marine guard on the door as the ship 'was entering a war zone'! Ten days later, he reported to what was then called HQ British Element Korean Base.

By early December British forces covering the withdrawal had reached roughly the 38th Parallel and the Brigade took up a far from ideal defensive position north of Seoul, with 55 Squadron based in Yong Dong Po, a suburb to the south of the capital. After a brief pause on Christmas Day, the Squadron moved up to an area just north of the city where they prepared a defensive position against a possible Chinese onslaught. Christmas, however, was not entirely uneventful, in that John Page's 2 Troop managed to burn down the otherwise deserted Tax Office where they were hoping to spend a few days. The cooks had started to prepare Christmas lunch when their petrol cooker set fire to the paper-thin walls, followed by a speedy evacuation. Fortunately nobody was hurt and the Troop Sergeant's shout of '2 Troop **will** have a Christmas dinner' resulted in an empty school being found, accommodation allocated, tables and chairs scrounged and a sit-down meal took place, in itself a unique occurrence. Morale was speedily restored and indeed enhanced in some perverse way.

The onset of winter brought untold misery to the thousands of refugees fleeing south, all freezing, many sick and starving. The sub-zero temperature was bad enough for the troops who at least had transport, rations and medical support, but they were traumatized by the plight of the refugees. Horror stories abounded and Tony Younger was particularly affected when he was reconnoitring a road in his scout car and, passing through a derelict hamlet, he came across a harrowing spectacle. There had evidently been an air attack as, in and out of ditches along the road, sprawled across it, were hundreds of bodies – almost all women. The scout car slowed to a crawl to avoid the corpses. Tony tried to blank out the carnage in the foreground but did not entirely succeed: his eye was caught by a young mother with a dead baby on her exposed breasts. Twice he had to climb out of his vehicle to shift a dead body blocking the road. He had seen refugees strafed by Stukas during the Second World War and only at Belsen had he seen an atrocity comparable to what he saw that day.

Passing through Seoul on Boxing Day, Tony Younger had another unpleasant experience. The streets were quite crowded with pedestrians and some bicyclists, but little other than military traffic drove along the main streets. On one wide avenue he overtook a surprising procession of about fifty people in a long file, three deep. The first half of the group had their heads concealed in straw coverings, similar to those in which champagne bottles used to be packed. As he got nearer, he noticed that they all had their hands tied together with electric cable, and that there were guards with rifles scattered round them. About the first dozen files were men and the last four or five were women, several of whom were obviously in great distress and were being roughly treated with rifle butts by the guards. On enquiry, it turned out that what he was looking at was a group of condemned people going to their execution, which was to take place in one particular valley to the north of the city. It was a sobering sight.

A few days later, on a visit to the Glosters, he was told that their reserve company had been astonished to see a group of about fifty people, all wired together, being marched into their valley. There was a Korean officer in charge and the Gloster company commander asked him what he thought he was doing. The Korean commander explained that this particular valley was, by ancient tradition, the execution ground for the city of Seoul and that this group would now be executed. The Korean officer had then been brusquely informed that if so much as one person was executed the second person to die would be himself. He was then ordered to release the prisoners from their bonds and to clear off. The wretched prisoners, however, were then marched south in the bitter weather, sleeping in the open, without anything more than the clothes they stood up in, and a high proportion cannot have completed their journey. And where was it to? Though the value placed on human life is not the same in all parts of the world, it is nevertheless shattering to be faced by what it really means.

A new Chinese offensive had been expected and this was launched against 29 Brigade on 3 January 1951. Though the attacks were repulsed, nevertheless the Brigade was ordered to pull out and withdraw south of the River Han. Many of the rivers were quite shallow but wide, with gravel bottoms, and thus could be forded. They were not of great importance as obstacles, particularly in winter when they froze over or dried up completely. There was one dramatic exception, the River Han, which flowed deep and strong past the southern capital city. Colonel Ike, the Engineer Commander of the American I Corps, allocated responsibility for the demolitions over this strategically important river – an American unit was to attack the pontoon floating bridge at the western end of the city and 55 Field Squadron would prepare the other three bridges for demolition. One was a roughly made affair of empty oil drums with a timber deck which was in continual use by civilian refugees as they moved south to avoid the war. As it was just a foot-bridge it presented no problem, and when everyone was ready the guards were withdrawn from the northern bank, a barbed wire obstacle was put on the bridge to stop any refugee trying to make a final dash for it and the bridge was blown. Though the river was already frozen at this point, the ice was not yet thick enough to take a marching soldier.

21

The second bridge was more complex and carried twin railway lines with huge bow-string girders mounted on massive piers that dominated the skyline of the stricken city. There was a problem here, in that the last train from the north was still standing about a hundred yards from the near side of the bridge and it was literally covered with Korean civilians, both men and women. There was nobody in the engine and the wood fire for the boiler was very low. An interpreter explained to the passengers that the bridge was going to be demolished and that those on the roofs of the carriages must descend and take cover to avoid the mass of lethal debris that would be hurled through the air by the explosion. Nobody moved. The interpreter then turned to the Squadron Commander and explained that no one would ever give up a hard-won place on the roof of this train, especially as it would be the last going south. A high probability of death waited for those left behind, so they were quite prepared to take their chance of being hit. With a heavy heart, Tony Younger told Bertie Bayton-Evans to go down to his firing point and press the exploder.

With a deafening roar the single bulk charge of 3,000 pounds of high explosive went up, to be followed a few seconds later by a whole series of thumps as bits of the stone pier landed all round them. On the train was utter silence. Then all the people on the carriage roofs started waving. Amazingly, not a single person had been hit by the terrible rain of stones and masonry. As for the bridge, one pier of the enormous bridge had disappeared and two huge bow-string spans had dropped into the river while a great yellow dust cloud drifted slowly to the east in the light air. The passengers then reluctantly gave up their places.

The third bridge was a much more formidable affair. This was the 'Shoofly' (an American term for a rail bridge over which you can also drive road vehicles), a wooden pile bridge of sixty-six spans carrying both road and rail across the 1,000-foot-wide river. Its demolition was made all the more difficult by an edict issued by the Americans that when bridges constructed with wooden piles were to be demolished, the piles must always be cut below water level. This made engineering sense because it is comparatively simple to 'cap' a pile if it is out of the water and thus re-use it to replace the bridge. The difficulty that arose from the edict this time was that the river contained numerous ice floes, mostly quite small but quite sufficient in size to knock off any less than perfectly tied on explosive charge. Also, working in water at freezing point was no joke, particularly when the air temperature was many degrees colder still. As this immensely complicated task proceeded, Bertie Bayton-Evans was forever dangling under the Shoofly, checking what had been done and testing that all was secure while the traffic still passed across overhead. Disaster almost occurred in an unforeseen and sudden manner when a spark from a train fell through the decking and landed on some explosive, which caught fire and started burning with a brilliant blue-white flame. Bertie was too far away to do anything so he shouted to the two Sappers nearest the fire. Corporal Gross and Sapper Hannon, well aware of the fact that more than five tons of explosives had been placed on the bridge, rushed to the scene and wriggled their way towards the flaring menace, knowing that the burning explosive would detonate when it reached a critical temperature. If this happened there would be no hope for any of them working there, or for the train that was still rumbling across the bridge. A hearty kick and the charge fell hissing into the icy water to disappear in a stream of bubbles. But for their bravery, this vital bridge might have been destroyed before United Nations forces could cross. This was particularly appreciated by the Americans who rewarded both men with the American Bronze Star.

After a few days the preparatory work was completed and defensive positions prepared on both banks to prevent a surprise attack, while day after day the traffic poured across.

But before this bridge was blown, Tony Younger left to visit John Page north of the city where he had prepared two other bridges for demolition in order to block the main road from the north before it reached the city limits. The city was silent and utterly deserted. Dawn broke and along street after street, normally teeming with an oriental profusion of men, women, children, bicycles, cars, lorries and the odd cart in from the countryside, there was nothing. Instead of the usual bustle, shouting, gear-changing, horns and bicycle bells, there was silence. Even the flags and bunting that bedecked the main streets had gone, as had the washing from the side streets. No light was visible in or on any building. To start with it was like a deserted film set, but this was one of the major cities of the world with a population well into seven figures in peacetime, and the cumulative effect of driving on and on through deserted avenues and passing huge deserted buildings was most eerie.

It was a confused and confusing situation. North of the city, the gunners gave covering fire for as long as they could before they had to move south and in the very cold temperatures their shells made a crackling sound as they passed overhead, almost as though they were forcing their way through ice crystals. As the guns fell silent, the infantry knew they were on their own, apart from the Sappers, and must reach safety behind the line of demolitions as quickly as possible.

John Page was waiting with John Shaw of the Royal Ulster Rifles for his final platoon to come through and was struggling to recall the correct drill for a Final Demolition and hoped that someone might turn up to sign the appropriate form and authorize the firing. Somewhat surprisingly, someone did and an officer from Brigade HQ bringing up the rear of the convoy condescendingly got out of his vehicle, handed over the relevant form with the injunction to blow the bridge once everyone was across. John asked him when that might be and how might he know, to which he helpfully replied, 'John, that's your problem. Good night' and drove off. The last of the Ulster Rifles were expected any minute and duly arrived carrying two wounded and, after a short pause, pressed on southwards. There were no signs of imminent attack by the leading Chinese troops, so the two Johns decided to wait another half-hour. It was just as well they did because soon a truck appeared from the north carrying the Adjutant of the Glosters, Tony Farrar-Hockley, who was able to confirm that no other vehicle from his Battalion was left on the wrong side of the bridge.

There were rumours that an American tank company was still in the vicinity so John hung on – wondering. They lived with this uncertainty in the darkness of a bitterly cold night, the thermometer recording well below zero, patrolling the area and investigating every suspicious noise or movement. At first light John spotted some tanks moving fast towards them – they could not be British and it was not thought that the Chinese had any there either. It was a relief to find out that they were in fact American. Taking a leaf out of the Chinese book, they had painted the front of each tank with the most grotesque dragon's face and to see a dozen or more of these truly horrific sights approaching at 25 mph was enough to frighten friends, let alone the enemy. Their commander, calm and relaxed, stated categorically that they were the last troops travelling down that road, so electric connections were quickly completed and, with a final nod from the Ulster Rifles, the bridge disappeared and the cliff to the right collapsed into the ravine on the left. Though a perfect demolition, it would not stop determined infantry for long as they could clamber over the resulting boulders, but it would certainly stop any wheeled vehicle until a repair could be effected. John still had another bridge to blow, after which they packed up their bits and pieces and headed back through Seoul to cross the great Shoofly bridge before it was blown.

Back at the Shoofly all was quiet and vehicles had now been crossing at their planned times, well spread out and alert, ready for anything. A platoon from the Argylls was dug in on the north bank and Bertie Bayton-Evans had established a firing point about 150 yards back from the river bank. This was a slit trench with some sandbags round the top to give extra protection. It was about five feet deep so that the surrounding area could be observed comfortably when people stood up, and could crouch down quickly for protection when necessary. The electric cable leading from the charges had not yet been connected to the terminals on the exploder as a safety precaution to avoid premature firing.

Tony Younger arrived back and jumped into the firing trench to be greeted by Sergeant Ball, smiling and calm, who thrust a hot mug of strong tea into his hand. This tough and reliable man had a firm face which broke into a ready smile whomever he spoke to, old or young, rich or poor, senior or junior: a man of great potential. Sadly, he was to be killed a few months later, along with Bertie Bayton-Evans, his Troop Commander. Colonel Ike arrived shortly after, his steel helmet contrasting with the blue berets worn by the squadron; American regulations enforced strictly the wearing of this awkward headgear, but for British troops the decision was left to each commander.

The Brigade Major was also at the firing point, methodically checking the sub-units of the troops still crossing the bridge and when he was satisfied that the last one had crossed safely, he drove off, wishing them luck. Sergeant Ball fired a Very pistol and a green ball of light hung in the sky, denoting the recall of the infantry guarding the far side of the bridge. They wasted no time. Before the burning light had even hit the ground men appeared from their weapon slits. Two groups marched back at a smart pace, looking remarkably fresh after their long and fortunately uneventful vigil. When they were safely over, the final group came, not quite at a run, but obviously keen to leave their exposed positions as quickly as possible. Although they had had no trouble, they knew that the advancing Chinese could not be far away.

In silence, they waited as the infantry moved out of the possible danger area for flying fragments. The moment of truth was approaching fast and the squadron was in the traditional position for the Corps of being 'First In, Last Out'. There were no friendly forces in front of them. The tension was palpable. Colonel Ike, the senior man there, had already signed the brief order for blowing the charges and he gave the final order to blow. Sergeant Ball, at the exploder, connected the cable and pressed the handle.

The result was quite unexpected. There were more than five tons of explosive distributed along the bridge and instinctively everyone expected a colossal bang, the blast from which would punch everyone in the face. Instead there was more of a rumble, nothing too loud at any time but spread over a couple of seconds or so. There was a gasp of horror from Bertie but he was reassured as everyone clambered up onto the parapet. There in front was the wide sweep of the Han River. The Shoofly had disappeared in a huge smoke cloud, leaving innumerable bits and pieces on the ice floes. Where there had been sixty-six trestles, each of four or five wooden piles, all capped by the decking of the bridge, there now remained two solitary piles sticking out of the middle of the river. Clearly the hundreds of underwater charges, all connected by miles of cable and detonating fuse, had produced the strangely unnatural rumble of an explosion that everyone had heard.

During the withdrawal to the south of Seoul, the Squadron had been responsible for the demolition of numerous bridges in the face of the enemy, which had called for great courage and resourcefulness. The Shoofly demolition in particular must be ranked amongst the biggest ever attempted by the Corps and there cannot have been many bridges demolished with more than sixty-six spans, and very few would have spanned a river as wide as the Han at Seoul. Colonel Ike, in his warm drawl, paid a generous tribute: 'Well, that is the best demolition I ever did see. You British sure should be proud of yourselves.'

Having withdrawn from Seoul the squadron rejoined 29 Brigade to establish a new defence line at a place called Pyongtek, some thirty miles south, roughly on the line of the 37th Parallel. It was a long and very dreary drive to get there, through a frozen and almost featureless landscape. The occasional clusters of brown mud huts were deserted and open doors indicated that strangers had already been through them to search for food or temporary shelter. The hills to the east were under a mantle of snow and looked uninviting. The journey took seven hours and on arrival at their destination they were allocated a bare patch of ground. These were still early days and they had not developed the art of moving the whole unit to a new location smoothly and without unnecessary discomfort. They made themselves as comfortable as possible and crept into their sleeping bags, dusty and dirty as they were, after a cold supper of biscuits and bully beef, to sleep fitfully in the arctic conditions. Tony Younger remembered seeing one man getting into his blankets for the night. As there might have been an alarm and since boots froze like concrete if left in the open, he had all his clothes on including his boots. There were plenty of sandbags around and he had one on each foot to keep the bedding clean. Each of his feet looked enormous and ridiculous, bound in the coarse hemp of a sandbag. 'If my old woman could see me now ...'

In theory, troops were not supposed to live on tinned 'Compo' rations for more than three months, but 29 Brigade existed on them for nearer six. Not until the spring of 1951 did fresh rations start to appear. During the whole of this time the Army Catering Corps performed wonders, using hydro-burners and oil-drum field ovens. A brew-up was, of course, essential at all times and with little fuel or wood around, plastic explosive became the normal source of boiling water. An 8oz stick would boil a gallon of water in five minutes, but larger amounts of Plastic Explosive (PE) were considered dangerous.

During this 'redeployment' the morale of the US Forces was rock-bottom and the Squadron was able to acquire much cast-off equipment, including Jeeps and 0.5-inch anti-aircraft guns, which they mounted on their Bren-gun carriers and proved their worth later. Conversely, the morale of the ordinary sapper became increasingly high. They may not have wanted to die for Syngman Rhee, but they were determined to fight to the best of their ability for their unit and way of life. On 1 January 1951, General Walker, the Army Commander, came to see 29 Brigade and on his way back to his own Headquarters he was killed in a road accident. The arrival of the new Army Commander, General Matthew Ridgeway, and the subsequent sacking of several Corps Commanders, came like a breath of fresh air and the situation changed dramatically. An attempt to restore morale in the Eighth Army by giving political talks on UN aims in Korea had completely failed but General Ridgeway adopted a different approach, much more aligned to British thoughts. He believed that disciplined, well-trained men who took a professional pride in their toughness and ability to fight, needed little in the way of ideological inspiration.

There was only one road in the western half of South Korea that would have qualified as a major road by European standards and that was the trunk road running south, connecting Seoul, through Taejon and Taegu, to the main port, Pusan. The surface of all minor roads quickly disintegrated. This meant that in dry weather there was a permanent dust cloud coming off road surfaces, while in wet weather the roads became slushy and the numberless potholes would fill with water as drivers avoided them, only to be emptied later as someone splashed through them. An unusual sight occurred when the roads were frozen and the traveller could come across the awesome sight of a 40-ton tank sliding sideways across the road and into a paddy field. The thaw which followed such a deep frost led to the complete collapse of many stretches of road.

Sappers had, somehow or other, to overcome this hopelessly in-adequate road system to enable the army to move. This was a never-ending task and 55 Squadron alone dumped 500 tons of broken rock in two days on many occasions. Working in a combination of dust and cold resulted in a number of cases of pneumonia and throughout the winter frostbite was a serious hazard. Working conditions on the roads were terrible, but for some reason many men developed a perverse amusement from the situation. It was a harsh time for them though, working in the open, day after day, and British battledress offered little protection from the biting wind. Greatcoats and blankets were similarly not designed for such a climate and troops were reduced to scrounging the better winter equipment of the US Army. Squadron tasks also included preparing fourteen bridges for demolition and help to the battalions with wire and mines, as well as the construction of a parking apron and connecting taxi-way and road at Suwon airfield. Though the bridges were all small and rather insignificant, they were located in succession along the only reasonable road and if they were to be blown it would be important to get the sequence right – otherwise everyone would be in the soup! Two or three sappers were left on each bridge acting as guard or firing party, little realizing that the poor chaps would be sitting on their bridges for a week or more. It was not surprising that cases of frostbite and pneumonia started to occur and John Page's twice daily visits to each bridge with hot food and a tot of rum provided little solace.

The winter not only took its toll on the health of soldiers in Korea; back in England a flu epidemic was rampant. John's driver was a reservist and an excellent and cheerful soldier, but his family ran an undertakers' business in Leeds and one day he produced a letter from his father which said, 'Hurry home, son. Business is booming, they are dying off like flies and I need you badly'!

Meanwhile, John Hackford was at Taegu, but there was little Sapper work in the Headquarters and in January the British Base moved back to Pusan, and then to Kure in Japan. On 15 January, he was sent to HQ 27 Brigade, who still had no Sappers, as their Engineer Liaison Officer to the US IX Corps. He was very embarrassed when he attended his first morning HQ briefing: as he entered the big marquee wearing his captain's badges of rank, everyone stood up for the three-star general.

All was still not well in the US Corps, perhaps not surprising after 'redeploying' over a total of nearly 200 miles, and discipline was very slack. Though the Headquarters was large, there was only one mess hall, an ex-Korean school, and everyone from senior officer down stood in a big queue for food. The Corps Commander was soon replaced by the Commandant of West Point, General Bryant E. Moore, who quickly got a grip of things and also instituted separate messes. John was ordered into A Mess and, when not travelling, had to be standing behind his chair before 7.00am for breakfast and only sat down when the General did. Sadly, two or three months later the General died from a heart attack after his helicopter crashed into the River Han and he had rescued his pilot.

Though some people, both in Korea and at home, may have questioned why they were in Korea, Tony Younger, commanding 55 Squadron, had no such doubts and at Christmas, 1950, wrote:

> *Just what are we doing here?*
> *Ice cold on a ridge in a foreign land,*
> *Chilled by winds from the ends of the earth,*
> *Far, very far from the homes we love,*
> *Just what are we doing here?*

The Korean peasant, gentle but strong,
Is swept up in a desperate fight;
His livelihood smashed by land engines of war,
Whilst death seeks him out from the skies.
Just what are we doing here?

Refugees trudge southwards below us,
With faltering, shuffling steps.
Do they know we are here to protect them,
That we hope they've the strength to survive?
Just what are we doing here?

In a Muscovite palace a tired tyrant sits,
Whose words mean these people must die.
A few hours more and their breath will be stilled,
But he'll never know, never care.
Just what are we doing here?

Someone, someday, must face up to his power
And say 'no' to that tyrant's greed,
Then peasant and wife can enjoy their old age;
Those of us who survive can go home.
That's what we are doing here!

Following the arrival of General Matthew Ridgeway to command the American Eighth Army, UN forces advanced steadily north again between mid-January and mid-April 1951 to the approximate line of the 38th Parallel. The remainder of 29 Brigade had arrived by this time and were involved in some serious fighting, breaking a massive head-on attack. The Turkish Brigade, quite close to 29 Brigade, also met a vicious Chinese attack, held it and then counter-attacked with the bayonet. It was reported that their terse signal to Divisional Headquarters, 'Chinese attack; two hundred and sixty-two killed with bayonet; four Turks dead', was disbelieved. In a rage the Turkish Brigadier demanded that the staff officer concerned should visit him at once, and when he did, forced him to count the Chinese dead. The poor man was sick before he reached three figures. Certainly there were four neat graves beside the road with Turkish helmets on them and each with a little red star and crescent flag.

During this period 55 Squadron were allocated 300 labourers from what later became known as the Korean Service Corps (KSC). This figure varied from time to time and they became extremely loyal, brave and hardworking, and added considerably to the squadron's capabilities. With the thaw came the rain and every paddy field, which was every flat piece of ground, became the colour and consistency of custard. The roads built for a dozen bullock carts a day were being subjected to a thousand vehicles and once the thin surface of stone was ruptured a seemingly endless supply of fill was needed for repairs. Bridges and culverts also needed repairs and there were frequent calls for assistance in mine and bomb clearance, including occasional Russian 'Krapper' mines. But at last the weather changed and the countryside began to dry out. The nights remained chilly but the days were cool and invigorating, with bright sunshine and the skies turned from grey to blue. Spring was absolutely beautiful and the hillsides were covered in azaleas.

As our troops closed up to the Imjin river, and its tributary the Hantan Gang, small rearguard parties and mines delayed our advance but by 7 April the south bank was in our hands. The overall Army plan was to swing our forces from a line running east and west across the 38th Parallel to a line running in a north-east and south-west direction, hinging on the confluence of the two rivers. In order to protect the hinge for this movement, the high ground dominating the river junction had to be secured, especially as it gave excellent observation over the hills to the north-west. It was decided to attack with one battalion, the Royal Ulster Rifles, supported by one squadron of the 8th King's Royal Irish Hussars. The engineer aim was to enable the force to cross the river and to maintain itself on the far bank. The first intimation received by 55 Squadron that such a crossing was projected was at midday on 7 April. The day given for the crossing was the 10th.

The Squadron was completely extended at the time, improving the exceptionally poor tracks in the Brigade area. The Troops were bivouacking independently on the stretches of road assigned to them and were about ten miles south of the river. Some assault boats were being operated for infantry night patrols, but otherwise no bridging material was available.

Preliminary infantry reconnaissances had been done of the river bank, but these had all shown that the Imjin was unfordable and that no vehicles could get down to it. However, the reconnaissances had been carried out under observation and occasional small arms fire during the day, whilst the confirming patrols at night had found great difficulty in crossing the river due to the current, lack of watermanship experience, and the cliffs. With the knowledge gained from reconnaissance, six RASC 3-tonners were made available for bridging materials and left at 4.00am on the 8th, with Keith Eastgate and a loading party, to fetch as much foot-bridge as possible, 300 feet as it turned out, from the nearest dump. This dump was at Ascom City, about sixty miles away near Inchon, and he was back by 6.00pm, a very creditable turn-round time considering the state of the roads and the traffic.

Reconnaissance parties continued to search for a suitable place to cross, without success, but on the afternoon of the 8th one was found, though it was not entirely satisfactory as the home approach for the last mile was a cart track, crossed and re-crossed in many places by a fast flowing mountain stream, and impassable to Jeeps without work. It was above the junction of the two rivers, so involved crossing both, initially with a foot-bridge, to be followed by a Class 12 Assault Bridge for vehicles.

There was no road or track on the far bank of either river and there was a steep bluff just to the north of both crossing places, up which it was obviously going to be difficult to drive a road. Furthermore, due to a low island in mid-stream, the Imjin was constricted and flowed at four to five knots, a very fast current for a foot-bridge.

The width of the Hantan Gang was calculated to be 156 feet and that of the Imjin 144 feet: this left no reserve of foot-bridge and necessitated wading over the shallow portion of the Imjin. However, it was the only place that offered any possibility and it was a relief to find, as a result of a confirmatory patrol, that the depth of the Hantan Gang was two feet six inches to three feet and the Imjin four feet, just within the wading depth of a Centurion tank and an Oxford carrier.

During the 8th, Squadron HQ and 1 Troop under Captain Desmond Holmes and Lieutenant Danny Cadoux-Hudson moved up to within three miles of the river and established a bridge harbour area for all the equipment. Enough Class 12 Assault Bridge, American pattern, was available to bridge the Hantan Gang, and this was moved forward in American transport. Even if any more had been available for the Imjin we did not, at this stage, know what our requirement would be, as it was still in enemy hands and had not been fully recce'd. A request for a further 300 foot of Class 12 Assault Bridge for this task was made.

Ten Oxford carriers were borrowed from the other two battalions in the Brigade, as being the only vehicles capable of carrying stores to the sites and for use as anchors on the sandy far bank. An armoured dozer of the 8th Hussars, the only machine available at that time, was put to work on the home approach the same afternoon, and on the next day, 1 Troop, with the Squadron D7 (American) and D4 dozers made a very presentable two-way track to within 200 yards of the river, where it came into view of the enemy.

Also on the 9th, 2 Troop under Captain John Page and 3 Troop under Captain Bertie Bayton-Evans finished off their road-making and night patrol activities and moved up. All three Troops did a rehearsal on dry land with the bridging expedients, none of which had been seen before. The Squadron O Group was held at 6.00pm and though all Troops had been briefed about their tasks earlier in the day, there had been no time to put them in the 'big' picture. During the remaining hours of daylight final preparations were made and a hot meal cooked before the men were able to rest for a while.

It was a dark night with the temperature at about freezing point and, promptly at 2.00am, 2 Troop with their foot-bridge loaded on Oxfords moved out of the harbour area, followed ten minutes later by 1 Troop. As planned, they went up to the last corner in the road, out of sight of the enemy and paused there. By this time the Royal Ulster Rifles had put covering parties over the rivers, silently, to give local protection to the Sappers. 2 Troop moved off again and their Oxfords started to ford the Hantan Gang at 0300hrs. The noise of the engines was covered to a certain extent by an intermittent barrage of artillery and heavy mortars. The Brigade Vickers machine guns, firing directly over the heads of the Sappers, were not popular!

An Oxford was sent over to the island in the Imjin to carry the standing cable and to act as an anchor. The launching site was a very steep slope down a fifteen-foot bank, which became more and more slippery with use. However, successive sections of the foot-bridge were built, manhandled down the slope, connected by bridles to the standing cable and launched. The standing cable was under water for most of its length and, due to the force of the current, was under such tension that the Troop Commander could not tighten it further to take up the slack. He was the first to admit afterwards that it is essential in these circumstances to keep standing cables absolutely taut and out of the water, but at 2.00am on a dark night in a war zone it is tempting to cut corners and to hope for the best. To this must be attributed the catastrophe that occurred when the bridge was 75 per cent complete and about fifteen minutes before the infantry were due to cross it. The fast current caused one float to dip under water, thus twisting a central section of the bridge. Before this could be righted the weak footwalk snapped and the bridge broke into two halves.

The current forced each half of the foot-bridge away at an angle to the other, and considerable difficulty was found in chopping away the broken sections and joining the two halves. After much effort the joint was repaired and the bridge completed by 6.45am. Due to this mishap the waves of attacking infantry could not use the bridge for the assault so the Oxford carriers, which had brought up the bridging stores, were used to carry the infantry over, dryshod and to time.

At the same time as this, 1 Troop were progressing with their own foot-bridge over the Hantan Gang. They had moved up to the river ten minutes behind 2 Troop as planned. Also using an Oxford carrier as an anchor they progressed in a similar fashion to 2 Troop, but without mishap. The current in this river was running at three knots, considerably slower than the Imjin but fast enough to necessitate great care. The width of the river at the selected place turned out to be 189 feet instead of 154 feet as previously calculated; also some of the bridging from this site had to be put in to replace the damaged items on 2 Troop's bridge.

In the end sixty-nine feet of improvised causeway had to be built out from the banks to ensure a dryshod crossing. The bridge and causeway were completed at 6.00am, as planned, and the long line of infantry started to cross.

At 7.30am 3 Troop started on the task of replacing the 1 Troop foot-bridge with a Class 12 Assault Bridge. Anchorage was provided by a 3-inch Steel Wire Rope (SWR) standing cable positioned about twenty-five feet upstream of the pontoon bows. The cable itself was anchored on the home bank by boring into the cliff face, and on the enemy bank by two buried baulk hold-fasts.

Previously prepared eye-spliced bridles were run onto the standing cable before it was anchored to allow easy movement along the SWR during booming out. This whole operation went very smoothly and the bridge was completed at 10.30am. British Class 12 equipment was not available and though the American equipment was undoubtedly good, the practical details were so poor that building time could have been almost halved if the component parts had been properly thought out.

Promptly at 10.30am, 1 Troop started to dismantle their foot-bridge and this was completed by noon. During the whole of this morning, the Divisional Engineer Officer from 3rd US Division had been attempting to find enough additional Class 12 equipment to bridge the Imjin itself, an estimated gap of 300 feet. In addition, Lieutenant Keith Eastgate was searching the bank with the leading tanks to try and find a suitable bridge site. By 1.00pm it was clear that bridging was not available anywhere in the Corps area so improvisation would be necessary. To make matters worse, Keith Eastgate reported that there was no suitable site as far as the Brigade boundary to the north. The only hope was to bridge near the existing foot-bridge. This had the advantage of a narrow gap, but the disadvantage of a rapid current, bearing in mind that the bridge would be improvised and not up to Class 12.

During the afternoon the D7 dozer waded the first river and started work on the home approach. At the same time some tracking, previously spotted in a railway yard in Seoul, was collected. At 5.00pm, as a result of the energy of the American Divisional Engineer Officer, stores started to arrive at the site. By spacing the boats at ten-foot centres, instead of the normal six feet, there were sufficient to cross the 150-foot stream to the island. For decking, enough Treadway equipment was found to deck one side but none for the other side. However, sufficient foot-bridge walk was found to provide another tread. In an attempt to strengthen this, walks were roped back-to-back, also providing ribands for wheels. A simple experiment soon proved that the walks would take a Jeep, but broke under a 15cwt truck.

The improvisations necessary, the current and the fact that the men had had little rest during the previous thirty-six hours, made this a slow job. However a lot of preliminary work was done on the approaches during the evening and the Troop did exceptionally well to open the bridge and approaches for traffic by 2.00pm on the following day, 11 April.

This completed the work of the Squadron for the assault over the Imjin. 2 Troop dismantled their foot-bridge without major incident, and next day more Treadways and boats were obtained to bring the Imjin bridge up to Class 8. 2 Troop worked continuously for a week on jeep tracks over the completely trackless country west of the rivers.

While the UN forces advanced against light but stubborn Chinese rearguards to the 38th Parallel, 29 Brigade, under command of 3rd US Division, had been allotted a sector about six miles wide, through which the River Imjin passed, with 1st Republic of Korea (ROK) Division on our left and 3rd Division to our right. The Belgian Battalion, under command of 29 Brigade, was in a bridgehead on the north bank, in a loop of the river supplied by the two Class 12 bridges built by 55 Squadron and about five miles of road driven by them through the hills.

To the left rear of the Belgians, and on the home bank, the Northumberland Fusiliers held about three miles of river and, to their left again, the Glosters held a similar stretch. The Royal Ulster Rifles were in reserve, concentrated about four miles behind the Fusiliers. The only roads in the area were mountain tracks; one led to the Glosters and another to the remaining battalions, both these 'roads' converging at a point six miles south of the river. There was one lateral road leading east from this convergence to the main north-south supply route. The only other lateral ran roughly along the riverbank. In addition to the never-ending road-bashing, the squadron searched conscientiously for fording places, but in all the dozen miles of the river for which the Division was responsible, there was only one place which was different to all the rest. Since this was just north of the Gloucestershire Regiment's position, it became known as 'Gloster Crossing'.

Following the foray across the Imjin in the first half of April, extensive and deep patrolling was carried out by all-arms columns to a depth of ten to fifteen miles north of the river. Only small bands of the enemy were found, so there was in effect an extensive no man's land over which our troops roamed at will. 55 Squadron was fully extended in these forays as they not only involved reconnoitring routes but also meant providing a section or more of sappers to look out for mines. They found several, loosely covered with earth, consisting of wooden boxes, undetectable by mine detectors, and containing about 15lb of explosives, quite sufficient to shatter the track of the largest tank or remove the wheel of a scout car or heavy truck. They were also busy with bridge and route maintenance, in construction of separate tank routes and in several smaller jobs, such as the brigade water point.

Individual Troops were spread out in suitable paddy fields, each of course with its own defensive perimeter. Little was known of enemy intentions and still less of their dispositions on the ground. The whole countryside north of the river was a maze of trenches, but observation of these from the air proved nothing as the camouflage discipline of the enemy was so perfect. Nevertheless, a sense of unease prevailed.

Chapter 3

The Imjin Battle, 22–25 April 1951

How fair and noble a thing it is to show courage in battle.

Thucydides 471 BC

Although well trained, the Chinese forces were not, in the early stages, so well provided with heavy equipment as they were later. Most of their soldiers were illiterate peasants, very fit, tough and prepared to undergo hardships without complaint. They relied on large numbers of men who did not require most of the amenities which Western soldiers had come to regard as necessities, and consequently a very high proportion of men were actual combatants. They were able to dispense with a long administrative tail as many of the administrative duties, particularly porterage, were performed by civilian coolie labour, mostly locally enlisted.

Chinese forces nearly always attacked by night and they showed remarkable aptitude for night patrolling. Owing to the United Nations air superiority, all deliveries of enemy supplies and ammunition, reliefs and troop concentrations were carried out under cover of darkness. For the same reason they were prodigious diggers and became very expert at camouflage. Their men displayed remarkable courage.

Towards the end of April, across the silent Imjin river, down dusty paths and tracks, through silent villages and dark foothills, a mighty mass was moving through the darkness. In platoons and companies, a huge force was advancing steadily, the lead element of over 300,000 men. Across a forty-mile front the greatest offensive of the Korean War was about to start. 29 Infantry Brigade stood directly in their path.

On Sunday 22 April, at about midday, isolated reports of enemy movement in no-man's-land started to come in. One of the first of these was from the pilot of a US artillery observation aircraft who was fired on whilst taking Tony Younger, the Squadron Commander, on a route reconnaissance. The plane was hit, the pilot cursed but landed safely with a dozen holes in his fuselage. By nightfall there was a certain tension in the air as the artillery fire increased, but still there was no definite indication of what was to come.

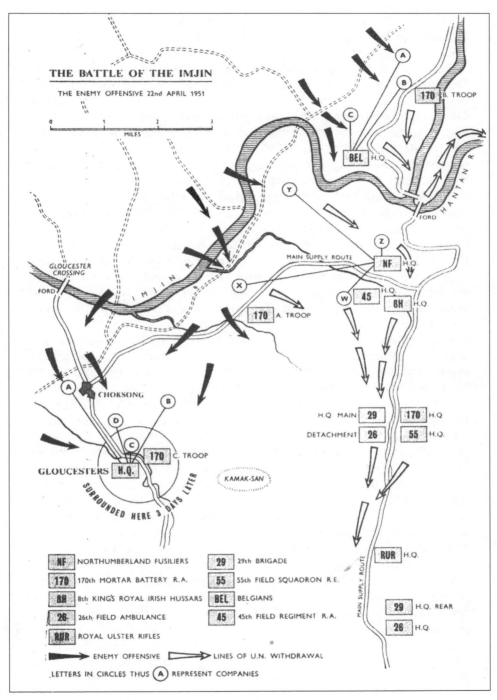

THE BATTLE OF THE IMJIN

THE ENEMY OFFENSIVE 22nd APRIL 1951

0   1   2   3
MILES

170 B. TROOP

170

HANTAN R.

A

B

C

BEL H.Q.

FORD

Y

Z

NF H.Q.

MAIN SUPPLY ROUTE

X

W   45   H.Q.

8H   H.Q.

170 A. TROOP

GLOUCESTER CROSSING

FORD

IMJIN R.

A

CHOKSONG

D

B

C

GLOUCESTERS   H.Q.

170 C. TROOP

KAMAK-SAN

SURROUNDED HERE 3 DAYS LATER

H.Q. MAIN   29   170 H.Q.

DETACHMENT   26   55 H.Q.

MAIN SUPPLY ROUTE

RUR H.Q.

29 H.Q. REAR

26 H.Q.

NF   NORTHUMBERLAND FUSILIERS

170   170th MORTAR BATTERY R.A.

8H   8th KING'S ROYAL IRISH HUSSARS

26   26th FIELD AMBULANCE

RUR   ROYAL ULSTER RIFLES

29   29th BRIGADE

55   55th FIELD SQUADRON R.E.

BEL   BELGIANS

45   45th FIELD REGIMENT R.A.

ENEMY OFFENSIVE   LINES OF U.N. WITHDRAWAL

LETTERS IN CIRCLES THUS (A) REPRESENT COMPANIES

Map 2. Battle of the Imjin, 1951

37

The HQ officer, Keith Eastgate, took a message at 10.30pm that the Belgians were being attacked and wanted protection for their bridges. This was arranged with the Ulster Rifles who sent an officer and fifty men, with Eastgate as a guide, to the bridges. The Glosters and the Northumberland Fusiliers were also being attacked by this time, but not heavily, and the artillery was firing continuously on DF* tasks. The bridge protection party crossed both bridges but were ambushed and engaged heavily on the far side by a large group of enemy who had infiltrated behind the Belgians. The bitterness of the fight that developed can be judged from the cold statistics of the action. Fifty riflemen and about a dozen sappers were involved and of these only twenty-seven got back, with ten wounded, and they took up a defensive position on the home bank, along with Keith Eastgate and the sappers of the bridge parties. In the early hours of the morning, a straggler from the Ulsters was hit by rifle fire in front of Keith while crossing the bridge. He fell into the river and immediately swirled downstream in the fast current. Keith dived in and with a few powerful strokes reached him and was seen to be holding the man's head out of the water as they were swept out of sight in the darkness. They were not seen again.

The Chinese, however, had crossed the river farther upstream and soon brought fire to bear on the small party of Ulsters and Sappers from both front and rear. The party then withdrew over the hills and all the Sappers, fourteen of them, returned safely.

In the meanwhile, the Commanding Officer of the Glosters arranged for a strong patrol to go down to Gloster Crossing. It was an obvious danger point and if the Chinese were planning a major attack they could dispense with boats and ferries and just wade through the water here. At 10.30pm, as the cold night air crept over them, the men lay still, listening and, thinking they could hear splashing, called for a mortar flare to light up the crossing. The sight that met their eyes was as unexpected as it was startling. Hundreds and hundreds of Chinese soldiers were approaching the crossing and others were halfway across. The patrol did not know it at the time, but this was the 187th Chinese Division, 9,000 strong.

While his men opened fire, the patrol commander called for artillery fire support and made sure the mortar flares continued to give light for his men to shoot. Lesser men could have made a bolt for their company position back in the hills, with such odds against them, but the Glosters were made of sterner stuff and, with the extra ammunition they were carrying, they exacted a terrible toll from their attackers as they fired into the masses below them. Bodies started to float downstream, but

* Defensive fire

still the enemy came on, showing undoubted courage. Before long, ammunition began to run low and the patrol was forced to pull back, but not before their actions had alerted the whole front, as well as inflicting a significant number of casualties on the Chinese.

Attacks soon started on the main battalion position and went on inexorably for three long days and nights. By the morning of the third day the 700 men were down to 400, with another hundred wounded, and hardly any ammunition, food or water left. Two strong task forces had tried without success to break through to them before the battalion was overrun.

While the Belgian battalion was withdrawing over the Imjin, the remainder of 55 Field Squadron was 'Standing To' as the small arms fire got closer. Just before dawn the hill overlooking 3 Troop's location was occupied by the enemy who had come through the Northumberlands' line. This particular hill overlooked the whole of the gun areas and the tank harbour area. Immediately he realized the position, Bertie Bayton-Evans with Lieutenant Larry Lamble and 3 Troop started to attack up the hill. With supporting fire from their own Brens, and from some Bofors LAA guns, they successfully gained the height, killing twenty Chinese and killing or wounding a further twenty on another hill which they overlooked from their own. They had called for help over the radio and at the same time the CO of the Northumberland Fusiliers, Lieutenant Colonel Kingsley Foster, met up with John Page and asked for his help too, explaining that one of his companies had been knocked off the hill above them. John told him that he only had about forty men but that with the help of Bertie they would see what they could do. They set off up a very steep hill, expecting to meet up with some of the Northumberland Fusiliers but somehow missed them and, after a long, hard slog, established a rather basic defensive position on the top of the hill with a wonderful view of hundreds and hundreds of Chinese below them. They soon realised how inadequate their infantry training was, but their weapons did include a 2-inch mortar and a few boxes of grenades. They used both. Though they did not see many enemy close up, there was much movement in the scrub and long grass while they gradually improved their positions and gained in confidence. Brief patrols a few hundred yards forward were risky ventures, not so much from the enemy as from the fear of being fired on by jittery sappers as they returned. The hours passed, it was very hot and news was scarce but eventually they received orders to withdraw and a company of the Northumberlands took over responsibility for 'Sapper Hill'. They descended 'with alacrity', having once more learnt the old lesson that if sappers are required to act as infantry the call will come at very short notice indeed and they must be ready for it. Fortunately, our casualties in this action were only three wounded.

Being St George's Day, the regimental day of the 'Fighting Fifth', the battalion had followed their tradition of wearing red roses, flown in specially from Japan, but their CO was in a despondent mood. Outside his Command Post that morning he confided to Tony Younger that he had a premonition of his own death. Tony tried to reassure him but was helpless to ameliorate his anxiety. Sadly, he was killed only a few hours later.

By this time one company of the Northumberlands had been overrun, and the Belgians and Glosters were surrounded. Also, the gun area was virtually untenable, so the Brigade Commander decided to withdraw his HQ, with the gunners and sappers, about five miles. After the Northumberlands had taken over the responsibility of the 'Sapper Hill', the squadron withdrew in small parties. By about 2.00pm slit trenches had been dug in the foothills overlooking the new Brigade HQ area, and the men were able to rest.

At 6.30pm the squadron was ordered to attempt to retrieve the River Imjin floating bridges. A tank and infantry force left with Desmond Holmes and 1 Troop to attempt this. It was realized from the start that this was likely to be an abortive effort as the bridges were already about two miles behind the enemy lines and, at 11.15pm, the force returned as it was unable to break through. Artillery fire was put down on the bridges, breaking one up completely and damaging severely the other. An American force coming down from the north-east at the same time held a stretch of the river long enough for the Belgians to pass through them, to everyone's relief as their position had been very exposed. However, attacks continued on the Northumberlands and Glosters, particularly the latter, also on the Ulsters, three companies of whom had been put into the line near the Northumberlands. Some idea of the intensity of the fighting is given by the sight of just one company of the Northumberlands who at dawn found their position carpeted with brass cartridge cases, looking like a 'firing point' on the ranges. There were some ninety enemy dead to the front and many more bodies had been dragged away.

The Squadron was not troubled by the enemy during the night, but sleep was virtually impossible as three regiments of artillery were firing over their heads, the Brigade's own Field Regiment alone firing 5,000 rounds. By this time it was obvious that the Chinese had no new tricks for this offensive. The Brigade had been warned that they would use air and artillery; the first of these never materialized and, as regards the second, although we did not know it at the time, twenty horse-drawn 75mm guns had been knocked out by our own artillery, between the Gloster position and the Imjin.

The enemy successes were being achieved by a mass of infantry, some of whom had no rifles but only grenades, and who surged like a wave in the general direction indicated to them. Wherever they bumped into opposition that did not give way in front of them they surrounded it, brought down mortar and small arms fire, and subjected it to attack after attack during the hours of darkness.

At 7.30am next day, 24 April, the Squadron was warned to prepare to lay a 'very extensive anti-personnel and tank mine belt'. Nothing further was known about this task but preparations were made to carry it out immediately details were available. The project was cancelled at 11.00am.

A very tense situation developed in the Gloster area during the day. The battalion had been attacked heavily during the night and suffered severe casualties, particularly in officers. They had closed in to both sides of a ridge and were surrounded by a very large number of Chinese (later estimated at two brigades). A force of one squadron of 8th Hussars and a battalion of Filipino infantry was sent to relieve them. The force started out at 5.30am and against considerable opposition they gradually fought their way up the long mountain track towards the Glosters. The infantry found the going very slow and, at about 2.30pm, the 8th Hussars abandoned them and pushed on unsupported. However, at about 3.30pm, a new situation developed when the Commander of 3rd US Division ordered the Glosters to remain in their positions for a further night pending an attack to restore the situation by an American tank battalion and two infantry battalions. At about the same time the leading tank in the relieving force was 'brewed up', blocking the road.

The position of the Glosters was very serious by then. They were short of food, water, arms, ammunition and radio batteries. Also an attempt to get helicopters to them for evacuating wounded had failed. An air drop could not be arranged until the next morning. In an attempt to alleviate their position, Desmond Holmes and Bertie Bayton-Evans from the Squadron contacted their second-in-command and arranged for light aircraft to 'free drop' some of their needs. Five trips were made but, due to the steepness of the ridge they were on, only one was successful. This success was due to Sapper Fairway, an ex-RASC air-drop expert who travelled with one plane and managed to hit the target.

On the same day an American Regimental Combat Team (RCT), three battalions with full supporting arms, moved in on the exposed right flank of the Ulsters to thicken up the front in that area. During the evening another American RCT started to move into the Brigade HQ area in preparation for restoring the Glosters' stretch of the front next day. The 8th Hussars and Filipinos also withdrew to the Brigade HQ area and the Belgian battalion came back there too.

On the night 24/25 April all the battalions, and the US RCTs, were attacked during the night. The situation began to get very confused with small arms fire all round and flares and artillery fire continuing throughout the night. The Squadron was dug in, preparing to defend itself against a mass infantry attack and was put on a 50 per cent 'Stand To' at 2.05am and 100 per cent at 3.00am. The situation obviously was getting out of control so all vehicles were loaded. The unit heavy equipment, i.e. Park Troop, less one dozer, had been sent south to Yong Dong Po the previous day.

The road to the Northumberlands and Ulsters was cut during the night and a force of 8th Hussars was warned to break through this block, starting at 5.30am. However, all the infantry were engaged so the only support available was from ourselves. 1 Troop under Desmond Holmes was warned for this and Lieutenant Brian Swinbanks, the Park Troop Officer, voluntarily attached himself to the force as the second officer of the Troop was on leave. This force succeeded in clearing the ground on either side of the road up to a gorge which dominated most of the road. At 7.00am Swinbanks took the men of one of the sections and put them in position on either side of the high ground overlooking the road. Daylight showed countless thousands of Chinese troops, mainly in small groups of twenty to thirty men, advancing towards them. At 12.30pm these positions came under attack but they managed to hold their own, largely due to the efforts of Brian himself who personally led three men up to a machine-gun post that was causing most of the trouble and silenced it.

As the morning wore on the firing became intense, with the 8th Hussars carrying out a highly professional withdrawal action by leapfrogging their Troops back down the valley. With the two infantry battalions painfully slowly moving southwards, exhausted by three days and nights of continuous action, the tanks destroyed literally hundreds of the attacking groups and kept the valley open. The Chinese were everywhere, among the rocks and bushes flanking the main valley, in the hills overlooking the valley, and in the paddy and on the road itself. They carried pole charges and anti-tank grenades and succeeded in knocking out six tanks and numerous smaller vehicles, albeit at a prodigious cost in life to themselves. They would have done a great more damage had it not been for the superb discipline and training of the 8th Hussars who remained completely unperturbed, with enemy swarming all round and even on top of their tanks. Trooper Barber even drove clean through a house to brush the enemy off the sides.

For some seven hours Sergeant Orton, Desmond Holmes's Troop Sergeant, was in charge of a party of nine men acting as local protection to a Centurion tank. He and his men were engaged continually by enemy small arms and mortar fire, but they were successful in breaking up the formed bodies of Chinese troops that attacked them. His tank was the last to withdraw to the ridge held by Sappers, where he picked up the remainder and came under violent attacks from Chinese using grenades, Molotov cocktails and automatic weapons. He organized and controlled the fire of all the tank passengers into two effective fire banks, showing a coolness under heavy fire that was an inspiration to them all. The tank finally caught fire and fell off the road.

By now in a dazed condition, Sergeant Orton was ordered, in English by a Chinese armed with an automatic weapon, to surrender. He attacked the man with his fists and laid him out cold. He then gathered the survivors together and led them to another tank through a large number of Chinese who fired and threw grenades at them. When this tank was also halted by Molotov cocktails, he immediately went to the front and put out the fire with his own clothes, thus saving the driver from being burned and blinded. The tank commander was wounded severely at this time so Sergeant Orton moved to the turret and took command of the tank. Under his direction the tank gunner successfully engaged several groups of the enemy, and Sergeant Orton succeeded in bringing back the tank with its passengers, the majority of whom were wounded by then, to safety.

During the whole of this period Sergeant Orton acted in the most cool and courageous manner, taking on the responsibilities of infantry NCO and tank commander confidently and efficiently. His actions undoubtedly saved the lives of many British soldiers and almost certainly a tank from being lost whilst at the same time inflicting the maximum damage possible to the enemy. There were many brave actions that day, but those of Sergeant Orton were in the very top flight. In particular, his coolness under intense enemy fire provided an inspiration to all who saw him and his extreme gallantry was subsequently recognized by the award of a much merited, and extremely rare, Distinguished Conduct Medal.

By 2.00pm the Northumberlands and Ulsters had withdrawn through the gorge, covered by the 8th Hussars with their Sapper support. An Australian officer, Lieutenant David Boyall, was commanding the last tank and picked up Desmond Holmes who had been holding the saddle with his sapper detachment. Under heavy fire, he and Brian Swinbanks went round and passed on the order to withdraw; the wounded were shoved onto the rear deck of the tank and the sappers then clambered aboard. There were Chinese all around and others were coming down the hillside. The last Centurion tank was now the sole focus for hundreds of Chinese and Desmond stood in the turret next to Bavid Boyall, firing his rifle as they set off. Bullets thwacked into the bundles of men clustered round the turret, explosives rang against the armour and bursts cracked overhead. Revving the engine to maximum pitch, churning up great clouds of dust behind them, the last crew of Hussars thundered south through the funnel of fire. As the Official History of the Korean War records, 'The last troops fighting as infantry to withdraw from this battle were, therefore, Royal Engineers'.

At no other time since the Second World War has a whole unit, the Glosters, been written off; the companies of the other infantry battalions suffered grievously too, losing around half their strength. It was not just the Glosters who were 'Glorious' and in fighting like this rank was no defence. Of the Commanders of the four infantry battalions involved, one was wounded, one captured and one killed; only one made it out in one piece. The encounter was no less intense for the Gunners and the gun positions themselves came under infantry attack. Each gun fired off approximately 1,000 rounds, twice as many as were fired in the entire Falklands War and about the same as were fired at the Battle of Alamein, all within less than three days.

The job done by the Sappers played a considerable part in enabling the two battalions to pass back down the road to safety, but sadly Brian Swinbanks was hit by a bullet and mortally wounded. The desperate nature of this battle is difficult to describe adequately, but one statistic gives some idea of its fierceness: 29 Brigade casualties amounted to 1,091, or about 25 per cent of its full strength. The total Sapper casualties in this action were three killed, four missing and fourteen wounded. For their part, the Chinese Sixty-third Army, which had attacked with great courage, lost ten times that number and the delay gave the Americans enough time to establish a defensive line north of Seoul and block any further Chinese advance. The Imjin Battle stands up there with Rorke's Drift or Arnhem: a stand against monumental odds by men whose orders were simply to hold fast.

Just to the west of all this, the last act of the Glosters was being played out. Lieutenant Colonel James Carne, the CO of the battalion, who later received the VC, was told that there was no hope of relieving him, and was authorized to break out to the south. He was captured, along with the Medical Officer and the Regimental Sergeant Major who had stayed behind with the 200-odd wounded. Only one company escaped intact, under their Company Commander, Mike Harvey, who struck out north with the ninety remaining men from its original 120, swinging west and then south before eventually returning to our lines thirty-nine strong.

One final detachment of the 55 Field Squadron is worthy of special mention. This was known as the 'ROK Troop' and consisted of 150 South Korean civilian labourers. These men were medical rejects from the conscripted South Korean Army. They were unpaid, clothed with the cast-off clothing of the Squadron, but fed daily by the Squadron with rice and dried fish. They were billeted in a village right up in the front line and, daily, under Second Lieutenant Smith RE, they were put to work on the roads and tracks being made by the Squadron. Around midnight the village came under small arms fire and a few minutes later the first element of the Chinese came into the village. They did not spare our Koreans and any caught were shot down without mercy.

Their leader, by the name of Oom, rallied his men and, during a lull and whilst it was still dark, led them out into the hills. Two days later, they rejoined the Squadron, fifty-nine strong, after a hazardous march across the hills and through both lines, having suffered many casualties en route. This was a good effort on their part as they could easily have disappeared and hidden until all the trouble had finished.

At the conclusion of the Imjin Battle, Terry Moore, serving with the Ulster Rifles, wrote:

> So this is the Land of the Morning Calm!
> Is this the Land of the Free?
> No! This is the Land where my soldiers have died,
> In search of your Liberty.

As a sequel to this battle, Captain Craig of the Ulsters, who had been missing since an ambush on the north bank of the Imjin, returned over the hills to our lines about thirty-six hours later. He said that he had been taken prisoner in this fierce action and marched at bayonet point into the hills immediately overlooking the south bank of the Imjin. As dawn came he arrived at the top of the hill to join a group of other prisoners, some riflemen, some Belgians, and Keith Eastgate. As the most recent arrival, he was put at the end of the line of dispirited prisoners and noted that Keith was at the other end. When the sun had risen a bit higher, there came a noise of aircraft approaching and soon it turned into an American air strike with rockets and napalm on the area, near enough for them to feel the heat. The Chinese appeared to go wild after this and opened up with their 'Burp' guns on the prisoners, starting from one end. Craig, at the other end, sprinted down the hillside with the energy of desperation and was lucky enough to get away. He held out little hope of any chance of survival for Keith.

It was May before we had edged forward again and were back on the south bank of the Imjin. At the first opportunity Tony Younger collected a small party, including Desmond, and set out to find the hill on which the prisoners were alleged to have been slaughtered. Prepared for the worst, and carrying picks and shovels, they eventually reached the top of the hill, very hot and sweating profusely. An awful sight of un-recognizable remains met their eyes. Tony and Desmond looked for clues as to which body was Keith's and eventually found confirmation in the pocket of a battledress jacket. They hacked a grave for him from the rocky hill top. It was back-breaking work but it was finished in the end. The pathetic remains of what had been one of the finest of men were laid to rest at last, but not before they took off their hats and stood humbly round the simple grave for a final prayer. It was a very tragic end to a most promising and popular officer.

Though the Imjin Battle was over and both sides paused for breath, there was much work to be done. Initially, further Chinese attacks were expected and preparations were made to demolish the bridges north of Seoul which had been blown in January and built again in March. Luckily such drastic steps were not necessary once the full extent of the enormous Chinese casualties had been fully assessed and UN Forces had been reinforced. Confidence was restored and gradual advances were made, with the Brigade determined to have really strong positions which could be held properly against any Chinese assault. Thousands of tons of wire and mines were brought forward to battalion and company positions. As things began to settle down more, the squadron concentrated near Brigade HQ and the officers and senior NCOs enjoyed being together after leading independent lives for so long. With the squadron concentrated, it was also able to work more efficiently and economically. An added bonus was the increase in social life with friends from other units dropping in for a chat and a drink.

The approach of summer brought with it major changes in the life of the Brigade as plans took shape for the introduction of a Commonwealth Division.

Chapter 4

Consolidation

The Commonwealth Division
Both British brigades, particularly 29 Brigade, had had a torrid time during the Chinese offensive and were withdrawn into Corps reserve while the Chinese withdrew northwards for some miles out of contact, no doubt in part to avoid the considerable artillery fire of the United Nations forces, but also to lick their wounds after sustaining heavy casualties. 29 Brigade took up a reserve position in the Yong Dong Po area with responsibility for defending the Kimpo Peninsula, just west of Seoul. The brigade had suffered very heavily and more than 25 per cent of its fighting men had become casualties. Much equipment had been lost and a period of relative calm was welcome. At midnight on 25 April 1951, 27 Brigade changed its name and became 28 Commonwealth Brigade.

With the halting of the Chinese offensive at the end of April 1951, the Eighth Army line ran from the west, north of Seoul, then due east to the east coast, just north of the 38th Parallel. Early in May, Republic of Korea (ROK) forces in the east took the offensive, accompanied by an attack on the western flank by 1st ROK Division. Soon after these operations had started, the Chinese began a counter-offensive of their own which was contained by UN forces with very heavy losses to the Chinese who were forced to withdraw again by 21 May.

Early May had found 28 Brigade to the east of Seoul, on the left flank of the 24th US Division and, on 14 May, the 1st Battalion King's Shropshire Light Infantry (KSLI) relieved the Middlesex Regiment, who returned to Hong Kong, thus completing the relief of the original units of 27 Brigade. 29 Brigade meanwhile spent the rest of May on the Kimpo Peninsula before moving to the left sector of its old position on the River Imjin, where they found that Gloster Crossing, where the Chinese had crossed some two months before, had been damaged badly by shellfire. A lot of work would be necessary before vehicles could use it once more and it was strongly suspected that there would be mines in the ford. Tony Younger, OC 55 Field Squadron, decided to waste no time:

> We cut ourselves some long sticks to mark any mines we found and then Bertie Bayton-Evans and I, together with Sgt Ball and two of their sappers, carefully edged our way into the water. Sure enough, there were mines for us all. I soon found one, lightly covered in sand, so I stuck my marker in near it and exposed the top of it with my hand. Working round the square sides of the box, I scooped out sand and gravel to feel the bottom. Soon I could feel all round it, so I slowly lifted the mine out of the water, took it back to the bank and removed its detonator.
>
> While I was doing this, my driver shouted down from the top of the cliff to say that I was wanted on the radio. This turned out to be a message that I was wanted elsewhere so I explained to Bertie that I had to leave and then drove off. That evening I was working in our office truck when Bertie came in.
>
> 'Do you know what this is?' he said, laying a thin tarnished metal tube about four inches long on my desk. I inspected this object, which had a plunger at one end. There were no visible markings on it to give a clue.
>
> 'I have never seen one before,' I said. 'Is it some form of release mechanism?'
>
> That is exactly what it is,' said Bertie. 'It has to be a Chinese release switch which they use to booby-trap anti-tank mines, because I unscrewed it from a mine. Guess where we found it.'
>
> 'Tell me.'
>
> 'It was sticking out of a second anti-tank mine underneath that mine you took out this morning. You are a lucky man, you know.'
>
> How stupid, how very, very stupid of me. I knew I had been a bit casual in just feeling round the bottom edges of that mine and not scooping out a larger hole in order to test the whole bottom surface. If the mechanism had gone off as planned both the mines would have detonated, probably killing us all. Certainly I would have been reduced to very small pieces.
>
> How could I have been so inexcusably careless? Perhaps some of the answer at least lay in the cumulative strain of the previous months. It would hardly have been human to have passed through all that without losing the keen edge of alertness, and mine had obviously been blunted. At the time I felt a sense of relief at my good fortune at coming unscathed from this close brush with death, and I also felt disgusted with myself at putting others at risk unnecessarily.

The door of the office truck opened again, allowing a blue twist of cigarette smoke to escape. Two clean-looking American officers, complete with the inevitable steel helmets, stood there. They explained that they had come from an Engineer Intelligence Team that was collecting items of Chinese equipment. Without a word, I handed one of them the release switch.

'Good Lord, incredible. This is at the head of our list. It is our prime objective to find one. How could you have known?'

'Don't worry yourselves about that,' I replied. 'Come and have a drink. I think we all need one.'

A few days later Tony Younger handed over 55 Squadron and left Korea. The day after he left, Bertie Bayton-Evans, Lieutenant Robinson, Sergeant Ball and Sapper Higgins were killed at Gloster Crossing, a terrible blow.

There was particularly close cooperation between the American and British Engineers, so much so that the former named their upper Imjin bridge after Bertie Bayton-Evans.

With only one Field Squadron for the whole of 29 Brigade, troops were affiliated to forward battalions where they set about assisting with the task of digging, wiring and mining the defences. There was always a lot of routine maintenance too and everyone was constantly alert, particularly during the hours of darkness. Damage from shelling needed repair, as did minefield gaps and perimeter fencing, and there were always patrols going out, with Sapper support. Jeep tracks up to company positions had to be kept open, drains and culverts cleared, and there was a constant need for trenches to be kept at the right depth and sumps cleared. In summer the vegetation grew quickly and fields of fire had to be cleared, tasks which some units were better at carrying out than others who had to be prodded, often by quite junior Sapper NCOs attached to forward companies to give advice on field defences.

During this relatively quiet period, 28 and 29 Brigades provided help with the arrival and assembly of 25 Canadian Brigade and the formation of 1st Commonwealth Division. There were the usual teething problems inherent in welding together numerous disparate units and formations: who was under whom, and that sort of thing, but nothing that could not be put right with a bit of goodwill. These teething problems also extended to the administrative support from the new Divisional Headquarters. The opening entry in the Divisional War Diary observed the difficulties of the Assistant Director of Medical Services in eating the two lightly boiled eggs he had ordered for breakfast. Among the domestic stores missing – items had been looted during the loading of the stores ships in England – were teaspoons. Watched keenly by his brother officers and the mess staff, the Colonel had to dispose of his eggs with a dessert spoon, which led to a series of mishaps, not the least being cutting off the tops of the egg. Several of the onlookers made the unkind observation that they were not going to submit to the Colonel's surgery on the battlefield.

By the end of May all three Commonwealth brigades (25 Canadian Brigade were now operational) had taken up positions along the line of the Imjin river, and arrangements were in hand for them to be reinforced with supporting Arms and Services to complete their formation into the Commonwealth Division. No longer would 55 Squadron be the sole Royal Engineers unit; indeed, they now ceased to be independent and were taken under command of 28th Field Engineer Regiment, while their Park Troop was transferred to 64 Field Park Squadron.

The formation of 1st Commonwealth Division took place formally on 28 July 1951 with the Engineer component of the Division being:

> HQRE. Colonel Eddie Myers CBE DSO, who had already made his name in the Second World War when he was dropped into occupied Greece to undertake sabotage, was appointed Commander Royal Engineers (CRE).

> 28 Engineer Regiment. The Commanding Officer was Lieutenant Colonel Peter Moore, a legendary figure with two DSOs and a MC, who was renowned for his personal bravery and prodigious energy and was to earn a third DSO.

The sub-units were:

> 12 Field Squadron RE in support of 28 Commonwealth Infantry Brigade.

> 55 Field Squadron RE in support of 29 British Infantry Brigade.

> 57 Independent Field Squadron RCE in support of 25 Canadian Infantry Brigade and under them for administration, but under 28 Regiment for operations.

> 64 Field Park Squadron RE.

The nucleus of 28 Regiment had been raised in Libya from 22nd Field Engineer Regiment, 12 Field Squadron being transferred as a unit and 64 Field Park Squadron and RHQ being formed from scratch. Over 100 volunteers from 22 Regiment extended their overseas tours or their period of National Service to go to Korea and, on 30 May 1951, the Regiment embarked for Korea on board HMT *Empire Orwell,* arriving in Pusan on 24 June with a strength of nineteen officers and 414 other ranks. To this must be added the men from the Korean Service Corps (KSC).

Field defences on the new positions were rudimentary and access was difficult, some companies being supported by a porter carry of two miles with a steep climb at the end. With no Sapper effort available, the Korean Service Corps (KSC) was invaluable. Growing out of the auxiliary force which 55 Squadron had found so useful, the KSC, consisting of men unfit for the South Korean Army, was organized on military lines, a regiment of three battalions each of four companies supported the Commonwealth Division, and sub-divided to provide support to the forward battalions. 28 Regiment had over 1,000 Koreans employed on engineer tasks. In porterage they could carry extraordinarily heavy loads and some learnt elementary engineer skills. They worked under their own command system, normally supervised by quite junior NCOs, and often showed considerable loyalty and courage. They provided an extremely useful addition, were hardworking and a number were killed, wounded or taken prisoner while working for the squadrons. They even helped in carrying defence stores right into forward positions.

The KSC were entirely self-supporting and usually pitched their camp in the next re-entrant to the Troop they were supporting. Though unarmed, they had a military rank structure with a Lieutenant in charge of a company of about 200 and a Captain in charge of a battalion, a youngish graduate from Seoul in the case of 28 Regiment. Whilst the field squadrons looked after the maintenance of forward jeep tracks, the KSC looked after the remainder. The companies only had hand tools and wheelbarrows, though they could call on 15cwt compressors when necessary. They also had the support of a British corporal with a 3-ton truck and there was a Sapper Liaison Officer from RHQ who had a jeep and a radio. The units under command of 28 Engineer Regiment steadily became more effective and a number of their officers soon acquired front line experience. They had shown that if they were left to work independently on task work, under their own officers, a fair measure of success was achieved and three of the six companies were formed into an independent battalion. They became proud of their work and got on well with British Sappers whose sense of humour always broke down difficulties in communication.

There were many miles of roads to look after, with the divisional airstrip thrown in for good measure. One of the LO's jobs in bad weather was to go round the whole area at daybreak and report on the 'going'. Green was okay for all normal traffic, Amber was for operational and essential administrative vehicles and Red was for urgent tactical traffic only: ammunition replenishment and so on. This information was passed to Division HQ, who put out a daily broadcast. The LO toured all the roads again before dusk, giving orders to the corporals for the next day's work and arranging for any regular support from the Field and Field Park squadrons and the RASC transport unit as necessary. The

Regiment was also provided with a contingent of 500 men from the Seoul Fire Service for road repairs. This was changed every ten days.

By this time, the end of July 1951, the Chinese had withdrawn to a line some 7,000 metres to the north of the Imjin, with a light outpost screen some 2,000 to 3,000 metres north of the river. Their standard weapons were the rifle and the Chinese stick grenade, to which were added some light machine guns at company level. Then there was the Chinese Burp gun, modelled on the Soviet sub-machine gun, with its very high rate of fire, though no great penetrative power – one Sapper took six bullets in his thigh and lived to tell the tale. They had very little artillery to begin with, but this deficiency was soon remedied and by about the middle of 1952 they were capable of putting down very heavy concentrations.

The engineer problems in Korea were huge as, in addition to the usual tasks of mine warfare, demolitions, river crossings, field defences and water supply, were the particular problems posed by the country itself. The mobile campaign of the previous twelve months had ended and the campaign became one of limited set-piece attacks with heavy artillery support. There was intensive patrolling and barbed wire, field-works and mines began to play an increasingly prominent part. There was also the perpetual problem of roads. Once the division started offensive forays north of the Imjin, it became necessary to put tanks across, but none of the ferry sites had roads leading to it, so, in the middle of the rainy season, it became necessary to construct long approach roads over very poor ground, as well as to construct exit ramps from the river.

Should the Chinese decide to attack across the Imjin again, a means of setting the surface of the river alight was devised, thanks to the ingenuity of an Australian Sapper. This was done by anchoring below the surface a number of oil drums filled with a mixture of napalm and petrol, bringing them to the surface and setting them alight by means of small explosive charges by remote control. During trials, there were some anxious moments, especially when an experimental drum, fully alight, accidentally broke loose from its anchor and started sailing down the river towards a bridge across the Imjin on the front of the neighbouring American Division! Fortunately it was successfully sunk by rifle fire in time. Another device which was installed in quite large numbers was a flame or illuminating *fougasse*. Basically this consisted of a container filled with napalm which could be propelled some fifty yards to light up areas or deny their use to the enemy. This was thought to be particularly useful owing to the wide front for which sappers were responsible and the distances between all-round defended localities. Both these devices sounded extremely dangerous though, especially to the user, so perhaps it was just as well that neither had to be used operationally as the Division soon advanced across the Imjin and drove the Chinese well back from the river before full production had started.

The Chinese troops usually wore rubber-soled shoes or were even barefooted, so 64 Field Squadron were tasked to produce yet another deterrent in the shape of welded steel tetrahedrons with two-inch-long spikes. Again, before mass production had started, the Division had moved forward and the Chinese were more interested in strengthening their hilltop positions than in marauding by night between the lines.

Individual reinforcements to keep the Divisional engineers up to strength continued to arrive. In the last week of August, Tony Kendall, together with Peter Hutchings, Oliver Keef and Alec Jackson, were posted from a Young Officer (YO) batch at Chatham and on their way to Korea stayed overnight at the Goodge Street Deep Shelter, the London Transit Camp. Access was by a circular staircase, which seemed to go on and on, carrying all one's kit. Reveille was at 4.30am, up the stairs again, this time also carrying a paper bag containing their lunch, and on to Paddington to join a troop train for Liverpool. After a rather circuitous journey, Paddington not being the usual departure station for Liverpool, the train reached the dockside shed for embarkation on the troopship *Empire Orwell* for the four-week voyage to Korea, disembarking at Pusan. It could equally have been the *Empire Halladale*, which earned the soubriquet of being the original 'Slow Boat to China', when the voyage took six weeks, or the *Asturias*, which was host to Second Lieutenants Mike Bruges and Sam Sowton. For young subalterns it was the adventure of a lifetime, though many a tear was doubtless shed amongst wives and girlfriends left behind.

The grim reality of the troop decks, to which one was assigned as a YO, was soon brought home to them. The *Asturias* in particular had gathered a plague of cockroaches which made their presence felt below decks, and every soldier had an odour of his own, particularly when heading through the Red Sea. However, the first task after sailing was always to devise a comprehensive training programme for the Sapper draft on board which would keep them occupied, with time for recreation as well. It included instruction in the field engineer tasks that were likely to be encountered as well as some infantry skills and fitness training. There was no shortage of small-arms ammunition and so there was plenty of target practice with suitable targets dropped over the stern and utilizing the infinite space of the ocean as a range. Many sappers became expert shots, much appreciated when called upon to act as infantry in Korea. Boxing, 'Housey-housey' and 'Crown and Anchor', the latter usually run (illegally) by the crew, did much to keep morale up and monotony at bay. Many officers played bridge every night to keep the brain cells alert.

Arrival in Pusan was always greeted by the ubiquitous American Army Band shuffling their way onto the quayside and most arrivals disembarked straight onto a train which took them to the railhead at Uijongbo, passing the remains of burnt-out tanks from the fierce battles around Taegu in the previous autumn. Others went on to Japan and disembarked at Kure from where they headed off to the Divisional Battle School before returning to Korea. Tony Kendall's main recollection of the twenty-four-hour journey up the Korean peninsula was of enjoying the novelty of American C Rations, though the enthusiasm for these rather dry packets soon evaporated and the British Compo was much to be preferred. On arrival at the Regiment's B Echelon and welcomed by Major Bill Woods, the Second-in-Command (2IC), Tony was allocated to 55 Field Squadron, commanded by Derek Fletcher. John Firth also joined at the same time and his first task was to check a suspect minefield at Seoul airfield but, sadly, he was killed almost immediately. Evidently the mines had been laid under a barbed-wire fence, making it hopeless to use a mine detector. This was a tremendous shock but the effect was relatively short-lived in that people soon got used to the inevitability of casualties. Two more officers in the Regiment died in the same way in the next few months and Colin Carr, one of the Troop Commanders, lost a foot from a mine.

The transition from peace to war mode was often slow with new arrivals, and this was something that was not confined to Sappers. One day a Centurion tank was moving up a narrow track towards a new position in a forward area when the CO radioed to ask why the Troop Leader wasn't getting a move on. He replied that there was a jeep ahead of him which was holding him up. He rapidly switched on to 'Active Service' mode when the CO gave the command 'Drive on'. The buckled remains were left there as a reminder to everyone that this was war and one didn't have to fill in Accident Report Forms.

To begin with, the Division was concerned mainly with improving the strength of its positions to prevent penetration by the Chinese but as the summer wore on it became more confident and began active patrolling across the Imjin for up to four or five miles. Contact was limited to patrols, which had to cross the river by ferries or rafts and, to meet the need for movement across the river, 55 Squadron had established a Class 9 ferry at a crossing known as 'Teal' on the divisional left, while 12 Squadron had established another ferry at 'Pintail' on the division's main axis, and 57 (Canadian) Squadron operated a Class 50/60 raft. By August the rains had started and, on the 6th, six inches of rain fell in just seventeen hours. The ensuing flood isolated Divisional HQ and left two battalions cut off north of the river, and maintenance of the ferries became a constant battle. On the 24th, after heavy overnight rain, RHQ recorded in the War Diary that the river rose ten feet in fifteen minutes at a point fifteen miles upstream of the 'Pintail' crossing and by 4.00pm it had risen to a depth of forty-two feet at 'Pintail' and thirty-five feet at 'Teal'! Three days later and the river flow was sufficiently low to enable rafting to start again at 'Teal'.

Some idea of the problems faced, and some of the incidents (described below), may remind Sapper readers in particular of the pleasures (and frustrations) of being a Troop Commander.

Imjin Ferry

Captain Vernon-Betts was involved heavily in the ferry operations across the Imjin. Fortunately there was no enemy activity in the immediate vicinity at the time, but the country around 'Teal' was almost all paddy or ploughed fields, with a two mile fair-weather approach track from the main road. Movement off the track was usually impossible due to our own minefields on either side. The ferry was for personnel only and the track was therefore only required to carry a small amount of traffic. Fortunately, there was a large un-mined ploughed field at the ferry site which served as a parking and off-loading area.

At this point the River Imjin was about 550 feet wide and the home bank was a cliff, 150 feet high, down which steps had to be cut. The cliff continued below water level, giving a minimum depth of six feet at the water's edge. The far bank shelved gradually at a slope of about one in ten and was of coarse, sandy gravel, interspersed with large rocks.

It was decided that the site was suitable for a 'flying ferry', the equipment to be used being the American M2 raft. This was composed of open bipartite wooden pontoons with box-shaped treadways clamped to the handrails of the pontoons. Three piers were used with sufficient treadways to provide a six-foot ramp at each end. This type of raft could carry a Class 9 load.

Two troops were engaged in the operation, each relieving the other in turn. These reliefs were very necessary owing to the extremely uncomfortable living conditions on the site.

The Rocket Propelled Holdfast, then in its early days, was considered the best method of getting a cable across a gap. It was a fearsome instrument, with a rocket on the end of its six-foot spike. The RAF balloon cable attached to the end of the spike was coiled down in a series of tubs with the rocket mounted on its launching rack, pointed in the general direction of the other bank and fired electrically. On the first occasion, the rocket reached the top of its flight, curved over and fell on the far side of the river; the spike failed to stick in, but at least the cable was across and could be made fast.

After attaching the traveller and guy ropes, the cable was tensioned until it was about ten feet clear of the water at its lowest point, which was near the enemy bank, while on the home bank the cable was about seventy-five feet clear of the water. By the following morning the river had dropped sufficiently for a power boat to operate but though the quantity of debris had diminished the current was still too swift for a raft. Information now came through that this was the only ferry in operation on the divisional front and that a patrol of about 700 infantry and porters, who had been trapped on the enemy bank by the flood, were to return over it.

At about 2.00pm a successful trial run was made with the current running at about five feet per second. This speed was undoubtedly excessive and the raft required careful handling to avoid straining the cable and the guys. An hour later the infantry started to arrive on the enemy bank and the ferry operated continuously for the next five hours without a stop and without a hitch.

Ferrying now continued spasmodically for about a week, but again the weather broke and torrential rain brought another flood. By dawn the river had risen sixteen feet and was still rising. Current speed was up to ten feet per second and very large quantities of debris were coming down, including parts of an American M4 rubber pontoon bridge from farther upstream. The sheer legs on the far bank were three parts submerged.

At 7.00am next day the cable started to dip in the water and fifteen minutes later it caught the first piece of debris. This was a large log about twenty feet long and about twelve inches thick. The cable 'played' this log for about five minutes, alternately allowing it to float downstream and then, as the tension took up, whipping it clear out of the water and hurling it far upstream like a leaping salmon. Eventually the log was thrown off and in rapid succession two more were caught and 'played', often being tossed twenty feet or more into the air. The last was a massive log which, after a few minutes, caused the sheer legs on the far bank to overturn. About 200 feet of the cable flopped into the water. Every few seconds the cable was swept downstream, tightened, and leapt out of the water in a sheet of spray only to fall back in again. It was a most impressive sight with the cable behaving in almost human fashion. Time and again it leapt clear over a mass of debris until it eventually parted under a large load of debris at 1.00pm.

Word now came through that, emboldened by the initial success of the ferry, another patrol of nearly two companies would also be coming back across it as soon as they could get there. This was the largest party for some time and as things turned out they could not have chosen a worse time. Repairs were carried out quickly and a new cable replaced the one that had been swept away but, by 6.00pm, when the first bedraggled figures began to appear on the enemy bank, the river had risen eighteen feet and the current was up to ten feet per second.

Considerable amounts of debris were beginning to appear and the river was rising at a rate of nearly three feet an hour.

It was decided to try to take the raft across to the enemy side on a trial run in spite of the conditions. Under careful control it made the first crossing successfully, although there was constant danger of water coming in over the bows. Both the Commanding Officer and the Squadron Commander were on board (every subaltern's nightmare!). In spite of the successful crossing, however, it was obvious that with any worthwhile payload, the raft would be too dangerous.

The return trip started with six infantry as passengers. Halfway across, with water heaping up round the bows, one of the guys snapped. The raft immediately swung head on to the current and stopped, held only by the safety line. For half-an-hour the raft hung in the middle of the river with the water rising and increasing quantities of debris swirling past on both sides. By some miracle the raft was not actually hit, although there were some very close shaves. Eventually a jury rig was organized with the safety line and the remaining guy. Slowly the raft edged towards the bank until it was close enough for a breastline to be thrown. The raft was pulled in and a slightly shaken crew and passengers stepped thankfully on to dry land.

The time was now 7.30pm and the river had risen twenty-three feet. Current speed was up to twelve feet per second and all hope of ferrying had to be abandoned. During the night the river rose to a record height of thirty-two feet, with an estimated current speed of at least fifteen feet per second. At 4.00am, in spite of all precautions, the water reached the cable and the fierce current soon parted it. Large Chinese log rafts, bits of bridge and innumerable other logs were pouring downstream in an endless flow, including a complete Korean house, riding the flood well! There was no shortage of other less spectacular debris – whole tents floated down and the QM acquired a few spares.

Soon after dawn the river started to go down and at about 10.00am a successful crossing was made with an American operated powerboat, dodging debris on the way over. The patrol started to come back six at a time and by 3.00pm all were safely across.

Chapter 5

Advance over the Imjin

By September 1951 the Commonwealth Division had a very extended front of some five miles in width, comprising a series of mutually supporting localities, each capable of all round defence and normally of company strength, in the foothills south of the Imjin. Though much work had been accomplished on the divisional front, it was now felt that, further to raids across the Imjin, the Corps defensive line should be pushed forward, so in conjunction with 1st Republic of Korea (ROK) Division on the left and 1st US Cavalry Division on the right, the Commonwealth Division was ordered in early September to secure a new line of dominating features north of the Imjin. This was to be the first offensive operation by the Commonwealth Division since its formation. It was termed Operation COMMANDO and, put simply, it consisted of two broad phases: 28 Brigade was to cross the River Imjin to establish a bridgehead and then to advance to contact against Chinese positions on Hill 355 and Point 317, among others. The main tactical reason for launching the operation was to seize the ground held by the Chinese, which gave them observation from hilltops over some of the Imjin crossings and numerous stretches of roads. Considerable preparatory work was required before the operation could be launched: guns had to be moved over the Imjin, additional ammunition and other stocks had to be brought forward, the telephone network was expanded and the casualty and evacuation system was amplified.

On 1 October, 12 Field Squadron constructed a jeep track for the Australians, the first 200 yards being completed in darkness as the area was under enemy observation. At the same time, heavy rain made newly constructed roads difficult to maintain and 45th Field Regiment were unable to move their guns until 55 Field Squadron had repaired the road leading to their position.

Lashed by intermittent rain, forced at intervals to take cover from shellfire, the divisional engineers maintained and pushed forward the road network with dozers, graders and dumpers, together with

58

compressor tools, picks and shovels. They kept open the bridges and ferries. Not infrequently they were delayed by the discovery of mines, some laid many months before by one side or the other. In these conditions the roads and tracks for Operation COMMANDO were prepared.

Captain John Cormack had joined 12 Field Squadron, commanded by Major Howard Stephens, a few weeks earlier and his first task was to build an aerial ropeway over the Imjin, assisted by Danny Cadoux-Hudson and his Support Troop from 55 Squadron. They used a wild-kite winch with a large timber baulk with a corrugated-iron wrapping to run the cable and build a safe anchorage which they buried in a deep trench. The cable was crossed over the river, again using a Rocket Propelled Holdfast to a pair of sheer legs installed on the far bank. The first rocket disappeared into the far distance. Shortly afterwards, the first tentative peace talks with North Korea were called off abruptly, prompting Danny Cadoux-Hudson to suggest that the rocket must have landed near Kaesong and interrupted the talks being held there.

In the bridgehead, which was effectively a Forming Up Place (FUP), John Cormack with six sappers met up with the 8th King's Royal Irish Hussars (KRIH). Two other similar detachments from 12 Field Squadron were to accompany the leading tank troops and search likely places for mines. Infantry support was provided by the KSLI from 28 Brigade. John soon transferred to the leading Centurion tank, leaving the remainder of his troop with the KSLI and appropriate instructions. They set off along an old Japanese metalled road with John riding on the turret of the leading tank, but when they turned off the road they hit a well-concealed Chinese anti-tank mine. The tank stopped abruptly and John was blown upwards and landed down inside the tank in some discomfort, especially to his back. For the rest of the advance he walked. Soon afterwards the tank ahead of him slipped off one of its tracks while trying to manoeuvre round a hill. All tank crews had explosive charges to cut the tracks when this happened but, as the crew seemed a bit uncertain, John blew a charge and cut it. It was then rolled out as level as possible so that the tank could drive over it. This was done successfully, the broken track repaired and the tank carried on as though nothing had gone wrong.

As the advance continued they came under sporadic shellfire and fighting was severe in several places. When they leaguered for the night John tried sleeping inside the tank, but this proved too cramped and uncomfortable so he took to sleeping under the tank, making sure it was parked on solid ground. Next day the infantry cleared the Chinese forward position, which the Sappers were invited to occupy in case of a counter-attack. In addition to their normal weapons, their Troop Commander managed to acquire a supply of No. 36 grenades and they prepared themselves for action. The expected attack failed to materialize and they were relieved in due course and returned to more normal duties.

Sappers were always more than happy to revert to their normal tasks, but for the infantry there was no respite and Private Roy Carswell of the KSLI, defending what he thought of as 'A Worthless Hill', and with plenty of time to think, and to be afraid, committed his thoughts to poetry:

> *Dawn is nigh, when it comes, they will come!*
> *Am I to see tomorrow's dawn? Feel tomorrow's sun?*
> *Yonder appears the first pale streaks of light!*
> *Is this to be my last day? Was that my last night?*
>
> *Last night, filled with sound, a night of fear,*
> *Rising to a crescendo, now dawn is near.*
> *Tuneless bugles, crashing cymbals, a hideous sound.*
> *Am I to die here, for this worthless mound?*
>
> *This worthless mound that war's laid bare.*
> *What are they like, those strangers out there?*
> *Do they sweat with fear, as they wait to kill?*
> *Wait to kill or die, on this worthless hill.*
>
> *This is not my war! Not my dear land!*
> *Why have I been guided here by fate's cruel hand?*
> *For my country, my loved ones, I'd willingly die!*
> *Is this the foreign soil where my body will lie?*
>
> *Now I can see him, my fellow being.*
> *Daylight has sent the last shadows fleeing.*
> *A grey clad multitude has appeared into view.*
> *'Dear God! There are so many! We so few ...'*
>
> *'Look to your front!' A calm voice rings out.*
> *So this is what war is all about.*
> *'Pick out your targets! Fire at will'.*
> *Is this where life ends, on a Korean hill ...?*

Oliver Keef, who had arrived just in time for Operation COMMANDO, was posted to 12 Field Squadron and joined 1 Troop, as the Troop Officer under Captain Barry Pollard. His first job was to join a troop of 8th Hussars who were clearing the road to the south of Hill 355, which was being attacked by 1 KSLI. All was going smoothly until they came under artillery fire. Oliver was standing talking to the tank commander who promptly slammed down his hatch, leaving him and his driver

60

looking a bit foolish standing in the middle of the road. They dived for cover under the tank, where Oliver takes up the story:

Driver: 'Get yer head beside the bogie and you'll be okay, Sir.'
Oliver: 'Thank you.'
Driver (nervously): ''Ope it doesn't sink, Sir.'

The thought of 50 tons of Centurion descending on me seemed infinitely worse than the odd Chinese shell and I emerged just in time to see the RSM of the KSLI removing Chinese prisoners by the simple expedient of booting them up the road. He was over six feet tall and the Chinese were barely five foot and couldn't wait to get out of the way, the odd kick in the backside keeping them going.

For the next few months we were occupied in finding routes for jeep tracks to get supplies up to the newly won positions, improving them and checking them constantly for mines as the Chinese tended to infiltrate between our positions at night. Once it became clear that we were likely to stay in our current harbour area, we set to improve the Troop's domestic arrangements. These included a timber bunker below ground as a Mess for the officers and sergeants – in its way it was quite palatial with an open fire. All was well until a battery of American 'Long Toms' moved in behind us. They fired directly over us with a thunderous roar, shaking our prized bunker and eventually causing the fireplace to collapse. Inevitably they attracted counter-battery fire, most of which fell round us.

We then moved and I found myself sharing a tent with our New Zealand officer, Malcolm Velvin, who had commanded the NZ Base Engineer Section, composed mostly of reservists, highly qualified and older than the rest of us. They had been told to remain in Japan, but this was not what they had come for, so they had hitched a lift to Korea and arrived at 1 Troop of 12 Squadron 'on leave' and declined to go back to Japan at the end of it!

The main engineer problem was one of access roads and a new road into the 28 Brigade area from the right was vital. New gun positions north of the Imjin were also needed and were not easy to prepare at the end of the wet season in areas consisting largely of paddy fields. Since most tracks had to be side-hill cuts to avoid the paddy, much plant work and a great many culverts were needed. Everyone quickly became expert in choosing a line and in constructing a jeep track, and D4 angle-dozers were not infrequently worked right up to the forward company positions, so it was important to maintain close liaison with the local infantry. One of the best bulldozer operators, a reservist, had spent much of his Korean tour in a Squadron cookhouse until one day he admitted that he might be able to achieve something with a dozer. With this proliferation of roads and tracks and a dearth of villages and signposts, indeed there weren't even any villagers, it became essential to give them all nicknames. The major arteries were given colour codes, with numerals for the tracks leading off them, e.g., Purple One or Amber Three.

The slightly more settled existence also led to a rash of signs. Traditionally, they were usually restricted to bridges, but amateur artists abounded and were only waiting to display their talent. 'Windmill Bridge' was soon accompanied nearby by a smaller 'Windmill Papoose Bridge', suitably embellished by a comely papoose. A particularly dangerous piece of twisting road had a large 'Dangerous Curves' notice board, but most accidents were caused by drivers distracted by the lines of the accompanying curves.

Tanks were often used in twos and threes, in hull-down positions, to strengthen forward positions. The supply of ammunition to them became a problem, due to the lack of suitable tracks, and the Field Park Squadron solved the problem by manufacturing heavy timber sledges, strong enough to be towed by tanks across all but the roughest country. One was seen being dragged through a ford over the Imjin, reportedly at 20mph, with no ill effects to sledge or load.

Few would have expected at that time that the line then reached was to remain virtually unchanged for the rest of the war. This is not to say that some very fierce fighting was not still to come. The positions occupied by the Division were more commanding than the enemy's, but the troops were spread very thinly on the ground and initially the battalions occupying such hill features as Hills 355, 217 and 317 felt exposed as they waited for the inevitable Chinese attack. Being so short of infantry, it was no surprise to John Cormack when he was told to act as infantry once again. Forming his Troop into a proper infantry platoon this time, he was ordered to take up a defensive position in support of 3rd Battalion, Royal Australian Regiment (3 RAR), a position he held for over a week. Supporting the Australians was always quite an experience and, when he asked for advice on his platoon layout, he was visited by an enthusiastic Australian captain who turned out to be a well known character, one of the first Aborigines to receive a commission. He was quite a soldier, with plenty of experience and a great sense of fun: one warm day he produced a water bottle and invited John to have a drink. He took a large swig and nearly fell down – the bottle was full of rum!

At first his platoon was only lightly armed with three Bren light machine guns (LMGs) and one 2-inch mortar. He later acquired a further three LMGs, three more 2-inch mortars and a Browning medium machine gun. They soon had the best barbed wire obstacle, as well as an anti-personnel protective minefield, in the Brigade. John, however, felt very conspicuous armed with a pistol and took to carrying a Russian rifle he had taken from a Chinese soldier whom he had captured. This was his first experience of being a fully-fledged rifle platoon commander, something he was to repeat with 1st King's Own Scottish Borderers (KOSB) and later with the Norfolks.

By 8 October all the Division's objectives had been reached and work to consolidate the new line began in earnest. 12 Squadron was made available for a large minelaying programme for 28 Brigade on the right flank of the Division. Mines were laid between defensive positions to hamper Chinese infiltration but some could not be covered by small-arms fire. Nevertheless, they undoubtedly helped to confuse and delay the Chinese troops when they attacked eventually in early November 1951. Intense fighting took place over the next few days but the enemy was unable to achieve any advance. For a critical twenty-four hours during this period two Troops of 12 Squadron occupied fall-back positions during the night in case of a Chinese breakthrough.

Captain John Page was also involved, commanding two Sapper detachments in the vicinity of Hill 317. When one of his Sappers was wounded seriously, no stretcher bearers being available, he carried the wounded man several hundred yards across the hillside under small-arms and mortar fire and placed him on one of the supporting tanks which were about to leave the position. He undoubtedly saved the wounded man's life, having shown great coolness under heavy fire.

The Chinese clearly now had a great deal of artillery, plus the expertise to use it, and were well provided with ammunition. Effectively they had breached our wire and nearly every slit trench not on the steepest reverse slope had received a hit near enough to blow in the overhead cover. Telephone lines had been cut early on, something that seemed to happen at the start of every battle, and radio sets could not be relied on unless sets were well protected.

Meanwhile, behind the forward units, attention was being paid to the crossings over the Imjin. A secure supply line was of paramount importance and it was decided that the crossings had to be upgraded sufficiently to withstand the next monsoon rains in the summer of 1952. In the meanwhile, in September 1951, US Engineers had built a Class 50 pontoon bridge across the river at the 'Pintail' crossing, with a further floating bridge at 'Teal'. Until the longer term projects were completed, in the summer of 1952, the Division had to rely on these two bridges, 'Pintail' and 'Teal', together with a fordable crossing farther upstream and a causeway on the western flank, originally constructed by the Korean army and known as 'Widgeon'. There was also a cableway, with a 500lb load capacity, upstream of 'Teal' to be activated in case the bridge became unusable. It could carry across two-and-a-half to three tons an hour over long periods and up to nearly five tons an hour in emergencies.

Snow fell in November and frost came with a vengeance during December. The Imjin, now a placid river, only 300 feet wide at 'Pintail', froze on 12 December 1951. More snow fell on Boxing Day and the landscape was white for the next five weeks. With increasingly low overnight temperatures, everyone learnt to pay attention to a number of necessary precautions. For instance, to ensure that heavy plant and vehicles would start up in the morning, fuel tanks were refuelled to the brim to prevent water condensation and then ice formation in the fuel systems. Vehicles were never parked on soft ground. All mud was cleaned off tracks and rollers which were then fully greased to push water out of track lubricating systems. At water-points all storage tanks and filters had to be housed in heated tents or shelters, where pumps and emptied hoses also had to be placed before nightfall.

It was a considerable relief, therefore, when a new range of winter clothing began to reach units. The clothing had actually begun to arrive in September, but a disastrous fire at the Ordnance Depot destroyed everything and resulted in frantic re-supply efforts. Units had to submit detailed sizes for everyone, but the War Office (as it then was), in its infinite wisdom chose this moment to alter the system of sizing! Distribution was further delayed ... However, the clothing when it did arrive was first class. Compared with the clothing that the first arrivals had in the previous winter, everybody was well dressed to cope with the winter: string vests, which took a bit of getting used to, long drawers were handy for their Y rears as opposed to their Y fronts (with an overlapping slit in the rear for you know what), thick shirts and the first of the Army's excellent 'woolly pullies' with draw strings at neck and waist. The boots were CWW (Cold Wet Weather), with a plastic honey-combed insole to provide good insulation. The insoles had to be shaken out whenever the boots were taken off to get rid of the perspiration which always seemed to accumulate no matter how cold the weather. If this was forgotten, the boots became even harder than usual when it came to putting them on in the morning. The best winter item, though, was undoubtedly the fur-lined Parka with its enormous hood with a soft wire edge which could be bent to keep any required shape. It also had a large 'tail' which could be buttoned up between the legs to keep in the warmth. The Parkas kept everyone warm and the wind out but, though much appreciated, often had to be discarded, along with their gloves, by men on minelaying duties who had to keep fingers free and needed the ability to hear. Sergeant 'Dai' Evans, of 12 Field Squadron, had been seen the previous winter encouraging Sappers to put their hands in their trouser pockets, quite contrary to normal army practice.

The dress code was in fact pretty relaxed and men wore cap comforters, berets (worn in many different styles), or even ski caps, whichever they felt was most comfortable. Steel helmets were supposed to be worn in many areas, but they were uncomfortable and heavy. Early type 'Flak Jackets' began to arrive and took a bit of getting used to as they were cumbersome to work in but good to keep the cold out.

Even more important, and a great morale raiser at the end of a hard day's work for all Sappers not on night work, such as accompanying patrols into no man's land, mine-laying, booby-trapping or strengthening our forward defences, was the provision of a hot drink and a warm and reasonably comfortable *hoochie* to go to. It was equally important to officers, who often had to think and write late into the night after an active day in the open.

Chapter 6

Life in the Line

Being largely static by this stage of the war, life behind the line was a great contrast with what went on in the forward area. Perhaps little less than a mile back, there were regimental signs, Messes, military police and an almost palpable air of normality. Men slept in tents, often rather gloomy affairs, lighting being reserved for the canteen. Wherever possible they would be placed on the north side of a re-entrant where they could be relatively safe from long-range artillery fire and were standing on platforms dug out of the hillside. Ammunition and explosives were stored in bays excavated into the side of the hill, well away from the tents. Drink was rationed strictly to Asahi beer from Japan, though the ration had a nasty habit of dwindling away during its long transit through the Lines of Communication. Improvised showers were welcome and men soon got used to twin, or even foursome, deep trench latrines (DTLs), often a source for exchanging gossip.

Though there was little time for recreation, each Troop invariably made a volleyball pitch on the nearest patch of flat ground where any number of men could take part and also benefit from the exercise. There was always plenty to occupy everyone and there was also the chance to see a film in one of the larger camps and even the occasional concert party. There was also plenty of opportunity to improve the standard of small-arms shooting. With no peacetime concerns about range safety, it was comparatively easy to use a neighbouring re-entrant as a range and full use was made of the abundance of ammunition. Care had to be taken, though, not to set the hillside on fire and unmarked minefields were an added hazard. Working by day and often by night throughout the divisional area, Sappers had to live close to their work and seldom remained in one locality long enough to make themselves comfortable. Every Field Squadron and, in fact, each of its three Field Troops moved more frequently than the infantry brigades and battalions to which they were affiliated.

In the forward area, under constant observation, food, ammunition and stores were brought up under cover of darkness. After dark, particularly on a position like the Hook and its adjoining hills, a procession of carrying parties would make their way along trenches, the walls of which seemed designed to catch on every protuberance. They were helped by the KSC porters, few of whom understood more than a word or two of English, but who were, for the most part, uncomplaining and absolutely invaluable.

In the early days after the Commonwealth Division was formed, the main Sapper task was still road construction and repair, but there were numerous other tasks as well. From the most forward positions, and often in front of them where Sappers were on patrols and laying mines, right back to the rear of the divisional area, Sappers were forever busy, seven days a week. As static conditions continued, and the size and quantity of Chinese artillery increased and their techniques improved, emphasis was placed more and more on the construction of field works. Shell-proof bunkers and dug-outs were designed and constructed on all defended localities. Meanwhile, nearly one hundred miles of roadway were constructed in the divisional area and many thousands of mines were laid around the forward positions.

During the depth of winter there was less work to be done on the roads as everything was rock hard and the roads stood up to the traffic. Throughout the winter, though, existing roads had to be kept free of ice and snow, no small task in itself. However, the situation changed dramatically in the spring when the thaw arrived. Roads could start disappearing under even quite light traffic, almost while looking at them, and the Divisional airstrip was a constant pain. The main trouble on the hilly roads was that the culverts were the last to thaw, so the run-offs overflowed at each one with drastic effects. Empty oil drums were often used for culverts; the tops and bottoms were easily cut out using a cold chisel and mash hammer, though a more popular method was a couple of turns of Cordtex explosive fuse. The drill was to blow or dig out the whole culvert with a compressor hammer or small charge of explosive, remake it and then move on to the next one. The British NCOs found that the KSCs were not strong enough in the arm to work the hammers (though they could and did carry immense loads on their A-frames on their backs), so they had to do most of that work themselves. Gradually a system was built up which the Regimental LO had to control. Excavators dug out loads of Imjin rock and stone and loaded it into trucks driven by an American transport company, which was brought up from the rear of the Corps, and taken to the collapsed road. KSC gangs then repaired the road at any time of day or night, especially if there was a flap on. Ammunition convoys had to get through and this produced problems on narrow roads, especially if half the road was

67

being repaired at the same time. When the weather improved, a New Zealand Sapper used to go round virtually all the roads with a grader and did a tremendous job. Nobody ever seemed to know who he was or where he came from – he was just known as 'Kiwi' and was a really cheerful chap.

Another of the LO's tasks was to obtain and supervise the KSC's pay. This was in the local currency, the *Wan*. There had been intense inflation since the war started and it took fourteen sandbags of *Wan* to pay out the three companies. The acquittance rolls were made out in Korean script and there was no way that a British officer could check anything. The system was that that the LO handed what he understood to be the right amount to the KSC company commander, who supervised matters thereafter. If there was a surplus at the end, so well and good and he kept it with no questions asked. If there was too little and the 'tail end Charlies' did not get paid, well that was just too bad, and it was supposed that he did something about it. The LO never had to account for the money to the Field Cashier from whence it came as he was only too glad to get rid of it. Later on there was a devaluation of the currency and one *Whan* became worth ten *Wan*. This was much easier for the LO as he now only had to carry one and a half sandbags of money.

Dug-outs and trenches were hard to keep clean. The effects of shell-fire and subsidence were repaired during the hours of darkness, but the erosion of shell splinters, mortar bombs and bullets often gave the trenches a pretty shoddy appearance. Under such conditions it is terribly easy for everything, and everyone, to get dirty and dispirited so it was important to maintain discipline and morale. Commonwealth Division units, on the whole, kept up their high standards and commanding officers insisted that trenches and dug-outs had to be spotless: rubbish had to be collected and taken back by porters to rear areas for disposal, tins were buried and empty beer bottles (in great demand in Seoul) were sold and the proceeds put into unit welfare funds.

Latrines and urinals had to be kept scrupulously keen, not at all easy on hill positions near the enemy, but essential if infection was to be avoided. Most of the former were sited on the reverse slope and once a man reached the 'thunder box' he could relax and relieve himself in conditions of reasonable security. To get there, though, often meant a hazardous journey along communication trenches and it was not desirable for all the occupants of a weapon pit to be stricken with a simultaneous urge. Urinals were let into the sides of trenches so did not present the same problem but a distinct odour of war permeated the whole area.

Primary functions aside, the hardship of dirt was difficult to overcome. Gone were the days when soldiers wore serge shirts for days, even in the hottest weather, leading Queen Victoria to ask what the strange aroma was when reviewing a parade. 'Esprit de corps, Ma'am,' was the reply.

Even on the coldest of days in Korea, soldiers stripped to the waist to wash and had a proper shower once a week at the Mobile Laundry and Bath Unit. Cleanliness, foot inspections, DDT and anti-malaria pills all contributed to the health of units, and shaving was good for morale. The danger of disease in these living conditions was ever-present and it was important to keep inoculations up to date. Men would be lined up for their jabs in front of the Medical Officer and there was always an unseemly rush to be in the front of the queue. The first served always got the needle when it was sharp and nobody ever seemed any the worse for receiving the same one. Dentistry was also important and though fillings were carried out using what might seem to have been primitive foot-operated treadle machines they were remarkably efficient. In addition to the usual health hazards, Korea harboured an unpleasant and potentially fatal tick-borne disease, Haemorrhagic Fever, or Scrub Typhus. Clothing had to be treated regularly to ward off the carriers, a tedious process to say the least.

While sickness was kept to the minimum, those who were wounded received prompt and efficient treatment. Helicopters were available to fly seriously wounded from Regimental Aid Posts direct to the American or Norwegian MASH (Mobile Advance Surgical Hospital) where they were on the operating table in minutes. For Sappers and Infantry alike, this was a great comfort, especially on hills like the Hook where there was a constant danger from shell and mortar fire, with a steady stream of casualties.

The Korean way of installing central heating was to build broad flues under the floors of their homes. In Seoul there were some elaborate such systems. Even in the mud and lath-walled and thatched shacks in the poorest villages the principle was the same. They built a fireplace outside at a level lower than the floor. The flue from this led straight into one or more broad flues under and right across the floor of the living room, coming out at the far end into a normal vertical flue or chimney. Many of the locally enlisted Korean Service Corps built for themselves this form of under-floor heating in their hillside shelters and similar heaters were constructed in the rear areas where the heater itself was placed outside, say, an office truck with a double chimney constructed with different size shell cases (of which there was no shortage!), with the hot air between the two skins channelled into the offices through openings in the outer casing.

With a bit more time during the winter months, tradesmen often had a chance to practise their trade. Travelling in open vehicles in the severe winter conditions was punishing and Corporal Hawton was happy to winterize a Jeep for one of the Commanding Officers, especially as he was rewarded with 'a bottle worth drinking'. Another task was to build a brick fireplace for the Brigade HQ Mess, using second-hand bricks from a ruined building and a fine piece of timber for the mantelpiece, for which they received many compliments, though no bottle.

The extreme cold in the winter months led to the very real hazard of 'fire'. Petrol, of which there never appeared to be a shortage, was the main fuel. Although more dangerous, it was cleaner to use than paraffin or diesel, though a number of young soldiers, and not a few older ones, learnt that petrol, when warmed up not only vaporizes most efficiently but, when subsequently lit, doesn't burn – it explodes, with surprising force. A combination of improvised stoves and tents was a sure recipe for disaster and there were endless courts of enquiry into the many fires, including one where the Court itself was sitting at the time. It was late in the winter of 1951 before proper diesel-burning 'space heaters' became available for heating shelters, tented offices, messes and caravans. In the meantime, every conceivable type of improvised stove had been installed in tents dugouts and *hoochies*, but the official space heaters were a great improvement and it was not long before most tents were equipped with an oil-fired space heater with a pipe through the roof, but they could get very hot and ignite the canvas. A few weeks after arrival Tony Kendall returned to his bivouac after being out all day to find it was a pile of ash and much later on, when sharing a small tent with the other officers, they woke to find it on fire and had to evacuate very quickly indeed, taking whatever belongings they could grab. One of 2 Troop's Sappers, while farther back in a rest area, had a disturbing experience when he was in his sleeping bag and his *hoochie* caught fire. He felt he could hardly leap out as he was tucked up with a pretty Korean girl – fortunately his friends came to his rescue, doused the flames and saved him from embarrassment. He took some time, though, to live it down.

Looking back, Troop Officers for the most part were in blissful ignorance of how their administrative backing was provided. Everything was taken for granted. In the case of the Chinese soldier, he did not require most of the amenities which the Western soldier always regarded as necessities and, consequently, a much higher proportion of men were actual combatants. The West, on the other hand, relied on a staff and administrative organization of great complexity, whose numbers often far exceeded the front-line combatants. Every big move, or air strike, involved staff work in the form of orders, instructions or messages, sent over a complicated system of communications, manned by highly technical personnel using very elaborate and costly equipment. Thankfully, Troop Officers in the Field Squadrons had none of these worries and belonged to that very exclusive club whose members were those in actual contact with the enemy.

Though Troop Officers saw few outside people, apart from the unit they were supporting, one person who was always around was the unit padre and the Commonwealth Division was blessed with having some excellent ones. Apart from Sam Davies, the Glosters' inspirational padre, another well-known padre in the Division came from St Martin-in-the Field, by Trafalgar Square, and the Black Watch had a memorable, and much loved, chaplain who, before he took Orders, had been a company commander in North West Europe and had won a Military Cross. He was always available for advice and consolation, not always of a spiritual nature in the case of some of the company commanders who also valued his wartime experience. He conducted regular Services and it was always noticeable to see how many soldiers attended, particularly on the eve of battle when there were few unbelievers around. Another excellent Padre was with the Royal Tank Regiment, who endeared himself to everyone when he conducted the funeral of a member of 55 Field Squadron. It was taking place beside the road, with a lowering cloud base and deluging with rain, when an American Jeep stopped and asked the way, seemingly unaware that a funeral service was taking place. The Padre stopped, looked the Americans up and down, gave them instructions and then added 'Now, piss off!', or words to that effect. He had expressed what everyone felt, it broke the tension and the Sapper mourners were all cheered. His predecessor had been a RASC driver in the Second World War before entering the Church and wanted the Troopers to call him by his Christian name. The men didn't like this familiarity, reckoning that padres should be treated like officers, and had no intention of calling him 'Sid', or anything else. He left the Regiment very quickly, a rare failure in the Chaplains Department.

For some time the contrast between the UN and Chinese lines had been most marked; from the air, miles of trenches stretching like a road network were visible behind the Chinese lines. Some trenches were two metres deep, up to ten kilometres long and wide enough to allow mules to pass. While these communication trenches were not camouflaged, their dugouts, tunnels and gun pits were certainly well concealed. The Chinese simply had to dig to survive. As the weight of Chinese artillery effort increased and its accuracy improved, the need for a similar policy in the UN battle positions became obvious, and a much more comprehensive digging policy was laid down by Division. As a result the CRE ordered a lumber camp, known as Nuthatch, to be set up by 57 Squadron RCE at a site several kilometres to the south. The Canadian Sappers were naturally adept at this lumberjacking and HQRE produced designs for command posts and bunkers, which were to be dug to a depth of thirteen feet and carried five feet of overhead cover so that they could ensure survival from two direct hits from 155mm shells.

Captain John Hackford, who had already been in Korea for some time, took over 2 Troop of 55 Squadron on the sad death of Bertie Bayton-Evans. The Troop was 'in support' of the Leicesters and on a number of occasions John took their patrols out through non-recorded Korean or Chinese minefields, and became known as 'that mad Sapper who walked in front of them dangling a long twig (to try to feel, if not to see, any trip-wires)'.

Thought was still being given to the useful occupation of the Division's excellent tanks, many of which were employed as mobile pillboxes on the forward hills, but this was really no role for the Royal Armoured Corps. In the summer months it was virtually impossible for tanks to move cross country without sinking into the paddy fields, but in the winter the ground was frozen solid and movement was thought to be possible. In the middle of February 1952, 5th Royal Inniskilling Dragoon Guards (5DG), who had replaced the 8th Hussars, carried out a series of small raids to destroy enemy bunkers. John Hackford took a party of Sappers with him in a 5DG 'tug', a turretless Centurion tank. The tug's driver and radio operator, its only crew, explained how, lacking a turret, it was ten tons lighter so could go where other tanks couldn't and pull any disabled tanks to safety. Lacking a gun, it had no need for ammunition racks, so there was room for up to six men inside. They had not gone far when one tank slid into another on an icy slope, delaying the whole operation. Further progress was impeded by tanks being unable to operate on the frozen ground and the operation had to be called off, but not before Lieutenant Peter Park, riding in one of the other tanks, had been killed by an exploding mine. John Hackford related how he cringed whenever he felt an anti-personnel mine went off under his tank and thanked the Lord that it wasn't an anti-tank mine.

Sometimes 5DG would position a Centurion tank as a pillbox on top of a hill by the infantry forward positions. One day one slipped down the forward slope and John Hackford was ordered to go down to it with explosives and destroy the still-secret mechanism which kept the barrel aimed at a target when moving over rough ground. As he fixed the charge inside the turret, he was pleased that a mist had rolled in and hid their activities from the Chinese. When he blew the charge from the company position up the hill, it somehow started the tank's engine. Everyone stared down at it as it seemed so creepy and ghostly.

Chapter 7

Operation Dragon

On the left of the Divisional sector, the River Samichon came into the Imjin from the north and there was a wide expanse of paddy fields stretching into no man's land and then up between the Chinese-held hills on either side. Three miles up the valley lay the village of Ku-Wa-Ri which air-photos showed was the location of a considerable supply dump and so it was decided to stage a bold raid up the valley, codeword DRAGON.

The possibility of the Samichon Valley proving suitable for tanks had not eluded the Chinese, who had dug a substantial anti-tank ditch across it. With the frost, the walls of the ditch would be as hard as concrete so there was no hope of the tanks crossing it unless it was bridged or broken down. With no assault engineer equipment available in theatre, a small party of Sappers would be needed. The plan was that the party, led by Captain Angus McKay Forbes, would travel in a Centurion tug to blow down the walls and then get back to their tank, ready for the next task. Operation DRAGON was considered to be highly important, and was also highly secret.

It was decided to carry out trials behind the lines before launching the operation and a two-stage procedure evolved gradually, using a length of specially dug ditch. It was decided finally that a large special charge was to be laid against the far wall, detonated from the tank. This made a deep hole which was then stuffed full of further explosive and again fired. Though it seemed to work it was going to be pretty hazardous, especially for the Sapper party.

To destroy camouflaged dumps in the open, like those at Ku-Wa-Ri, would be much easier said than done. Both the CRE, Colonel Eddie Myers, and the CO, Lieutenant Colonel Peter Moore, had spent a good part of the Second World War with guerrillas, one in Greece and the other in Yugoslavia, and they knew from personal experience that to blow up an ammunition dump was remarkably difficult. Various boxes of ammunition and explosives were assembled for the trial and attacked with a variety of explosive devices but most of the stacks usually remained apparently undamaged but probably in a highly dangerous state. Explosive effects are not always the same and one of the experimental blasts, initiated by carefully placed charges, detonated very little of its intended target but lobbed a mortar bomb into our own positions in the next valley where stood a much-prized stack of ammunition, which was certainly not intended for destruction. The mortar bomb, falling entirely at random, set the lot off, causing considerable consternation.

Lovely warm days started to thaw the frozen paddy fields upon which the whole feasibility of Operation DRAGON depended and day after day the 'not before ...' date for the operation had to be put back. After about a fortnight, the days and nights became very cold again, but an officer returning from R&R leave in Tokyo reported that Operation DRAGON was being discussed openly in his hotel. Even with complete secrecy it would have been a very dangerous undertaking, so once it was out in the open, it was decided to cancel the operation, to the relief of several Sappers.

Chapter 8

Roads Again

During the early part of 1952 it seemed that a Chinese spring offensive was most probable. Although the Division was well established north of the River Imjin, an alternative reserve line of greater strength, called Line Kansas, was selected south of the river. Two access routes were started by 12 Squadron, both running through valleys with little top soil but lots of granite. Bulldozers could not touch the rock and the earth itself was frozen nearly as hard. A combination of explosives and bee-hives (shaped charges), using about four tons per mile, was employed to carve out a four-metre wide roadway. Meanwhile, three major landing strips in the divisional area were built by 57 Squadron of the Royal Canadian Engineers, including the Divisional HQ airstrip on the south bank of the Imjin. Minelaying continued and training courses were run for assault pioneer platoons in the infantry battalions. There was unfortunately never enough time for fully adequate training and a hard core of Sappers was always required for minelaying to ensure safety and correct procedures.

Patrolling, with the aim of capturing prisoners, became more intense and more skilful on both sides. On several occasions Chinese patrols managed to pass through our lines; one such patrol ambushed a mine re-supply vehicle from 12 Squadron. The NCO in charge evaded capture but was wounded, while the driver was taken prisoner. Thereafter night movement over certain routes was by convoy, under escort.

Towards the end of February a big engineer effort was once again mounted to prepare routes for the thaw. Route maintenance received an even higher priority. Ditch clearing, culverting and potholing, necessary but not exciting, became the order of the day. Even during the hard winter frost the heavy traffic caused a rippling, corrugated surface on the earth roads. Motor graders were the most suitable plant for smoothing out the 'wash board' effect on road surfaces, but they were in short supply. The most effective improvised device for surface maintenance was to drag a Bailey transom at an angle behind a 3-ton truck. 'Dragging', as it was called, was an exceptionally boring task but a sense of pride in the state of their own particular road was induced gradually amongst the Sappers engaged in this routine task, which had to continue all the year round. Many miles of low-gear work for this task added to vehicle serviceability problems.

The very severe weather during January through to March 1952 caused considerable damage to roads. The two main results were frost heave as the temperatures fell and the delayed result of frost boil when the thaw set in towards the end of March. In the case of frost heave the road surface broke up and constant pothole repairs were required; when frost boils occurred the road structure, already strained by frost heave, disintegrated into slush under the weight of the traffic. It was found that, with a prompt and reliable reporting system, it was possible to keep frost heave, or boil damage, under control by digging out the patch concerned and filling with stones, subject of course to operational use of the road. Regular sapper air reconnaissance of roads in the divisional area reinforced the reporting system but the troop commanders had to cover a proportion of their roads every day to check on surface and drainage.

Tippers pre-loaded with hardcore were on standby wherever operations permitted. Hundreds of tons of stone were quarried and moved daily by the Commonwealth Sappers using KSC labour, with *grizzlies* and *chinamen* for loading, and plant holdings grew far beyond the normal establishment. Prevention of frost damage was inevitably found to be in the proper drainage of roads before winter set in, requiring a combination of adequate side and catchwater drains, which together with culverts, needed constant maintenance to keep them free from obstruction.

Chapter 9

Spring Returns

The Korean countryside, so brown or snow-covered all winter, came to life again in April. The country took on a much kindlier aspect with the dead grass gone and the hillsides covered in purple azaleas and other flowering shrubs. This coincided with a divisional sidestep, coupled with a brigade redeployment, and Hill 355, to the north of the Divisional area, again came under our control, raising, once more, the minefield problem. Divisional policy had always been to count any friendly dominated area as safe unless marked as a minefield, but the Americans, who had been the previous tenants of Hill 355, had come to regard all areas as dangerous unless marked safe. This was not altogether surprising as the heavy fighting in the area had obliterated most of the perimeter fences and landmarks, as well as rendering most of the tripwires ineffective. As a result, though, it required a considerable and courageous effort on the part of many Sapper reconnaissance parties to plot and re-mark the minefields and any gaps. Courage was also required by those Sappers attached to forward companies who were invaluable in guiding infantry patrols through the numerous mine-fields. Prominent among these were Corporal Fox, who was awarded the Military Medal, and Lance Corporal Green, as well as Sappers Allen and Sheerin. Sadly, minefield casualties continued, including the death in 12 Field Squadron of Sergeant Morgan and the wounding of Sergeant Newman.

As a result of this experience the divisional minelaying policy was modified and the use of trip wires was abandoned. American M2 jumping mines, with pressure fuses only, were to be laid to the British pattern of four mines per yard of front – the immediate effect being a logistic one, with one and a quarter tons of mines being required for every 100 yards of minefield. Though trip wires were not to be used any more, existing ones continued to cause problems. Second Lieutenant Ian Thomson, newly arrived in 2 Troop of 55 Field Squadron, and with no previous experience, was sent out soon after arrival to gap three anti-personnel minefields for an operation, a hazardous task at the best of times and extremely daunting for a young subaltern. Shortly after dark he was informed that some soldiers had strayed into one of the mine-fields which consisted of Schu-mines as well as anti-personnel mines. In conjunction with the Assault Pioneer Platoon officer of the battalion he organized illumination of the area with mortar flares and then moved into the field himself, insisting on tackling the more dangerous Schu-mines and assisting in the rescuing of two men. A few days later, conducting a recce with his OC, Major Derek Fletcher, of a minefield of M3s in some long grass, his boot got entangled in a trip wire. Derek calmly traced the position of the mine, following the trip wire, disarmed the M3 and disentangled the trip wire from Ian's boot.

Being the man he was, Derek never mentioned the incident and indeed, with his quiet nature, he was largely unknown outside the Squadron. He was one of those men who needed no flamboyance or macho image to be admired and respected, but his men would have followed him anywhere. He was known affectionately by them as 'Granny' Fletcher due to his granny spectacles and his resemblance to an academic or aesthete, rather than a fighting warrior, but he had the reputation of a man who led from the front and his Jeep driver told of him standing upright with his Sten gun blazing away to cover his men's withdrawal from a sticky situation. He also carried out numerous reconnaissances in the forward area under fire and was subsequently awarded the DSO.

Each Troop had its own camp, with 2 Troop being just south of Hill 355 which was then occupied by the Welch Regiment. They were about two miles across the valley from the main Chinese positions, with Squadron HQ two miles farther back. The camp was occasionally shelled. Their general Sapper jobs included digging a reserve defence position behind Hill 355 and they were also tasked with building a road to support the Leicesters. This consisted of a six-inch rock base with a laterite top-coat, with material coming from the stone and laterite quarries operated by the Regiment. The Troop had its own detachment of KSC who worked on the roads or in the quarries under the super-vision of an NCO. They were particularly effective in wet weather when heavy plant tended to churn up the ground and create a sea of mud. The finish on a road worked on by them was often superior to that produced by machines.

Minefields continued to be laid, using American M2s and M3s, work-ing by night. The sappers first laid the mines unarmed and erected the perimeter fence. The Troop Commander or the Troop Officer then entered the minefield and armed the mines by removing the pins and then made sure that the minefield was correctly marked on the map. The CO, Peter

78

Moore, often visited minelaying parties, usually appearing carrying a heavy box of mines on his shoulder. His energy was prodigious and his personal bravery was renowned, so he was held in awe, and not just by the Regiment. He had the uncanny knack of turning up just when things were going wrong on a project or operation – but his wrath was often tempered with an encouraging word or two which saved the day. It was important not to make the same mistake twice!

When the grass had grown up in the summer, it was very difficult to locate the mines and many were set off by wandering deer and wild pigs. Minefields became the bane of our lives and more about them can be seen in Chapter 12.

On 7 July 1952, despite reservations as to the state of the 'going', a Squadron of Centurions from 5DG was sent across the Samichon valley as part of a daylight raid. One of the tanks was blown up on a mine which broke the engine mountings. The tank was bogged down and could not be pulled back as it had fallen over a bund into the field below. Ian Thomson was sent with a party of Sappers to clear the mine-field round the tank so that a dozer could excavate the bund behind the tank. This took several days in full view of the enemy and while they were doing this Ian was wounded in the stomach and chest by a Chinese mortar and had to be 'cas-evaced' to the MASH, via the Indian Field Ambulance. He was then airlifted to Japan, operated on and sent to the Rest Camp in Miyajima, getting back to the Squadron about a month later.

At about this time a much-needed second forward supply route was constructed from near 'Pintail' bridge to ease the supply position up to the vicinity of Hill 355. Construction took about six weeks, with special drainage arrangements across paddy fields.

At the same time 55 Squadron erected and manned a cableway for priority stores to Hill 355. It was powered by an ancient 15cwt truck, one of whose back wheels acted as a winch which hauled a trailer up and down a slope of about 1:1, on the end of a long cable which was reeved through innumerable snatch blocks. The winch station attracted a certain amount of enemy attention, but by taking advantage of early morning mist and the brief summer darkness, the service was main-tained for some weeks. Sadly, no sooner had they handed it over to another squadron than the enemy, most inconsiderately, cut the cable, much to the inconvenience of the driver who had to dodge the trailer as it came down rather more rapidly than it went up. After this, it was decided to blast a track up to the summit, which would not be quite so easy to destroy. Nevertheless, supplies to forward positions remained fraught and everyone, including visitors, carried something useful from the pile of stores at the jeep-head. Incoming mortar fire was always a problem and camouflage screens were erected along the more exposed roads and jeep tracks. Nevertheless, in dry weather a passing vehicle would throw up a cloud of dust which could still be spotted through the screening. One track leading towards Hill 355 was nicknamed the 'Bowling Alley'. It was often targeted.

Preparations for the 1952 rains had been made in good time. The CO, Peter Moore, was continually aware that a sudden rise in the level of the Imjin after rainstorms could sweep away bridges and ferries, leaving only cableways to supply the Division on the north bank. The engineer counter-flood plan, 'Noah's Ark', provided specified tasks at all critical points and the squadrons were ready to switch to flood control at short notice. Construction of a high-level trestle bridge, made entirely of timber, was undertaken at 'Teal', downstream from 'Pintail'. American Engineers also built a two-way steel and concrete bridge at 'Pintail' and completed it four days before the first major floods. Both crossings were supplemented by cableways and rafts, Class 50/60 at 'Pintail' and M4 American equipment at 'Teal'. Since the possibility always existed of a withdrawal south, either because of enemy pressure or of river conditions, demolition chambers were incorporated in both of the new bridges and demolition drills were frequently practised. In addition, special arrangements were made to keep the bridges open during times of flood. An organization was set up which included special observers and a troop of tanks to shoot up large pieces of debris. Unfortunately, ricochets from the tank guns were apt to cause consternation. This was particularly so in the case of 64 Field Park Squadron, who were the recipients of almost a score of 20-pounder shells landing in their squadron lines, some bursting within five yards of a group of sappers, fortunately without wounding anyone. A querulous call to Regimental Headquarters elicited a heartless reply of 'Dig in or get out'. The tanks themselves were quite upset that their firing had failed to hit anyone.

Sheers were designed and installed by 64 Field Park Squadron on the bridge piers, and motor tug teams stood by to guide debris through the spans, or to demolish obstructions in the gaps with explosives. 12 Squadron was made responsible for 'Teal' and a newly-arrived Canadian squadron for 'Pintail'.

Though 'Pintail' survived the floods, 'Teal' bridge was overwhelmed in the first major flood on 29 July 1952. Despite heroic efforts by Sappers to clear the debris with explosives, the bridge was swept away, creating a 280-foot gap. The real tragedy of the day, though, was the failure to land an American squad tent, complete with duck boards and shower unit, which came floating down from upstream and had just too much way on to be guided into the bank by motorboat. It touched one of the remaining piers as it sailed through the bridge and sank without trace. By midday on the 29th, the river had risen thirty feet and for the remainder of the flood season 12 Squadron had to be content with an

M4 ferry at 'Teal', backed up with a cableway for small stores. Some units were cut off temporarily by flood water, not just from the Imjin but also from the smaller rivers, and all the squadrons had to abandon other work in order to re-establish communications. The Army Air Corps were also called on to help with reconnaissance. Assault boats had to be sent to the KOSB with supplies and others were sent with 20-pounder ammunition for the tanks. Fortunately, the Korean labour force had acquired many skills and were able to make an important contribution to clearance and repair.

'Teal' had only been completed some three months earlier by American Engineers and it had been reassuring for British forces north of the Imjin to have what was believed to be a permanent bridge behind them. It was ironic that the bridge had succumbed to the forces of nature, rather than being demolished by our own side in the event of having to make a withdrawal. American Engineers however replaced it by a low-level, two-way semi-permanent bridge, designed so that it would be submerged quickly in flood to save it from damage by debris floating down as the flood reached its height. The Imjin rose again in August by forty-one feet in three hours.

64 Field Park Squadron was always a hive of activity, quite apart from being shelled by our own tanks, and carried out a wide variety of jobs. The Stores Troop, despite having only thirty-five men, handled prodigious quantities of stores: vast amounts of barbed wire, sandbags and other defence stores were unloaded at the Tok Chong railhead, some thirty tons a day being brought forward nearly ten miles to the squadron, and as much carried forward to the brigades every day of the week.

The Squadron was also responsible for repairs to engineer equipment, all of which was utilized to an extent that was never envisaged and suffered accordingly. Plant Troop held more than twice the normal scale for a squadron and kept their hard-worked equipment in working order themselves wherever possible. Repairs, far in excess of that normally carried out in a Divisional Field Park, were carried out in situ rather than sending them back for repair, but some repairs were inevitably beyond the capacity of the Field Park and were carried out by the British Commonwealth Engineer Regiment in Japan, which rendered invaluable assistance to the Divisional Engineers in many other ways as well.

Workshop Troop could turn their hand to anything, one task being to design and manufacture a roller as an anti-mine device. It was also rumoured that, despairing of the late arrival of the *Empire Halladale* troopship, they had laid down a keel behind the welders' shop. They did, however, also manufacture showers and heaters, and one of their more unusual requests arose from the adjutant of a certain Gunner regiment who rang RHQ to say that a flock of crows were fluttering round an anti-personnel minefield close to their position. Three mines had already been detonated and could the Sappers please help. This request was passed down to the Workshop Troop, who immediately made twenty scarecrows. The main burden of their work, though, was the prefabrication of standard bunkers from timber brought forward from the forestry camp established by 23 Canadian Field Squadron.

The Field Park's final sub-unit was Dog Troop. In early April, a detachment of about a dozen dogs was sent out from UK, reputedly trained to detect and 'mark' buried mines, by sitting down on locating one. They arrived with their handlers under command of a NCO, but it was felt that this was really an officer's job. Alec Jackson accepted the appointment with mixed feelings and on first acquaintance said he found them to be charming animals. Next day one of them bit him.

A greater worry than their teeth, though, was whether the dogs could actually find mines, not just some mines, but every single mine. One anti-personnel mine missed would be quite enough to reduce the attraction of canine friends, and the handlers took this point too. Dan Raschen thought they might be more useful for flushing out pheasants and even for retrieving, but sadly he found that pheasants had not been on their training curriculum. Indeed, some of the dogs turned out to be distinctly 'gun shy'. Though largely unemployed to begin with, not to say unemployable, the Troop persevered: one use for them was to accompany patrols on silent night patrolling, alerting troops to the presence of Chinamen, especially dead ones, rather than to the presence of mines.

Dog Troop changed a lot during the following year and only the best four were retained for mine-detecting. They dealt with the serious business of clearing doubtful areas of mines, while the remainder became Tracker, Patrol or Guard dogs. Dog 'Digger' was still considered to be in 'boy's service' and had to be forcibly restrained from joining the rum queue on the frequent occasions when the mainbrace was spliced during the wet weather. Dog 'Flake' was found to prefer finding Chinamen to mines and was attached to a forward battalion where he proved his worth on patrol. The battalion built him a shell-proof kennel. The four least efficient mine dogs were back-loaded to suitable homes amongst United Nations personnel in Pusan – roast dog being a favourite Korean dish precluded local disposal. Dog 'Query', a retrained mine dog, became an excellent tracker and once followed the cold scent of a thief for three miles over mountainous country. As a result the thief was captured. On another occasion he was used to track a patrol dog that had escaped in pursuit of a deer. The patrol dog was found but not, unfortunately, the deer.

One of 64 Squadron's sappers, Robbie Lancaster, used to recite poems he had written in the form of letters to his mother, to cheer everyone up. Here is one of them:

Dear Mum, it seems like ages since we came over here
To battle on for glory in this land they call Korea.
I've had time to settle in, the time to look around,
I've had the time to leave my mark upon this battleground.
But Mum it's hard to battle on, it's hard to make a show,
When you're frozen to the marrow and you're slipping in the snow.

Where your muckers all around you are dropping off like flies,
And the blindness comes to get you from the snow-glare in your eyes.
The grub is always frozen and your head is full of lice,
While the water in your bottle is a solid lump of ice.
When you grab your gun to fire it at some advancing Chink,
The steel it leaves a blister, well it kind of makes you think.

Oh to be in England where there's heat enough to share,
And the lovely dancing sunbeams cast a warmth into the air.
Where a man can live in comfort and find a helping hand,
I would give a lot to be there in my blessed native land.
With the sound of water tinkling in a quiet woodland dell,
Takes the place of banzai screaming which knocks your nerves to hell.

But first there is a war to win, to make our homeland free,
To make this world around us like one big family.
So I'll spit upon my bayonet and prime a new grenade,
And never let those Communists ever think that I'm afraid.
Oh to hope that I'll be good enough to see this job well done,
I'm sending you this letter
From your ever loving son.

No doubt greeted with ironic cheers from his fellow sappers!!

Meanwhile, 55 Squadron drove a tunnel, 184-foot long, through the hill under Divisional Headquarters. This had followed a warning, which fortunately came to nothing, that the Chinese Air Force might become active and that a nuclear attack could not be discounted. The tunnel was constructed in twenty-two days, working in shifts and starting at both ends, with two chambers eighteen feet by nine feet, with provision for other chambers. The tunnel was timbered throughout and despite lack of tunnelling expertise or survey techniques, the two ends met in the middle to within one inch of accuracy.

Although, by the late summer of 1952, there had been no major attacks by, or onto, the Commonwealth Division, for several months, neither side allowed the other to take liberties. The war reverted to the old sport of trying to catch prisoners and this usually took place while on patrol in no man's land. Small pockets of men were also kept forward of our defences in 'standing patrols' or in listening posts which the Chinese delighted in attacking. The Royal Norfolk Regiment in particular were very vexed when each time they put a listening post on a feature called 'Crete', it was attacked and the occupants sent home with scant dignity. After various efforts to deceive the enemy had failed, it was decided that an improvised explosive device, fired remotely, might cause the Chinese to think that the hill was still held. The device came to be called a 'battle blanket' and consisted of a selection of small explosive items pinned, sewn or clipped to an old blanket. For initiation, it required a length of safety fuse, a length of so-called instantaneous fuse, some detonators and a few 1-ounce guncotton primers which, if set off by a burning fuse and a detonator, made much the same noise as a hand grenade. By carefully cutting nicks in both types of fuse, pops and bangs could be initiated every few seconds. Corporal Ford built the battle blanket for use on Crete and laid nearly a quarter of a mile of electric cable, connecting it all up at dusk before quietly withdrawing. Two platoons of the Norfolks remained in ambush close by. Later that night, the Chinese were heard in the neighbourhood and Corporal Ford pushed down the handle of his electric exploder to ignite the safety fuse of his battle blanket up on the position. Within seconds there was the first bang of a guncotton primer, just like a grenade, then another, then crack, crack as a couple of detonators fired to represent rifle shots, then a quick succession of bangs denoting automatic fire. This was all too much for the Chinese who, thinking the hill must be occupied, promptly put in an assault. The two platoons of the Norfolks came up behind them, killed twelve Chinese and took six prisoners, at relatively small loss to themselves. An immediate award of the Military Medal was made to Corporal Ford for his part in this successful and unusual action, but sadly he was killed less than three weeks later. He was affectionately known as Ernie Ford and his Troop was much moved when early one morning his body was brought back, sewn tightly into a grey army blanket, his shape and form still clear to see. With great reverence he was laid on the ground and the Troop gathered round while the Padre said a few prayers and gave words of comfort and encouragement, following which the body was taken away quickly for subsequent burial in the Commonwealth War Cemetery at Pusan.

Towards the end of October 1952, the Division again side-stepped to the left, with one battalion of 29 Brigade moving west of the River Samichon, taking over from the 2/7 US Marine Corps whose 7th Marines were holding a horseshoe of low hills with its apex a hill later to become famous as the Hook. The hill was vital to the defence of both the Marines, and the left Brigade of the Commonwealth Division as a breakthrough here would make possible the systematic roll-up of virtually the whole western sector of the American Eighth Army front. Its loss would have been disastrous and almost certainly have resulted in a United Nations withdrawal to the south of the Imjin river.

Chapter 10

The Hook

The Hook itself was merely 150 yards broad and 300 yards deep, sufficient room for only one company. With so little room to dig positions, the company had two platoons forward and one in depth 150 yards farther back. The forward left-hand platoon had a good field of fire towards the closest Chinese positions along a connecting saddle. A dug-in flamethrower was available to assist them at the nearest point to the enemy, but it was never brought into action (possibly because there was never enough time to initiate it, or perhaps nobody knew how to operate it?!). The forward right-hand platoon had a good field of fire along a bare ridge to its north-east, and the rear platoon was well sited to cover both platoons, but the ground to the north offered the Chinese a possible approach via a convex slope in dead ground. This precariously held piece of real estate was connected on its right to a ridge known as 'Sausage' and on its left rear to Point 121, both set back from the Hook and less vulnerable. In view of its vital importance, the Hook was to be held through thick and thin until the end of the war, by which time more casualties had been suffered than on any other single battlefield in Korea.

Before taking over the Hook from the Americans, Ian Thomson and three or four sappers from 3 Troop of 55 Squadron were sent over in advance to join the Marines to recce minefields in the Samichon valley and the roads and defences in the forward area. They were dressed in American uniforms so as not to give away the intention to change units. The United States system of field defences seemed to be a long continuous trench from the west coast to the east coast (interrupted by the Commonwealth Division) with strongpoints every twenty yards or so. The strongpoints were nothing more than sand-bagged machine-gun positions and were not always mutually supporting, largely due to the hilly terrain. Prior to the changeover, the Marines were subjected to ten days of continuous bombardment and the day before the Black Watch were due to take over from them the Chinese launched yet another attack, preceded by a day of even heavier bombardment, and overran the position. Only after some very heavy fighting was the position restored.

The next morning, the Black Watch found that the Hook position had become a powdered, ragged hill with no bunkers intact and communication trenches almost useless. Trenches originally over six feet deep were now three-foot and V-shaped. These very inadequate defensive positions needed complete rebuilding and the Black Watch immediately requested Sapper assistance. 55 Squadron was given the task and 3 Troop, under Alan O'Hagan, with Ian Thomson as his Troop Officer, worked round the clock with each section completing an eight-hour shift. They could only work by night to avoid the mortar and small-arms fire from the Chinese, who were only about a hundred yards away across a small dip with a pimple called 'Ronson' half way, and 'Seattle' just behind it.

1 Troop under Peter Ball, with three platoons of Korean Service Corps labour, were tasked with digging a 400-yard communication trench on the reverse slope of the Hook, and to provide a Command Post and an OP with concrete lintel, followed by bunkers and LMG posts. 2 Troop under Dick Sullivan, also with three Platoons of KSC, were set to work on the neighbouring hill feature, Sausage, with similar aims. To support this deployment a tactical Squadron HQ and an administration area were to be established adjacent to the Black Watch HQ under the Squadron Second-in-Command. The policy of task work and better treatment and respect towards the KSC officers and men – extra rations and sharing tea with the British sappers – paid dividends. Although there was shelling and four KSC were wounded, they all worked hard. Three Sappers were also wounded, Corporal Hollick of 2 Troop seriously, and the Black Watch had six killed.

Soon after moving onto the Hook, Lieutenant Colonel David Rose, CO of the Black Watch, decided to copy the Chinese by basing his defence on tunnels and overhead cover. Thus if a position was overrun, his men could go to ground and airburst artillery fire be used to make the position untenable to any enemy in the open. He envisaged the forward position on the Hook and the platoon on the left of the Sausage being turned into fortresses with tunnels leading off the forward trench immediately behind the section positions. Each tunnel entrance was to be provided with a grenade trap and two dog-legs and would be four-foot high and three-foot wide, close-timbered and driven back into the hillside until the overhead cover was a minimum ten feet. Thereafter, a chamber would be dug large enough to hold a section, with a six-foot arched roof. The soil was hard decomposed granite (DG) but could be dug by hand.

Meanwhile, enemy patrol activity and artillery fire had increased greatly, pointing to a renewed enemy attack in the Hook area. It was feared that the enemy were using the dead ground at the base of the 'Warsaw' feature to make tunnels to protect troops forming up for an attack so as to be safe from UN artillery fire. On the night of 12 November, Dick Sullivan and twelve men from his Troop, together with a section of infantry for protection, set out to investigate. They carried prepared charges in large packs, some bound to the end of six-foot pickets. They found that reports had exaggerated the size and importance of the so-called tunnels, but nevertheless set off their charges using time pencils. Two men of the Black Watch were wounded, but otherwise there was little opposition.

Three nights later Alan O'Hagan and Adam Gurdon, a Black Watch platoon commander, together with a radio operator and a rifleman, were also tasked to carry out a reconnaissance to locate enemy tunnels, immediately in front of the Hook, to the left of Warsaw from where it was thought the Chinese were launching their attacks. Alan takes up the story:

> We set off well after dark, initially making our way as silently as possible in the direction of Warsaw. The night was dry and relatively still but on the breeze we suddenly became aware of the strong smell of garlic and knew we were either in the vicinity of a Chinese patrol with their penchant for that particular flavour or where they had just been. In case they were somewhere around, we felt it would have been impolite to have joined their picnic uninvited so we moved carefully away to ensure that we maintained our etiquette, to say nothing of our secrecy! As we continued over what seemed to be the vast expanse of Warsaw, we heard the sound of a cock pheasant some distance ahead of us. This was not unusual and, indeed, pheasant made a frequent appearance at our dining table having already provided good target practice as we maintained our weapon skills. It was, however, unusual at night and then we heard another – and another – until we became aware of a ring of pheasant calls, evenly spaced forming a semi-circular arc to our right and finally sounding behind us, somewhere between ourselves and our forward positions. Perhaps not surprisingly, we concluded that these particular pheasants were potentially hostile. It so happened that we had stopped immediately next to several deep and disused trenches in which we could take cover while our radio operator called for an artillery strike over the area. It came in quite quickly, but none of us had appreciated the allowance that should be made in judging the likely variation of the fall of shot from a 25-pounder gun. The net result was the arrival of a number of shells in such close proximity to our shelter that we

were just as pleased when the barrage stopped. We discovered that the pheasant calls had stopped too.

Having continued over the crown of Warsaw and well down and along its left hand reverse slope, just above the bank of the stream, and with, as yet, no tunnels discovered, we realized that since we were now well into the early hours of the morning, it might be expedient to consider beginning our return journey. We called up Battalion HQ on the radio and were told that the CO's specific need was that we should press on in the hope of finding something. We did so and, with a mixture of both relief and apprehension, we suddenly realized that we had found a hole in the hill, big enough to crawl into and with a mound at the mouth to protect the doorway from direct fire. There was complete silence from within and total darkness. With my fellow patrol members standing guard outside, I crouched down and headed literally into the tunnel. Halfway over the mound, with my head on the ground inside and my feet in the air behind me, I felt extremely vulnerable. Feeling my way along the tunnel walls, and able to stand now, I soon came to a T-junction and turned on my mine marking lamp to provide some subdued lighting. Whether it is possible for eyes to turn in opposite directions simultaneously I cannot be sure. All I know is that it was with profound relief that the two spurs of the tunnel, to left and right, were empty. They extended perhaps 20 or 30 feet in each direction and could have accommodated a sizeable number of men for a limited period.

With the satisfaction, and relief, at having found at least this tunnel, we began the long, careful climb back up the steep hill and then across the top of Warsaw. Dawn had already arrived over our forward positions before we reached them and it was with some relief that we re-entered the forward trenches at about 0500hrs. It had been a long night.

Any plans to deal with that tunnel and any others found in the meantime were put on hold when, three nights later, after a tremendous barrage, the Chinese launched their next major attack on the Hook from the direction of Warsaw and overran the position. Working on one of the accommodation tunnels that night were Lance Corporal Brown and Sappers McGowan, White and Wilkinson. Ian Thomson and Alan O'Hagan shared duties on the Hook between them, covering as much of each twenty-four hours as they could from their Troop location a mile or so to the rear. Ian was on the Hook that night and escaped the enemy charge by a narrow margin and just before our artillery began to bring down defensive fire, causing heavy enemy casualties. At dawn, the Black Watch recaptured the Hook and Ian was able to return to look for the missing Sappers, who turned out to have been captured. While he was there the Chinese again attacked and took the western half of the company position. The eastern half was still in our hands, with soldiers milling about in a dazed and disorganized way. Ian reported that

> I shouted in my best County Angus voice (my family come from there) 'Black Watch stand firm, turn round, face the enemy, aim and fire.' To my surprise they did just that! Fortunately reinforcements arrived and the Chinese were finally driven off the Hook. It was estimated that 4,000 to 5,000 artillery and mortar rounds had been fired on the position. The area was littered with dead Chinese – one body was so compressed that it fitted on to a 'Shovel RE'.

For his work on the Hook and his previous minefield clearing, Ian was awarded a well-deserved MC.

Next day, David Rose's gunner battery commander told him an enemy intercept had given Brigade HQ two hours' warning of the attack, but they had failed to pass it on. The Brigade Commander admitted that it was true 'but he really didn't see what difference it would have made'. David Rose replied that he did not think seventy-five wounded Jocks, not to mention the missing sappers, would agree with him and demanded to see the General. After seeing the Divisional Commander and on being assured that this would not happen again, relations with Brigade HQ were restored eventually with the arrival of Brigadier Joe Kendrew a week later.

Fortunately, few of the Command Posts, OPs, bunkers or tunnels suffered significant damage, although most of the communication trenches were half filled and parapets demolished. Between 19 and 23 November shift work continued on the tunnels and in assisting the battalion in repairing their defences, hindered by continuing heavy enemy fire. However, the communication trenches remained in poor condition and, on 23 November, it was decided to take the risk of heavy shelling or attack to repair them in one night as a Squadron task. All available KSC, 150 in all, and twenty-six sappers and NCOs from 2 and 3 Troops went up to the Hook at 11.00pm and dug until first light. Luck was with them as the night was completely quiet, almost too quiet since the KSC had been found to work better with a few shells around, with nowhere to run, their safety being the depth of the trench. The only enemy activity was a sniper who narrowly missed the OC, Major Bob Frosell, as the last of the working party left the position at dawn.

During the whole of the month, routine engineer support was afforded to 29 Brigade, including construction and operation of a waterpoint for the Hook area, and also the screening of those roads supplying the Hook which were under observation by the Chinese.

These screens, which were already in extensive use to the north of the Samichon, were made using twenty-foot poles, carrying rolls of chicken wire and scrim. However, due to a complete shortage of wire rope, the guys had to be made with barbed wire. Thus when damaged by enemy fire they became a prickly mass difficult to untangle and repair, often under fire. The Squadron's major effort, apart from work on the Hook, was to make six miles of new road to enable two batteries of the Field Regiment to move to support the new position. This was completed in two weeks by two Troops at the cost of three casualties from mortar fire.

After the communication trenches had been re-established on the night of 23 November, enemy activity diminished and the two Troops were better able to get on with the section tunnels and to finish the bunkers and defensive positions. Where possible, ventilation shafts were to be made for all tunnels. More attention could also be given to the other companies to the east of the Hook. Every effort was made to finish all tasks by the end of what had been a month of extremely hard work, an exceptional achievement in which they had constructed thirty-nine four-man bunkers, four medium machine-gun posts, a gunner OP, 1,500 yards of new communication trenches, repaired and deepened a further 1,000 yards, and started six tunnels.

Meanwhile, 12 Field Squadron was starting similar construction on Hill 355, a sinister position at the opposite end of the Divisional front, in 28 Brigade area. Bunkers were dug into solid granite to a depth of thirteen feet using 'beehives' and explosives and, not infrequently, hammer and chisel. Their other tasks included looking after some twenty-five miles of gravel roads requiring constant maintenance and repair. Captain John Elderkin had joined the Squadron in October and shortly after his arrival was able to fly early in the day with the Army Air Corps Reconnaissance Flight to report on the current state of the roads and allocate tasks to the KSC accordingly. The Squadron's KSC Company was in charge of an educated Korean with a good knowledge of English who was easy to get on with and their contribution was invaluable. Sadly, two of their men died when their bunker collapsed on them one night.

Snow fell in November, the frost came with a vengeance during December and the Imjin, now a placid river, only 300 feet wide at the 'Pintail' crossing, froze over on 12 December 1952. More snow fell on Boxing Day and the landscape was white for the next five weeks.

1952 had been an eventful year, but more was to come in the next few months. It was not all shot and shell, though, or even doom and gloom, and there were numerous episodes and tales of an amusing nature.

Chapter 11

On a Lighter Note

Early Days

Some fortnight prior to embarking with 29 Infantry Brigade for Korea as part of the UN forces in 1950, 55 Field Squadron had been sent on a final training exercise in Thetford. Peter Chitty, one of the Troop Officers recounted that:

> For three or four days and nights we tried to convince our Brigadier, and to lesser extent ourselves, that we were what he had called us earlier, 'Britain's finest post-war contribution to world peace'. Then on the way back to Tidworth it happened. Add a total lack of sleep to the trials and torments of trying to be something you weren't, had all proved too exhausting. Sitting in the lead Bren carrier, I was taking the massed might of our squadron's armoured element back to base in Tidworth. All the other officers had diverted for a 'night briefing' in London, but not me. Although the youngest officer, clearly I had blacked somewhere, somehow and with someone on the exercise.
>
> As we approached a magnificent new roundabout, or to be truthful, as the Council witnesses later reported, for I and my driver were asleep, we took it head on. Tracks churning and mud flying, we mounted peripheral London's latest traffic flagship at about 25 miles an hour. Loyal to a man, the other 13 carriers followed in their master's tracks in best Becher's Brook style. I think the roundabout had only recently been completed for, mixed with some massacred geraniums, some of the opening tape was later found in our tracks, and a pair of ceremonial scissors mysteriously appeared near the ammunition bin. Perhaps we had opened it? Suffice it to say, damned Council were neither amused, nor were they assuaged in any way by

the fact that we were Britain's potential heroes. As a gracious gesture befitting the dockside mood, an enormous bill was served on us in Southampton as we embarked on the troopship, and later increasingly menacing and more demanding letters followed the squadron around two retreats and one advance.

On arrival in Korea, 55 Field Squadron moved north from the port of Pusan to Suwon, just south of Seoul. Peter Chitty, now John Page's Troop Officer, was then told to return to Pusan to bring up the heavy baggage. This was put on a train carrying some of the newly-arrived Turkish Brigade, who leapt from the train every time it stopped at a station to hunt for and kill any dogs they could find there, which they would then cook and eat. Peter had to admit that dog is very palatable, as he came to find out later.

It was noticed that when they came to a 'repaired' railway bridge, the train stopped for some time then crossed over slowly and stopped again for a while before setting off properly. On investigation, it was found that the driver was getting off to cross the suspect bridge on foot and then the fireman would set the throttle at 'low', get off the engine and follow across on foot as soon as the train had been stopped by the driver at the other side. The passengers decided to follow suit, just in case.

A few weeks later and 29 Brigade had withdrawn south from Pyong-yang with the American forces. They had paused at Seoul, and Peter Chitty was told to recce for sheltered accommodation for 29 Brigade farther to the south. On the way down with a half-troop, he spotted a large hot springs/spa building just off the road so they went there to overnight if possible. There was no roof left above the large circular hot bath and snow was falling, but they stripped off and washed themselves. Very soon afterwards two Korean nuns came into the building together with about thirty nubile girls and, one nun excepting, they all stripped off and jumped into the water. This made it extremely difficult for the men to get out of the bath and into their clothes. Eventually, Peter led the scramble out with everyone clutching their personal possessions, much to the amusement of the girls – and the nuns.

Next morning Peter continued his journey south feeling rather like a modern John the Baptist to prepare the way for the Brigade. His story continued:

It was winter, and the cold was unbelievable in intensity. The troops needed somewhere dry and warm in which to rest and reorganize. I found a splendid winter base for the Brigade near the main supply route to the south which could house most of the Brigade: the country's only silk factory. It covered acres of

Taejon with fine, substantial industrial buildings and at first seemed to give us all that was needed – accommodation, garages, water and potential warmth. That being just what we needed after a long day, my recce party unrolled their sleeping bags as the cook tried to get the petrol hydro-burner cooker started for supper. During the next week we prepared and cleaned up the buildings to receive the Brigade. One night a 3-tonner turned up with two padres in the front, one C of E and the other RC, and in the back were about thirty very dead bodies they were taking south to bury near the Commonwealth Base in Pusan. That night the Padres and I slept together in my luxurious double bed in the former manager's house. It was dreadfully cold but the C of E padre got out and knelt in prayer. After about eight minutes I had to get out of bed to lift him back in as he couldn't move. After this the RC one prayed, 'Dear Lord, it is far too cold to kneel in prayer, so I will pray where I am. You may appreciate it the more this way as you will not have to hear my chattering teeth.'

Larry Lamble arrived soon after this so I decided to celebrate with a special dinner. Well, that was the intention, but hydro-burners being what they are, one exploded and first the cook-house and later the building, and finally most of the factory was burning well. Our base was on the first floor of the main building and pretty soon it was clear that we would have to evacuate the building fairly quickly. The stairs were already burning, so we lowered ropes from the windows and all but Larry and I left. I then told him to leave – one rope had already burned through – but he drew rank on me, saying that as he was Intake 1A at Sandhurst and I was only Intake 2, I had to go first. Being some-what fed up by this, I noted that the stairwell was no longer on fire so I went downstairs and outside, from where I called up to him that I had left the building. By now, the staircase was well alight again, so in the end Larry had to scramble down a rope, or perhaps he leapt into the nearest pine tree, I cannot remember.

Soon I saw the whole complex in a totally different light. The light of millions of yens-worth of buildings gradually brighten-ing the drab surrounding city, with a warmth of colour, blazing symbols of light, a beacon of welcome to the exhausted Brigade. In the cold light of dawn, I consoled myself that it had been touch and go whether or not all the Brigade could have fitted in. Even today I like to think that the fact that by removing the Brigade's winter quarters, there was now nowhere left for the Brigade to go, and that this somehow stiffened the resolve of the Brigade Commander to stand and fight it out where he was, which proved to be the turning point of the war. A hydro-burner cooker does not readily spring to mind as a war-winning invention ...

Getting on for the end of January, with bitterly cold weather, Peter Chitty rejoined 55 Squadron at Osan, south of Suwon. On entering the Mess, which was in a school building, he saw a very hot wood-fuelled stove and noticed that, hanging round the chimney pipe, there were a lot of wooden loo seats. These had been devised by Bertie Bayton-Evans: when you wanted to go to the frozen 'long drop' you warmed up your own named loo seat and, clutching it to your breast, ran to the 'long drop' and sat on it before it cooled. Brilliant!

In this connection, Peter was sent out one night with a carpenter and a tinsmith to the rear company of the Royal Ulster Rifles. No details of the task had been given and when he got there he was led to a wooden 'long drop' on which was seated a moaning rifleman. It appeared that when he had sat down his scrotum had touched and frozen to the metal splash plate so he could not get up. The 'chippy' cut through the wooden side and then the tinsmith was able to cut around the problem area and they were able lift him off, wrap cotton wool around the injured part, and send him to the Field Ambulance to thaw before later surgical trimming.

Village Transport

Outside the few large towns of Korea the only industry was farming and the normal vehicle for moving heavy loads was a long, low cart hauled by oxen. The villagers had no tractors and certainly no cars. If they needed to travel any distance they would just walk to their destination. Consequently, the main roads were only of sufficient width for two carts to pass, while the lesser ones were only wide enough for one cart. Civilians quickly learned to keep off the main supply routes used by the United Nations forces, but along other roads life still had to go on. Men and women, swathed in padded cotton clothing against the cold, criss-crossed the inhabited areas carrying loads of all sorts. More often than not they would be bent double under the ubiquitous A-frame, made of bamboo poles, which enabled them to carry on their backs a hundredweight or so of branches, their principal fuel.

Another common method of transport was a long bamboo pole with a heavy wooden bucket at each end. When properly balanced across a man's back he could jog along in a seemingly effortless manner, synchronizing the natural oscillation of the buckets with the rise and fall of his own shoulders. The popular guess about what these buckets might contain was confirmed one day when a driver in an open Jeep went too close and hit a bucket. The bucket was knocked forwards, so

that its mate, pivoting round the neck of the carrier, came from behind
to deposit a full load of night soil down the unwary driver's back.

The Whisky Distillery

Shortly before winter set in, Tony Younger had written to a Scottish
cousin about the wickedness of the Siberian wind when it swept down
the peninsula. It happened that he ran a whisky distillery and in his
reply he said he was sending a case and had arranged for it to be taken
by hand from Hong Kong to Tokyo by a member of the firm of Jardine
Matheson, whose commercial links spanned the Far East. Tony wasted
no time in summoning Desmond Holmes, his 2IC, and they concocted
an (un)likely story that he should proceed to Japan to purchase on the
open market a special bolt for one of their bulldozers.

Desmond had a marked gift of quick thinking and was capable of
producing as smooth a story as most, backed by plentiful twinkles from
his blue eyes and tugs at his military moustache. If he could not talk
his way back with his precious cargo nobody could, and sure enough
he returned two days later, laconically explaining that he had had no
problem. The man from Jardine's had been there, together with his own
bottle which he had generously shared with Desmond before taking
him out to dinner and showing him something of night life in Tokyo.
Desmond had the case, wrapped in heavy brown paper and clearly
marked 'Map Glue'. 'After all,' he explained, 'you can hardly expect
to be believed if you say you are carrying bulldozer parts and their
container goes 'glug' whenever it is moved.'

The squadron's Quartermaster had met an American truck driver
who offered anything they wanted in exchange for a bottle of whisky,
an unobtainable luxury in their Army. A couple of days later he came in
with a present for Tony. It was a puffy bundle that was obviously a
sleeping bag and when asked how many he had got, he replied 'Three
hundred and sixty, one for each member of the squadron!' Successive
bottles were to result in tentage and petrol-burning heaters for tents,
and in fleece-lined coats which made all the difference in the world to
sentries and guards during the long winter nights. The Quartermaster
also acquired a good number of caps with fur ear flaps, which could
only be worn at night for fear that the Brigadier would see them and
explode, and rubberized boots with beautiful thick insoles.

There were still several of those wonderful bottles remaining and
Uncle Sam was toasted deeply and sincerely.

Muddy Paddy

The winter of 1950/51 was hard and the early months of spring brought
rain with endless maintenance work on roads and culverts. This was

tedious work for the Squadron and the Brigade Commander felt they needed a suitable task to enliven their days. He promised a week's leave in Japan to anyone who could solve the problem of dealing with bogged vehicles. Tony Younger gave the job of collecting suggestions and selecting a winner to Keith Eastgate, a former heavyweight boxer at Sandhurst who had the 'right combination of reliability and humour'. Entries, marked 'Muddy Paddy', poured in. One proposed welding a spade-shaped extension to the exhaust pipes of all vehicles, which could then be reversed onto the paddies to dry them out. Another recommended a maypole, equipped with ropes and buckets on the end, which could be erected in the centre of a paddy field by the sappers, who could then run in ever decreasing circles – to the accompaniment of the Band of the Royal Engineers – filling and emptying the buckets. The competition amused Keith, but by mid-April, as the weather improved, the paddies dried up of their own accord and the terrible winter was really over.

The Concert

The writer Eric Linklater described his month with British forces in Korea in his book *A Year of Space*. One day he went to the ferry near Gloster Crossing to see the return of troops from the northern bank. The Imjin was still broad and running fast, but it had dropped five or six feet and the ferries were working again. The day was hot and beyond the river rose a chaos of seemingly empty hills, and two or three hours' search through field-glasses revealed no movement. The soldiers had had to remain in their forward positions, after a foray north of the river, to guard some American tanks which had bogged down, and though the Chinese had been avoiding action they might be tempted to intercept or obstruct the withdrawal back to the river. It was not a likely prospect, but it was not impossible. Then at last a long thin column came round the shoulder of the ridge, and on a downhill diagonal approached the river and gathered at the crossing.

The ferry consisted of three pontoons bridged by a light decking and attached to a cable by a wire bridle. It swung out onto the river, the cable sagging downstream, and lying at an angle to the current, took it on the beam and drifted over. The soldiers clambered aboard and stood close-packed as if in an underground train at the rush hour. They came ashore and silently, with weary faces, climbed the steep southern bank of the river. The first arrivals were a platoon of the King's Shropshire Light Infantry, nearly all of them young. They were heavily burdened, as infantry soldiers always are, and were tired but not exhausted. The ferry went back athwart the stream for its next load, and down the northern hills other columns were marching to the river.

Some of them arrived at Brigade Headquarters in time to attend a performance by an English concert-party. The Americans had sent professional entertainers to amuse their troops, but these were the first English artistes to visit Korea. They were lively and agreeable people, and they roused their audience to enormous laughter and loud applause. The soldiers, closely seated in a coign of the hillside under a sky that threatened more rain, leaned back and tumbled in their seats, rocking with delight. So much pleasure in such a land was a very moving spectacle. There was an adept, gay comedian in the party, a good conjurer who convincingly sawed an officer in half, and two attractive young women, one of whom played the piano. The comedian and the conjurer were applauded and laughed at, but the young women woke a sort of rapture in the soldiers. They sang their songs and played their pieces well enough, but their great appeal was that they seemed to be thoroughly 'nice girls'. There was adoration and longing in the soldiers' voices.

Other concert parties came out too. Jack Warner and a troupe of lovelies gave a show to the Brigade and 55 Squadron built an open-air theatre with Bailey Bridge chesses on tree trunks as seats and a raised stage on oil-drums. Danny Kaye also came out and kicked-off a soccer match between the Squadron and the Glosters.

The Top Hats
3 Troop of 55 Field Squadron was re-entering Seoul for the second time and stopped for a brew-up alongside some derelict shops. Coming the other way in his jeep was the Brigade Commander, Brigadier Tom Brodie. Larry Lamble and Bertie Bayton-Evans, his Troop Commander, saluted smartly and on turning back to the Troop were surprised to see that they had evidently found a store of Korean top-hats. These they raised politely to the Brigadier as he drove past, much to his amusement.

The Razor Blades
The British Army prides itself in expecting its soldiers to be shaven properly, no matter how difficult the circumstances. A prime example occurred on the road above Kaesong when 27 Brigade was covering the American 'withdrawal' from North Korea. John Page was standing beside an American colonel watching the companies of the Argylls coming off the surrounding hills, each led by the company piper as they marched smartly to their waiting transport. Incredulous, the American exclaimed 'Gee, those Scots have been fighting in the hills for days and every man is shaved and his boots clean'. Quite so.

A serious problem then arose in the early summer of 1951 when NAAFI experienced a major shortage of razor blades. 55 Squadron decided to go to the top, perhaps emboldened by their earlier success in the whisky business, and a carefully prepared letter was sent to the Managing Director of Gillette Razor Blades explaining their predicament. Almost by return of post came a large parcel of several thousand razor blades.

Such manna from heaven was worth celebrating and serious thought was given to the distribution of this largesse. It was decided that the OC, Tony Younger, should hand the package to a token recipient on a squadron parade and that the contents should then be distributed to the men. Much thought went in to considering who might be the most appropriate recipient and the selectors' eyes fell on Sapper Hapstein, who was a reservist and John Page's troop storeman. Hapstein came from Whitechapel and with that name and background his entrepreneurial skills can well be imagined. Hapstein's empire centred around the Bedford 3-tonner which carried the troop's quota of spare stores and was fitted out like a high-grade ironmongers. Though the vehicle sank lower and lower on its springs, Hapstein always innocently assured his Troop Commander that the ever-increasing contents had fallen off the back of the proverbial lorry and might come in useful one day. Not surprisingly, most of the more recent additions bore an American maker's label.

However, Hapstein's real claim to fame rested on his facial appearance. Like many of his race, Hapstein was a walking definition of the word 'hirsute'. Shaggy black eyebrows hung deep over his dark jowl and shaving for him must have been like trying to mow the Black Forest daily. The main players were briefed, the squadron parade went ahead, Hapstein played his part admirably, and the razor blades were duly distributed amid much laughter and cheers.

The Bath

While showers were available at the Ordnance Bath Unit, there were no actual baths. For this one had to wait for R&R in Japan or the conclusion of one's tour and departure via the Commonwealth base in Kure. There was one exception, though:

> We had just moved to Yong Dong, a quieter area with a wide valley between our forward positions and the enemy's. The Adjutant asked me if I would like a bath and, seeing my disbelief, directed me to an open piece of paddy a couple of hundred yards away. Sitting on its own, in isolated splendour, was a real enamel bath! I found out later that it had been 'liberated' by the Leicesters

while passing through Seoul. Either the Assault Pioneers or a previous Sapper Troop had fitted it with a water tank and an oil-fired heater and it had both Hot and Cold taps. I made immediate use of this unexpected luxury and revelled in the glorious hot water. After a good soaping to get rid of accumulated grime, I lay back for a good old soak. After a few minutes luxuriating, I heard shells landing near by, but I was in a cast iron, enamelled bath and I wasn't going to let a little matter of a few shells disturb my equanimity as I slid farther down into the warm water ...

The Intelligence Officer

'I don't think he gives a damn about Intelligence. My sole job seems to be to ensure that the Commanding Officer has Cooper's Oxford marmalade for breakfast. Doesn't he realize that we are in the middle of a war? And where does he think I'm going to find it? And to think that my Annual Confidential Report depends on it.'

Motor Graders

Plant Troop was deployed all over the Divisional area. Like everyone else, they were woefully short of domestic transport and took to using various items of plant. On one such occasion, a grader was despatched to collect the Troop beer ration. The grader was overtaken by a US helicopter which landed ahead of them, a three-star General got out and they found themselves the recipients of a speeding ticket from the Corps Commander.

Peter Chitty had had a similar experience on another occasion when he was ordered to take messages to Brigade HQ, some four miles away. Seeing an unused grader he decided to 'borrow' it. Unfortunately it took up rather a large slice of the Visitors' car park and there was nowhere for the CO to park when he arrived there. Peter was threatened with court martial for this but the Brigadier thought it highly amusing and got the CO to drop the charge!

The Engineer-in-Chief's visit

The General had spent the day touring units and as many officers as could be spared had assembled for dinner in the marquee doing duty as the Officers' Mess at Regimental HQ. At the conclusion of the meal, the Engineer-in-Chief was invited to address the officers. An essentially shy man, he had to be persuaded to stand on a chair so as to make himself heard. At the end of his speech, and just as everyone was about to start clapping, an unmistakeably Kiwi voice shouted from the back of the tent, 'Whacko Bluey, you old Beaut!' Nobody could be angry and the General took it in good spirit, amidst the gale of laughter.

Coronation Day

Daylight came on Coronation Day with the usual view of enemy positions across the valley, only this time right under their forward trenches were fluorescent aircraft panels outlining 'EIIR' for everyone to see. It was a great start to the day and led to endless speculation as to how they got there. An officer in the Durham Light Infantry had been out on patrol the night before ...

1100hrs was the signal for every tank in the Division to climb to the crest of the hill they were on and to fire a salute at maximum elevation over the Chinese lines. At the same time every gun in the Division fired smoke into no man's land in battery blocks, red, white and blue, across the whole of the divisional front. It was also the signal for every company commander to stand up in full view and call for 'Three Cheers for Her Majesty the Queen' and throw their hats in the air.

The enemy never fired a shot all day, so chivalry between armies is not dead yet.

The Steel Picket

The Troop Commander needed to make a hole in a picket and decided that the quickest and most effective method would be to fire a shot through it with his rifle. While this is a good way of making a hole, this is not to be recommended where the picket is a high tensile steel one. Happily, the Troop Commander was the only person to be hit by the flying fragments.

The Camp Fire

The two sergeants were tucked up in sleeping bags in their *hoochie* with their space heater burning, little realizing that the fuel was leaking. Suddenly it burst into flames and they were lucky to escape with their lives. The whole Troop was soon on the scene to admire the conflagration and to offer the two sergeants crocodile tears of sympathy, but they were standing too close when the troop's supply of ammunition, kept in the tent for security, started to explode. Then they noticed that the picric acid from a Chinese Bangalore Torpedo, which had been picked up a few days earlier, had flames shooting out from each end. This led to a hurried withdrawal, but not before one of the corporals had been hit in the shoulder by a flying cartridge from one of the sergeants' Sten guns.

There were no offers to try and salvage any kit.

Pheasants

Pheasants originated in Korea, a fact well known to Dan Raschen, which he always said was his prime motivation for volunteering to go to Korea. He felt that his own shotgun was probably too good to go to war with, but he found an old twelve-bore shotgun in his parents' garden shed, which previously had belonged to their gardener. With this under his arm, and 200 cartridges, he set off to war.

On 24 August 1951, he arrived at HQRE, courtesy of a friendly Movements Officer. Dan was duly thankful, having restrained himself from asking him whether he had seen any pheasants lately and whether it had been a good breeding season. There were indeed pheasants in Korea, plenty of them, but unfortunately many of them found safe haven in the numerous minefields. This did not deter Dan and he soon established where the most likely coverts were.

Everyone was out when he arrived, but a sergeant clerk filled him in on the various personalities. The CRE, Colonel Eddie Myers, had a CBE and DSO; of the five officers in the headquarters, four held the Military Cross and the other had been taken prisoner at Dunkirk. The Commanding Officer, Lieutenant Colonel Peter Moore, had two DSOs in addition to his MC. Dan now understood what the Posting Captain in England had meant when he said, 'We are only sending good officers to Korea', but did begin to wonder what he was doing there himself.

Undeterred, Dan continued to keep an eye open for pheasants and in mid-September he heard a cock pheasant calling only 300 yards away, but resisted the temptation to go after it 'as the shooting season had not yet started' – perhaps the Chinese hadn't appreciated this when they invaded the south. As it happened, he then found that the stock of his shotgun had broken, but an enterprising 'Chippy' in the Field Park Squadron soon fashioned a new one. Mr Purdey would have been proud of him.

Due to other (military) commitments it was nearly the end of October before he shot his first pheasant, using the Adjutant's shotgun as his own was still 'hors de combat'. Just before Christmas, the CRE came to dinner and was most appreciative of the pheasant that had been served up, saying that the General's Mess, where he dined, never aspired to such luxuries. He was much too polite a man to drop hints, but Dan thought it would be a nice gesture if a couple of brace could be dropped off at their Mess. As the next morning was lovely, they set about the task immediately, though not without a (small) twinge of conscience lest some operation should crop up. An hour and a half later they had shot a cock and three hens, with another brace of pheasants on the local marsh that afternoon. End result: one appreciative CRE and an even more appreciative Divisional Commander.

As the Intelligence Officer, Dan was expected to know where all the minefields were and this resulted in several invitations to shoot. On the last day of the season, which was strictly adhered to in accordance to British law (!), he was invited to shoot with the CRA, the Divisional Commander also being one of the Guns. On a previous excursion, the latter had found himself against a minefield fence and wasn't sure if he was coming out of a minefield or going into it. Sensibly, he then walked along the fence until he was sure where he was, but had found the experience detracted from the pleasures of his sport.

As a Sapper, Dan's trump card remained his assumed knowledge of the minefields and, though all areas were freely available to everyone, others tended to keep farther away from the minefields than was perhaps strictly necessary. However, an American helicopter entered the scene: the pilot had discovered that if, by flying low, he could put up a pheasant and then follow its flight precisely, the bird presented the equivalent of a sitting target to a crewman pointing a shotgun through the window. Quite apart from considering the practice most unsporting, it was felt to be poaching and the pilot was tracked down. It was pointed out to him that when he had landed to pick up a pheasant, he had been lucky to escape with his life as he had actually landed inside a minefield. Then there was the possible damage to the helicopter to consider as well. The practice ceased and the Divisional pheasants were safe.

Enemy Propaganda

Sappers, and indeed all troops in the forward areas, enjoyed the Chinese efforts to subvert us. Nightly broadcasts from loudspeakers promised safe conduct, interspersed with the latest Bing Crosby songs; then there were the Christmas cards, left in a 'letter-box' fixed to a post, for those who went on patrol, with a message inside wishing us a Merry Christmas and unfolding to send a letter of peace and adjuring us 'not to fight for the Yanks any more'. They were very attractive Christmas cards too.

Safe Conduct Passes, written in both English and Chinese, promised that the Bearer would be escorted to the rear where on arrival UN personnel would be guaranteed, 'in accordance with our policy of leniency to prisoners of war, the following four great affirmations:

- Security of life.
- Retention of all personal belongings.
- Freedom from maltreatment or abuse.
- Medical care for the wounded.'

Signed: The Chinese People's Volunteer's Headquarters

Then there were the propaganda leaflets, mainly consisting of 'reprints' of letters from home, but apparently American widows received $10,000 compensation if their husbands were killed, and their most popular leaflet displayed a lovely girl lying on her back, looking up dreamily and saying 'I don't want their $10,000, I want you'. The Sappers' reply was 'So do I'.

The propaganda could be quite alarming. Most of the leaflets were spread over forward areas by means of airburst shells. Leaflets would fall in a great cloud, but the canister fell to the ground with an alarming whirring sound, though it signalled the arrival of the leaflets and led to a mad rush to gather them up. Goodness knows what effect the Chinese thought it would have on our troops, but no one was interested by the enemy declaring, 'It's no disgrace to quit fighting in this unjust war'. The Chinese did have one quite insidious leaflet, though. This listed American monthly casualties on one side (over 100,000 in one year) and on the other were printed what they called 'Five Good Friends':

1. In every assault, keep as far back as you can. The first man forward is the first to get hit.
2. When our artillery is blazing away, shelter in a foxhole or some other place.
3. If surrounded, it won't do you any good to ask for help by radio or signalling. You may get killed before rescue comes. Remember, we pick up your signals too, and our men move fast. Your best policy is to surrender. We treat prisoners well.
4. On patrol, your chances of getting killed are high. So try to get out of it. If you are caught in an ambush on patrol, remember resistance may cost you your life. Lay down your arms and we guarantee your safety.
5. Many of your buddies know, 'The safest place is really behind the Communist lines. You stay alive that way and sooner or later you'll get home safely.' That's true! If you're afraid that we'll fire at you while you are coming across to us, follow these instructions: Choose favourable weather and come towards our side waving a white handkerchief or cloth. We will send someone to guide you safely through the minefields to our side.

Pretty good advice, if only we had believed it. It may have had some effect on other nations but our soldiers just hooted with derision.

Counter Propaganda
As a result of the Chinese incursion between our forward troops and Brigade HQ in December 1952, the 'powers that be' got in a panic and issued a form on what to do in the event of capture:

If you are captured you are required to give the enemy the information shown on the following certificate in order that your capture may be reported to your next of kin. When you are questioned, but not before, tear off the duplicate certificate and hand it to the interrogator. DO NOT ANSWER ANY OTHER QUESTIONS. ALWAYS CARRY THIS CARD IN ACTION. The interrogator may not take away your S.1511, S.43A, AB 64 or AB 439. It is important in your own interest that the particulars of rank should be kept up to date.

Write in BLOCK CAPITALS

BRITISH FORCES IDENTITY CERTIFICATE

Service Number .... Rank ....

Surname ....

Christian or Fore Name(s) ....

Date of Birth..

W.O.P. 33764

Goodness knows what the Chinese would have made of it.

Escape and Evasion
In the middle of 1952 Dan Raschen was one of a few officers selected for the doubtful honour of attending a course on 'Escape and Evasion', or 'What to do if you are taken prisoner'. Dan described what happened:

> I never claimed to be the Commonwealth Division's greatest asset, but had hoped that it would never be hinted so publicly that I was expendable. None of us on the course, needless to say, had the slightest intention of becoming prisoners but the theme, just in case we were, was that it would be much appreciated if we could please escape and then tell our friends where the thousand or so Britons already in captivity were. It was not

105

explained why none of them had escaped previously, nor with what super powers we were to be gifted to waft us back to our own lines. Our lecturer was a much decorated and tough airman who had made various escapes, the last one successful, from a German POW Camp. It took little imagination to see him in the part, especially as he had blue eyes and admitted that he spoke fluent German. None of us thought that we looked like Koreans, nor did we speak the language and, if the prison camps turned out to be in Manchuria, as was possible, nor did we speak Chinese. They were an interesting couple of days and made a change from our normal duties, but none of us came away convinced that we were born Houdinis.

An unexpected aftermath to that course, and certainly a matter of pure chance, was that two of our small number were the next two officers not to return from patrol. Unfortunately neither of them returned at the end of the war either.

Curry Lunch
India's contribution to the Commonwealth Division was to provide an Indian Field Ambulance. Every man was a paratrooper and it was the only unit in the Division to achieve the grading of 'Excellent', even for its vehicle maintenance. Apart from having a splendid medical reputation, the unit was the best possible advertisement for India five years after the departure of the British. In early 1953, the Division was in reserve for the first and only time and the Indians decided to have a Curry Lunch for 'all those who had served in the Indian Army'. It was just as well that they had prepared both the rice and the curry itself in large galvanized baths because it was astonishing how many officers claimed to be eligible. Sapper officers were well to the fore, many having quite genuinely served in the Indian Sappers and Miners. The Indians were victims of their own reputation though – always impeccably turned out, extremely friendly and generous hosts. They also produced excellent curry. Such a change from the British moan of 'What, turkey again?' as we received our, very generous, American rations.

Grumbles
Sapper Bloggins: 'Of course we grumble. It's the only f . . . ing privilege we have out here.'

The Rodent Course
It was impossible to bury rubbish in the freezing winter months with the result that there was an influx of rats. John Page, the Adjutant at the time, decided that Dan Raschen should go on a one-day, officers-only, rat-catching course, assuring him that he should be proud to have been

106

selected, so great was the demand for places. Off he went, with his Jeep and driver, back down the main supply route with its own minefields and ever increasing festoons of telephone cables on either side, past Rear Divisional Headquarters, past the massive ammunition dump with its lines of pre-loaded lorries and past the fuel and ration dumps, besieged by trucks from every quartermaster. Then came the NAAFI and the Interrogation unit, followed by odd American and South Korean units until one reached I Corps Headquarters at Uijongbu, halfway between the Imjin and Seoul.

The instructor on the Rodent Course was an American captain, who doubtless had Borgia ancestry, and delighted in making all but a literal meal of what anyone could have understood over the telephone. 'Rat poison' was referred to with reverence and if he found his British audience rather unappreciative, the Commonwealth element left him in no doubt. He went on to recommend that the mixture be wrapped in silver paper, when it became known as a 'sweet' and a long lecture followed on not giving them to children. That there were no children in the combat zone was immaterial. Lay a 'sweet' where there might be a rodent and, lo and behold, it might be nibbled and, if so, death should follow within a week.

The prize for passing the course was a small tub of the mixture and a small roll of an early form of aluminium foil. One week later and the stench of dead rodents in the rice straw roof grew so powerful that, in the middle of winter, the tarpaulin covering had to come off and the rice straw had to be replaced. Captain Borgia would have been pleased that rodents, rather than children, had liked his sweets.

The Strike

In late 1952 there was a strike by the Japanese work force in Kure and every available person in the Joint Reinforcement Base Depot was called on to help. A Sapper captain commanded an ad hoc platoon of the Black Watch and ran the Deep Freeze department of the Supply Depot, cold work but nothing compared to the Korean winter. The Canadians took charge of loading ammunition bound for Korea while the Australians were put in charge of loading supplies, including drink. It was extraordinary how cases of beer seemed never to be properly secured in the slings and crashed to the deck, spilling their contents. It was a wonder anyone in the Division got anything to drink during the strike, but it was thirsty work doing all that loading. Fortunately for everyone concerned the strike did not last long.

Battle School

The Battle School had three companies, Australian, Canadian and British, all part of the Commonwealth Division and towards the end of

1952 Lieutenant Colonel Pat Sholto-Douglas of the Black Watch took over command. The Instructors worked hard and played hard, with forays into the Hiroshima night clubs a regular feature of out-of-hours activities, but everyone was on parade next morning. The Commandant of the School reckoned that the way to integrate the Commonwealth was through the medium of alcohol and he did his best to set a good example. The Officers' Club in Kure was another good watering hole and after marching in the fifteen miles from Hara Mura with their intake at the end of their fortnight's training, a Turkish bath and a massage from an attractive hostess was *de rigueur*, following which the Instructors were ready for a drink, or two. It was a great opportunity to let one's hair down and one quite senior officer, after some serious drinking, woke up next morning to find himself in a large dirty linen basket in the gent's loo. He was probably more comfortable there than the Squadron Commander's driver, who was carried back to his bed after being found curled up in the urinal of a Tokyo nightclub. After one particularly exuberant party in the Kure Officers' Club, all the Instructors, including the Commandant himself, were invited to leave. Perhaps it had something to do with a thunder-flash exploding in an ice bucket? Quite spectacular anyway.

R & R

Five days' Rest and Recuperation was much looked forward to after several months in Korea. After the illegal but necessary action of swapping English pounds for American dollars (Exchange Rates: £1 = $2.8 = 16,800 Won = 1,008 Yen) and Korean won for Japanese yen, the night was spent in the transit building in Seoul. This was followed by an 800 miles flight to Tokyo Haneda airport in an American four-engined Skymaster and thence to the British transit camp where documentation was delightfully brisk and was followed by a taxi ride, at the Queen's, or King's, expense, to the Maranouchi Hotel, with its famed marble bar. This was run for Commonwealth personnel of officer status, which included a lot of girls from the Embassy. The rooms were excellent and a welcome change from a sleeping bag. It cost sixteen shillings a day (60p) and the dining room was thrown in. With an Australian Army Cash Office on the top floor, money was not a problem

For most people a tour of the shops was in order, starting with the American PX, which was huge and appeared to sell everything, and gave a good idea of prices elsewhere. Most of the shopping, though, was done at Takashimayas Department Store, on the Ginza, which liked to be considered the equivalent of Harrods. Noritake dinner services were a favourite and the shop packed them beautifully. They represented wonderful value. With a long final day to fill in, a walk round the Imperial Palace was a praiseworthy but not very profitable outing, and to cross a road in the centre of Tokyo was much more dangerous than being at war in Korea.

Night life in Tokyo depended on one's taste, but the girls were very friendly ...

Inevitable visits to nightclubs found taxi dancers and floor shows, perhaps with a naked girl taking a bath set up on a stage so that all you could see were arms and legs flailing over the side and covering the sex-starved audience in foam. Another was set out on seven floors and charged a different price for entry into each floor, the seventh being the most expensive and the ground floor the cheapest. The girls came down from above on a huge sort of lift. When the customers on the seventh floor had made their choice the lift descended to the sixth floor where a further selection took place. This ritual was repeated on each floor until by the time the lift reached the ground floor there were only the least attractive girls left, with dozens of customers vying to claim one.

For the Sapper other ranks, R&R was much the same. Some took occasional advantage of the rest camp in Inchon, near Seoul, which was comfortable enough but was just that: a rest of five days, sleeping late, having beers in the canteen and with all camp chores carried out by Korean house boys. There was no outside entertainment and a ten-minute walk along a dirt road brought one to the edge of what was little more than a shanty town. Tokyo, on the other hand, was spoken of as a sort of Shangri La, with everything placed at the disposal of sex-starved soldiers who were fawned over by gorgeous women anxious to help them spend their months of back pay.

Though hardly believable today, taking off from Kimpo airfield for Tokyo was the first flight for the majority of soldiers. Arriving at dusk, coaches took leave personnel off on the hour-long journey to the leave centre, with everyone staring out of the windows at the bustle along the roadside, brilliantly lit shops, restaurants and beer halls, and all the flashing neon signs pushing excitement and anticipation to barely bearable levels. The calm and ordered reception at the leave camp, with tea and buns provided by the Japanese Salvation Army, brought every-one down to earth, even more so when the next step was to be escorted to another building where they handed over their personal effects and were ordered to take off all their clothes. 'Just like going to jail,' someone remarked. 'The gas chamber's next,' came from another as they were lead off to a shower, but they came out smelling of carbolic and feeling cleaner than they had for weeks. After clean uniforms and the return of their personal effects, morale was high, but most people were too tired after a long day and though Tokyo was just outside the gate, a meal and the prospect of sleeping on a real mattress was even more tempting.

After drawing their back pay next morning – a Sapper's pay in those days was about £3.50 a week – it was time for everyone to explore the city. Attractive Japanese guides were organized by the British WVS to show the sights and help with shopping, a jaw-dropping experience to men accustomed to the austerity in England. The Ginza, the main shopping street in Tokyo, was a blaze of light and flashing signs from end to end and filled with tempting goods, cameras being the most popular purchase.

Though beer in the canteen was ridiculously cheap, the beer halls and clubs in the city were infinitely preferable. There was also the prospect of female company, with girls latching on to men as soon as they entered. Rather more insidious were the street photographers taking a quick snap and then handing over a ticket to say when and where the photograph could be collected. These invariably had an invitation on the back for a club or brothel, complete with location details.

The plentiful supply of beer was epitomised in:

'The Squaddie's Lament'

I'm lying here, drunk, in a corner
My head beating, just like a drum.
I spent last night in a boozer
And ended up flat on my bum.

My mates, they all lie in the gutter
Wondering just where they are.
Oh Lord, at last I remember.
We're in Tokyo – on R&R!

Though not a patch on Tokyo, it was also possible to enjoy R&R in Kure, the British base in Japan. Hiroshima provided experiences of a different kind by night. It was hard to realize that the city had been devastated by the world's first atomic bomb only a few years before and here were night clubs and wonderful street lighting with thousands of globe lanterns and enormous neon signs that would make Piccadilly Circus look pathetic.

The legendary Commanding Officer, Peter Moore, at that time still a confirmed bachelor, could not see the need for R&R, but he did go, and on return was heard to remark, 'It's good to be back', as he scrubbed Japan out of his hands.

A Special Occasion

Nothing could show the contrast more between those in the forward positions and those six or seven miles away than to find no fewer than seventy-three officers solemnly sitting down to a formal Guest Night, just south of the River Imjin. The occasion was the Annual Sapper-Signals Guest Night and in 1953 it was the Sapper turn to be hosts. They saw no reason why this should not take place and were determined to make it a memorable event.

Officers were despatched far and wide for suitable food and drink. Ice-cream came from some American gunners and someone found the whereabouts of the American ice factory, while the Canadians were able to provide dozens of items which weren't in British rations. A major in Seoul had a sack of potatoes – fresh spuds were, in the words of the country, 'Hav-a-no', but we had to have them with the meat ... Drink was not a problem and we managed to get some Australian hock at just over £1 a bottle and gin at £1.50. We calculated that half a gallon of beer per head would suffice and that we should all be able to forget the war for a few hours.

We had a huge marquee and General West, the Divisional Commander, was the Guest of Honour. Dan Raschen had by good chance found a catering warrant officer who was a real master and produced a memorable meal. Iced clear soup (he'd used two turkeys in it) was followed by some excellent beef steak with tinned asparagus in cheese sauce, peas and two types of potato, then ice-cream, fruit, and angels on horseback. We drank 'The Queen' for the first time.

Fortunately the front line was relatively quiet and the rains were late – the previous year the Imjin had risen thirty-six feet in twenty-four hours.

A Cultural Exchange
1 Troop of 55 Field Squadron were based in a small re-entrant just across the Samichon river, a tributary of the Imjin, on the main lateral road some three miles behind the forward positions. One afternoon they noticed a Jeep that had come off the road some three or four hundred yards towards the American Marine Division on our left flank. It appeared to be abandoned so it was towed in to the troop location and pushed into a secure shelter, dug out of the hillside, with the rest of the troop transport.

A few hours later a couple of American Marines arrived, driving a Wrecker, and asked if anyone had seen their Jeep which had come off the road nearby. Looking innocent, they denied all knowledge, standing in a cluster in front of the missing vehicle, sitting under a tarpaulin in the vehicle bay. After a few more queries as to what might have happened, the Marines switched to another subject, asking if the Troop had any beer for sale, explaining that US forces did not have alcohol. In turn, the Sappers explained that beer was extremely scarce and that they were down to their last crate. Not to be put off, the Marines offered

111

'good money' for the crate but the Sappers held firm and said that it could not be spared. After much haggling and an ever increasing offer, the Sappers reluctantly gave way and sold their 'last crate' to the Americans for many times its true value.

The delighted Marines loaded the beer onto their truck and set off with great glee. The Troop were well pleased too. Not only did they have a large sum of money, but the crate of beer was the one they had found in the overturned Jeep only a few hours before. They had also won a Jeep.

2 Troop had beaten them to it, however, in that they had already 'taken into care' an American Dodge ¾-ton truck which they had found 'abandoned'. Soldiers, particularly Sappers, are not thieves, though – just opportunists.

The Groin Protector

The only thing that really worries a soldier when he is wounded is if he loses his manhood. It would therefore seem to be a good idea if, in addition to their 'flak jackets', they were issued with 'groin protectors'. When the Black Watch received the first ones, a Jock held his up for all to see and, in a tone of derision, said 'What's this then, a fooking cock-box?' While the Sappers looked on in mild amusement, the Company 2IC grabbed it and proudly strapped it on over his trousers, explaining that he had been wounded in Malaya by a bullet that hit him in the thigh within an inch of removing his most precious asset, that he wasn't going to take a second chance, and didn't mind who laughed at him.

Send Port and Pyjamas

It was a dark night when Dan Raschen, returning to his office in Divisional Headquarters, stumbled over a steel picket which removed a small part of his thigh. He picked himself up and went back into the Ops tent to view the damage, which was not all that extensive, but there was a certain amount of blood, probably the only blood seen in Divisional Headquarters in the entire war. At last he could find a genuine use for the field dressing which everyone had to carry at all times. His companions were full of good advice on the medical channels he should now pursue, but Dan decided to go to the Indian Field Ambulance as, being a Saturday night, he would be well placed for their magnificent Sunday curry lunch. This was agreed by the Medical Officer and he was taken there via the Engineer Regimental HQ, where, knowing Dan's partiality to port, he was well fortified for the onward journey.

Sadly, the surgical unit was being reorganized and thoughts of curry lunch receded as he was moved by ambulance Jeep to the nearest MASH (which came off the tongue rather quicker than Mobile Army Surgical Hospital). By 2.00am he was on the operating table, about to be dealt with by an American captain, who sewed him up with six stitches before putting him in the main ward where he happily slept off his port. The male staff were helpful and pleasant but there were two very fat females in trousers (which definitely did not suit them) who taxed Dan's sense of chivalry. A third was more attractive and remembering, that nurses found it pleasing to be called 'Sister', he addressed her as 'Sister' in his most polite manner. That was evidently not the form in America, though. 'You call me Noice,' she said. 'Sister' was evidently altogether too fresh.

Now that his leg had been repaired, Dan asked to go back to his job, but the answer was firmly negative – now he was in the medical system, he would have to stay in it. For good measure, and to ensure he knew his place, one of the fat nurses rolled him over and gave him the most enormous jab of penicillin in his bottom. On recovering a bit from this onslaught, Dan hobbled to the end of the ward and was delighted to be able to make a short telephone call through to the Commonwealth Division where he managed to get hold of one of the Engineer clerks, told him where he was and asked him to send port and pyjamas. With amazing efficiency, both items were delivered early that evening. Luckily they had had the sense to disguise the bottle of port in a parcel as he had heard that alcohol was definitely not allowed in the MASH, or indeed anywhere else in the American forces. Unfortunately, his parcel did not include a corkscrew so, refraining from asking any of the 'noices' for one, he had to broach the bottle by pushing his thumb in the neck, causing a further problem of concealing a full bottle of port under the bedclothes. Ever resourceful, Dan solved the problem easily and without having to share with his fellow American patients.

Feeling rather frail next morning, and with his leg still hurting, he managed to return to Divisional HQ where he was invited by the Chief Clerk to fill in an official accident report form without delay. Against the question demanding details of the circumstances of the accident, he wrote 'I was sober', a statement which, many years later, was still on his personal file in the Ministry of Defence where the fact that he had been sober was so notable as to raise a few eyebrows among his friends.

The Tin Hat

The British soldier has always adopted an individual and idiosyncratic attitude to headgear, particularly in war. Many regiments, of course, have adopted their own particular headgear and there is no doubt that this fosters pride and is good for morale. Sappers in Korea adopted their own particular fads, despite the Divisional Commander's order that steel helmets were to be worn in all forward areas.

On a visit to one particularly forward area, the CRE, Colonel 'Paddy' Hill, upbraided the Troop Commander when he found a wide variety of headgear being worn by his sappers. Turning to the Troop Commander, who was wearing a blue beret, he said 'How do you expect your soldiers to wear steel helmets when you don't set an example yourself?', to which he replied, 'I feel they ought to be able to wear whatever they wish; it is good for their own well-being and many of them, including me, hate tin hats. They are hot, heavy and get in the way when they are working.' The CRE made it quite clear that he disagreed and felt that the Troop Commander should be setting a better example.

That afternoon, while the Troop Commander was talking with Sergeant Shirley MM, his Troop Recce Sergeant, a Sapper arrived and presented him with a brand new steel helmet 'with the compliments of the CRE, Sir'. With that he scuttled off back to Divisional Headquarters. Some time later, with the Troop Commander holding the tin hat in his hand and wondering what to do with it, he suddenly found himself being helped to his feet by Sergeant Shirley. 'What happened?', he asked. 'We were just talking, Sir, when there was a 'woosh' and you fell to the ground at my feet. Are you all right?' The Troop Commander felt a bit dazed and his head hurt. He took off his beret, rubbed his head and found some blood. The beret had a small hole in it and it was evident that he had been hit by a piece of shrapnel. He could vouch for the truth that they always say that you never hear the one that that hits you. He also realized that he was still carrying the CRE's brand new steel helmet and quickly swore Sergeant Shirley to silence, saying 'If the CRE ever finds out that I have been hit on the head while still wearing my beret, I shall never hear the last of it!'

The Stork Landing
It happened to Bill Moncur on the troopship to Korea. HMT *Lancashire* was steaming down the Red Sea, it was a very hot night and he was sleeping on deck when he was woken by a horrible punch on his chest which completely winded him. Gathering his thoughts, he looked down towards his feet and saw what he described as 'the most fearsome long-legged bird standing there looking at me through gimlet eyes. He had a long and most wicked looking beak'. Needless to say, there was much laughter and disbelief at breakfast, only partly assuaged when Bill opened his shirt to disclose the cuts on his chest. He swore that it was a stork that must have been attracted by the lights of the ship and that he watched it taking off again rather skilfully, with a short angled gallop, skimming over the handrail and disappearing into the inky night.

Additional flavour was added to the story by the belief (unproven) that one of the ladies on board might have been (or become) pregnant.

Chapter 12

The Final Months

The two weeks before Christmas 1952 were a quiet time, though the Chinese engaged in intense, though fruitless, propaganda with loud-speaker broadcasts, leaflets and 'Christmas Cards', the latter being left in 'Letter Boxes' in prominent positions in no man's land where our patrols would find them. Christmas Day itself was quiet and, as far as circumstances permitted, it was celebrated in the usual traditional manner. The New Year period which followed was again quiet, although in the second week of January there was a noticeable increase in enemy shelling and mortaring.

On 16 January 1953, orders were received that the Commonwealth Division would go into Corps reserve some ten or twelve miles to the south and be relieved in the line at the end of the month by 2nd US Division, which included the Dutch, French and what was then called 'Siamese' battalions. The Korean Service Corps units were to stay in place and the Divisional Artillery was to remain in support of the Americans as their own artillery was supporting a South Korean Division elsewhere.

While British units knew they were in the theatre for a year, the Americans had a system of rotation based on a points system. They had to gain thirty-six rotation points, based on four for each month in a battalion area, three per month in a less forward area, two in a place like Seoul or Pusan in Korea and one per month in Japan. Thus rotation could come as quickly as nine months for men in forward areas or after as long as three years for those stationed in Japan. This led to some odd situations and was the main topic of conversation in American units. American excavator and truck drivers soon found that they could deliver rock and stone to the KSC just as efficiently if they moved their camp to the north of the River Imjin, which was a three-rotation-point zone.

But before the final Commonwealth units withdrew, in the bitterly cold dawn of 24 January, a fighting patrol from the Duke of Wellington's Regiment, under command of Captain Rodney Harms, accompanied

115

by Captain Dick Sullivan and a detachment of 2 Troop from 55 Field Squadron, carried out a raid across the valley from positions east of the Hook. Their objective was a Chinese tunnel at the base of a hill known as 'Pheasant' and the assault took place in the early morning when the British positions were still in deep shadow from the Chinese to the west and the patrol was able to assemble and move across no man's land without being seen. Morale was high, and they were well prepared, with equipment kept to the minimum, faces blackened and pockets emptied of all papers which might aid identification. A sergeant checking one of his well-known characters said, 'I'll bet you've got some beer hidden away somewhere', and received the reply 'No, Sarge, but I've got an opener in case we find some over there.' Raids in daylight like this were unusual as most of the fighting was confined to the hours of darkness and surprise was achieved. The raid was supported by artillery, the tunnel was destroyed with a satchel charge and the body of a Chinese officer was recovered. There were no British casualties and Dick Sullivan was awarded an immediate Military Cross and Corporal Jenkins a Military Medal.

In Reserve

By 29 January the relief was complete and the Division withdrew out of contact with the enemy for the first time since its formation eighteen months before and moved into reserve behind the Imjin River. It was to enjoy two months' rest and a welcome period of training, though the Sappers were kept busy developing camps and winterizing accommodation and equipment in the reserve area. Everyone tried to make themselves as comfortable as possible and one squadron utilized a tent as an Officers' and Sergeants Mess, put in a false ceiling, and a wooden floor to keep off the frozen ground. They even had a brick fireplace, the brick conveniently falling into the back of a truck after it had accidentally nudged a tottering wall down in Seoul.

During the period in reserve each squadron rotated its troops fortnightly: one troop on local R&R, one troop on track construction on Line Kansas, the Divisional reserve position, and one troop on training. The training was divided into a week on general military and weapon training and a week on Bailey bridge training. Superimposed was a regimental wireless exercise, a divisional exercise in the counter-attack role and several brigade exercises. By the end of the ten week reserve period a lot of almost forgotten basic military skills had been re-learnt. The period in reserve was crowned by a Sapper Demonstration Day for the remainder of the Division to show the variety and ubiquity of Sapper tasks. As a final touch, 1 Troop of 55 Field Squadron, spurred on by a promise of a bottle of beer per man for every minute under fifteen, built a sixty-foot skeleton single-single Widened Bailey bridge

1. Sergeant George Orton DCM. He was awarded the Distinguished Conduct Medal for his actions during a seven-hour engagement with Chinese forces in the course of which he not only led local protection for Centurion tanks of the Irish Hussars but also took command of a tank when its commander was wounded severely.

2. From time to time tanks, such as this Centurion, got into difficulties on some of the natural obstacles of the Korean terrain.

3. In the winter months the earth froze solid and made life even harsher.

4. Roads had to be built or widened. Sappers work on strengthening and widening a bend while a mobile light anti-aircraft gun stands guard.

5. Footbridge across the Imjin river.

6. Sappers performed a wide range of tasks in Korea. Among them was the re-alignment of this stream in Violet valley to prevent flooding of the road.

7. Sappers strengthen a culvert to protect this roadway across a causeway before the rains come.

8. Sappers working on a 'wash-out' at Indigo 4.

9. To prevent enemy observation of roads Sappers erected screens such as these, using 20-foot poles, chicken wire and scrim.

10. Cableway on Hill 355, known as 'Little Gibraltar'.

11. Hard-core was needed for a range of tasks. These lorries are being loaded at a quarry in 1953. The loading equipment was known as 'Monster'.

12. Another loading operation.

13. A Grizzly being operated by 55 Field Squadron to separate large stones from the gravel needed for road surfacing.

14. *Storming the Warsaw Caves* from the painting by David Rowlands.

15. The Royal Engineers' Korean centrepiece depicts the South Great Gate of Seoul and commemorates all the engineer units of the Commonwealth Division which took part in the campaign.

16. Among the dangers faced by troops in Korea was that of crashing on the many bends on the roads. This sign was erected in an attempt to draw drivers' attention to the 'dangerous curves'.

17. Mines presented another danger and this sign, at the south end of Pintail bridge, once again uses a cartoon female figure to draw attention to the risks.

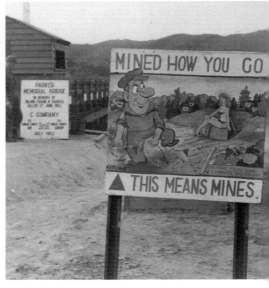

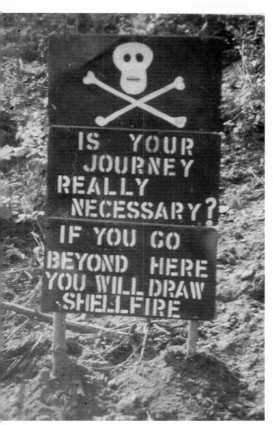

18 & 19. Other signs indicated the danger of shelling in stark fashion.

20. No. 55 Field Squadron built this Bailey bridge, codenamed 'Windmill' and proclaimed the fact to those who used it.

21. A shell bursts on the rear slope of the Hook position.

22 & 23. Two views of the Hook from the defenders' positions. A communication trench may be seen in the second view.

24. And another view of the Hook.

25. Some of the most vicious fighting of the war occurred around the Hook. This post-war view of the front of the feature was taken from about midway between the British and Chinese positions.

26. Living conditions in the front line were difficult and digging in was essential. This is the entrance to a tunnel on the Hook.

27. Pintail Bridge being constructed over the Imjin river by US engineers. This bridge replaced the original pontoon bridge.

28. Construction work underway on Teal bridge, also by US engineers.

29. (*Left*) Those wounded in Korea were often able to enjoy a period of convalescent leave in Japan. Some spent time on the island of Miyajima – where many *Kamikaze* pilots spent their last days – and enjoyed its tranquillity and scenery such as this pleasant harbour.

30. (*Right*) Window shopping in Miyajima.

31. Headquarters of 1st Commonwealth Division, 1953.

32. Colonel Arthur Morris speaking to a Sapper from Major Scott-Bowden's 12 Field Squadron in 1953, 'So how are you going to clear this minefield?'

33. Life went on nonetheless as these members of the Royal Engineers and Royal Signals demonstrate by holding their annual dinner in the field.

34. (*Left*) Some things haven't changed. This Korean peasant's lifestyle is similar to that of the 1950s.

35. (*Right*) And it was a typical Korean peasant with his heavy load that was modelled to represent the first United Nations' war in this presentation piece to mark the service of 55 Field Squadron with 29 Independent Brigade in Korea.

36. In April 1988 the memorial to those officers and men of the Corps of Royal Engineers who lost their lives in Korea was unveiled by the Chief Royal Engineer, General Sir George Cooper, and dedicated in the Garrison Church at Chatham.

37. The Sappers' Korean Memorial.

in eleven minutes dead, to get Sherman tanks across and into the attack. Stands were erected for spectators and one demonstration, of a bridge demolition under fire, with a sapper being 'blown' off the bridge into the water was so realistic that numbers of spectators rushed forward to help the 'wounded' sapper! The demonstration was further enlivened by the Press photographer who found himself almost too realistically charged by a tank amidst dummy explosions on all sides of him, and the Giant Viper whose hose broke in half to let the rocket and front portion travel nearly a mile to scatter, fortunately without damage, a crowd of innocent Korean villagers going about their normal business.

The Divisional Battle School

Meanwhile, training continued apace at the Divisional Battle School over in Japan, which had been set up immediately prior to the formation of the Commonwealth Division. John Hackford, who had been sent to the, mainly Australian, Engineer Regiment based in Kure, spent most of his time with some Canadian Sappers constructing the School, which was way out in the country some fifteen miles from Kure at Hara Mura. All the water was piped from a small mountain lake and a camp was soon set up, primarily to train the infantry reinforcements and to make them fit again after weeks on a troopship. A small Sapper wing was provided to train the Infantry Assault Pioneers and for battle simulation. Subsequently Sappers were taken on the Battle School establishment and All Arms mine training became a routine feature; Sapper reinforcements, too, were sent through the Battle School.

By the end of 1952 the Battle School was well established. The staff were all battle experienced and keen to pass on their expertise. The training was hard, with officers treated the same as the other ranks, starting off every morning with a run to the top of a nearby ridge – 'the last man up is a sissy' sort of thing. The firing ranges were covered with scrub pine and dwarf oaks similar to the hills in Korea but were prone to catching fire as the result of the plentiful supply of ammunition. Infantry platoon tactics and live firing with every type of weapon they might find in Korea, including mortars and tanks, was the order of the day and each man fired about 500 rounds from the different weapons during his Course. The Camp itself was far from comfortable, deliberately so as the Commandant was determined that every trainee should be really fit and acclimatized before proceeding to Korea. If they were tough, fit and well trained, they would be less likely to become casualties, or suffer from frost-bite or pneumonia in the harsh winter months.

While small arms training was most important, especially for Sappers who were often called on to act as infantry, many found that the Sten gun, and in particular the 3.5-inch Rocket Launcher, caused problems.

117

Then there were the hand grenades. They made everyone nervous, particularly the Instructors. Watching too many films where grenades invariably exploded at the opponent's feet, blowing him to pieces, induced a cavalier attitude which was as far from reality as it was possible to be. The correct method of throwing and the importance of throwing oneself to the ground, unless throwing from a weapon pit with plenty of protection, was dinned in to everyone's head. The effect of an exploding grenade, with its all-round danger area, was not always appreciated on first acquaintance.

With the constant use of live ammunition, especially by inexperienced troops, casualties were to be expected as an inevitable price to pay in the course of training for war, though every effort was made to avert them. One morning Captain Bill Moncur and his team fired off their fifteen 60mm mortar bombs and then stepped aside to let Captain Frank Murdoch and his team take over. As they walked off the firing point there was an almighty explosion followed by total silence. A 60mm mortar bomb had exploded as it lifted above the site and had showered its deadly shrapnel down on the firing point. Not only were those on the firing point affected, but a party of about sixty Sappers undergoing weapon instruction close by were also stricken. An infantry subaltern, his bag packed to return home the next day, was killed instantly and Frank Murdoch died of his injuries a few hours later. Rescue helicopters could not get through due to heavy hill fog and all the injured were evacuated by road to the Military Hospital in Kure. Many of them were injured seriously, one of them being Lieutenant Brian Cave who had his armpit ripped out by shrapnel.

Infantry training over, it was time for specialist training and for the Sappers this meant mine warfare and explosives in particular. Though basic training back in the UK had included both subjects, there was still much to learn when faced with close proximity to the real thing. Anti-personnel mines, including the Chinese wooden box mines, were particularly dangerous and it was important to avoid being killed. Korea was littered with minefields, many unmarked, and mine prodders and a pocket of safety pins were the Sappers' best friends. A good knowledge of explosives was also an important aspect as they were used in road building, quarrying, and demolition of stranded tanks, enemy tunnels and so on. Not the least of their uses, plastic explosive was the best way of making a quick brew or for catching fish. At the end of their course, anything up to four weeks depending on when people were needed by their units in Korea, the intake would march with their instructors the fifteen miles or so back to Kure to await posting to their unit in Korea.

One morning the Commandant sent for one of the Sapper officers waiting to go over to Korea as a Battle Casualty Replacement (BCR) and explained that he wanted to have a troop of Centurion tanks at the

School. While the tanks could be brought up by rail to the nearest station, there was only a very narrow track from there to the School. The officer promised to see what he could do and set off on a recce, reporting back that he thought it would be possible to get the tanks through, with a little strengthening of bridges and widening here and there. A day or so later he took a party of sappers with a selection of twelve-inch by twelve-inch timber baulks and set to work, strengthening each bridge as the tanks got to them. The bridges all creaked a bit and the odd parapet cracked as there was only an inch or so to spare on either side, demanding careful driving, but they all arrived safely at Hara Mura. He doubted though if they would ever get back again and they are probably there to this day. It was only when he came back that the Commandant confessed that the Australian CRE had done a recce himself and had declared that the task was impossible!

For new arrivals, waiting to go over to Korea, there was plenty of advice on the Japanese way of life and their attitude to sex. While the padres attacked promiscuity from a moral standpoint, the medical officers' approach was more pragmatic and emphasized the dangers of venereal disease and the methods of avoiding it. The Americans had a marching song which included the lines:

> *I met a girl and she was willing,*
> *Now I'm getting penicilling.*

It was hardly surprising, though, that barrack-room gossip centred round sex. There was plenty of it available in Japan, but there was little opportunity for it in Korea and the Division's period in reserve was soon over.

Mines And Minefields The Bane of our Lives
Though much attention was given to mine warfare at the Divisional Battle School, its importance was really brought home to people when they first came across a real minefield on arrival in Korea. Everyone's first sight of a red triangle denoting a minefield, and the sudden realisation that this one was for real, sent a shiver down the spine. There were plenty of stories of minefield casualties and all ranks were well aware of the dangers but nevertheless, there were always incidents.

———————————

Dan Raschen had joined 12 Field Squadron at the end of August 1951, shortly before the whole Commonwealth Division was to advance across the River Imjin and he was soon asked to mount a road recce for 3 RAR (3 Bn, Royal Australian Regiment). Anywhere else it would have been lucky to have been called a track, but in Korea it was a 'road'. The road turned out to be an unditched track of fairly flat earth, about twelve feet wide and completely unmarked by vehicle tracks, though on closer inspection there were what appeared to be Chinese rope-soled shoe marks. Borrowing a bayonet, Dan probed the area some three inches under the surface. Sensing resistance, and with increased care, it didn't take long to unearth his first Chinese Box Mine. (See illustration.)

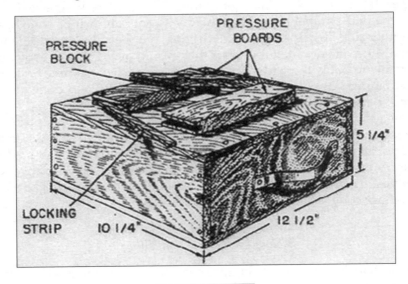

Having established a new line north of the Imjin, the Division consolidated their positions. Barry Pollard and his Troop were tasked with laying anti-personnel mines over on the right boundary of the Division and the Infantry were soon clamouring for Sappers to lay a minefield to stretch eastwards from the lower slopes of Hill 317 to join up with the minefield which Barry was laying about 600 yards to the right.

Dan Raschen was called on again and described what happened next:

> The hillside where my minefield was to start was steep and, with no form of track, would have been difficult enough had all the small pine trees been standing. As it was, the lower slopes of 317 had been subject to a napalm attack so the trees had all been scorched and we were constantly stepping over, or ducking under, filthy black branches. I had never laid a live minefield, but had been trained to lay anti-tank mines to a design I knew well, always in grass fields which were level and reasonably flat. Such exercises started with a lorry driving up to the end of the

proposed minefield and the mines, never in any great quantity, being unloaded. Great play was made, very sensibly, of recording exactly where the minefield was laid, so that, not just in training, we could lift it again if needs be. First a reference point had to be chosen nearby, perhaps the corner of a building, or any other prominent object sufficiently permanent as to be unlikely to disappear completely in war. It was from this reference point that the survey of the minefield, made with a compass, started. I was pretty sure that, on that napalmed slope which had gone out of its way to be featureless, I was never going to know to the nearest couple of hundred yards where I was, let alone pinpoint the end of my minefield exactly on the map.

Major Peter Leslie, my OC in 12 Field Squadron, told me not to forget to complete the perimeter fence before I armed the mines at the end of each day, meaning the removal of their safety pins. This was quite a point as the field was obviously going to take us several days so we would have to put up a temporary fence on the open end each night. Mines were still in short supply in Korea and I was told that the first hundred or so would be American M3 anti-personnel mines, then the rest of the 200 that we would need for laying with tripwires would be another type of American mine, the M2, and also some of our old British Mark 2s. I knew that the M3 was just a lump of cast iron filled with TNT, whereas the others were what we called 'bouncing mines' and much more complicated. Our Mark 2s had been obsolescent for years, so all this started to set an interesting scene, as did the news that the usual igniters for the M3 mines were not available and that we would be given items known as M1 pull fuzes.

In no time I had managed to find M1 pull fuzes in the excellent little American Mines book which we had been issued with and discovered that after withdrawing not one, but two safety pins, a pull of two to three pounds on the little ring at the end of the igniter would release the striker and fire whatever explosive charge it was connected to. Normal pull switches of the type one used with tripwire mines needed a pull of fifteen to twenty pounds to set them off, so the care needed in setting these booby trap switches would be comparable to that of playing a salmon on a trout rod.

As I set out the line along which the first row of mines would be laid, I found that I was walking along what must have been a Chinese defended position, which may have accounted for the attention the area had been given by the napalm. Amongst various items of rather dull equipment still lying around were a dozen or so small wooden boxes, which I knew must be the Chinese version of the old German Schu mine. These devices contained a small charge of TNT and a rudimentary fuze from which the safety pin was pushed out as the lid was pushed down by a walking man. The usual effect was not only the removal of a 'schu', but a foot and part of a leg as well. I kept well clear of them. (See illustration.)

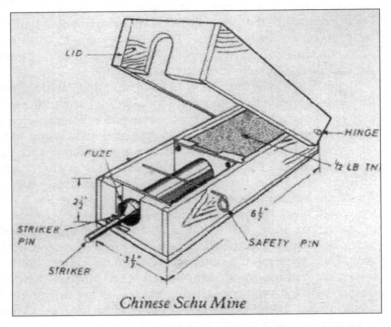

Chinese Schu Mine

I gave top priority to building a footpath for getting the stores up the awkward hillside and through the napalmed trees and by the next afternoon our Korean labour had hacked, picked and shovelled an excellent access route. As we had laid none of these mines before, let alone with booby trap switches, the consensus of opinion was that it should be the Troop Commander's honour to arm them. This involved pulling out the safety pins from the booby trap switches, which had been screwed in, one to each mine, and once done, meant that the mine would explode at a tiny touch of its tripwire. I was thankful that the wind was not blowing, and quickly appreciated that a hand as steady as one that spills no froth from a brimming glass of ale would be required.

My job in arming each one was to gently make fast the wires to the ring, making sure that they were just tight enough to be off the ground, but on no account exerting a pull of more than two pounds, then to ease out the safety pins. After that, it was a case of edging away extremely carefully without touching the tripwires, or rolling anything onto them. To start with, this was all rather hair-raising, but after the first few the main problem was to keep concentrating. The tripwires were specifically designed to blend with their background and, even after handling them a moment before, were extraordinarily difficult to locate. I was thankful that we were doing the laying and arming by day, and wondered how folk ever coped at night. After having learnt British minefield drills for eight years, here was I laying my first live minefield with unknown mines to almost unknown drills. All very strange.

The fence on the Chinese side had to run through thick trees, so some care was needed in aligning it to make sure that it kept properly clear of the forward mines, but the fence on the home side looked a much easier task and we were making better progress in setting it out when, close on the ground beside us, there was the characteristic plop, followed by the hiss of a hand grenade being ignited. I needn't have worried about warning my assistant, as he had got the message remarkably swiftly, but I still shouted loudly. Otherwise, I muttered 'Good old Mother Earth' and attempted to simulate an ever flatter pancake. Have you ever thought, when lying on your face, whether your bottom sticks up more with the muscles tensed, or when all floppy and relaxed? Until then I hadn't and am still not sure which I would advise. However, the hissing continued for an interminable time, and I was convinced that the bang at the end of it all was likely to be enormously large. It never came, so eventually I looked up very cautiously, to find that a trip flare had started the makings of a forest fire. Almost at the same moment an exceedingly irate Australian soldier arrived, who told us what a couple of Pommy sissies we were.

Soon after we had started the minelaying next day we finished the stock of M3 mines and had to start laying the M2 American bouncing mines instead. These were based on the principle of the much dreaded German S mines which were first laid in vast quantities in front of German positions at El Alamein. When detonated they exploded at about head height and a man lying down was just as vulnerable as one standing up.

The M2 mine needed to be laid upright, or the bomb would not be projected upwards. To fix them on the ground they had to be at least partially buried, and this was easier said than done amongst the large stones and pine roots. However, Sgt Marshall (my Troop Sergeant) soon had answers to the problems, and I left him with a party to do the job as I went off with two men rolling out the barbed wire through the trees for the forward fence on the Chinese side of the ridge line. Though there were no friends in front of us, the Chinamen had not been in evidence, but an adequate number of their shells, say one every couple of minutes, were soon arriving in our area. It wasn't long, however, before we heard an explosion with more reverberation than the crack of a shell and knew that another of yesterday's mines had gone off. We assumed that another branch must have fallen on a tripwire, and I was beginning to understand why the reliability of tripwire minefields was in question.

Meanwhile the minelayers had just topped the hundred mines for the day and I and Sgt Marshall stayed after the others had left to remove the safety pins. The hillside on which those mines had been laid, balanced would be a better word, was much steeper than the gentler slopes of the previous days and the act of arming the mines provided sporting occupation. To approach a mine from uphill, test the tension of the tripwires, very gently remove the safety pins and then climb or crawl up the slope again to regain the comparative safety of the line of the laying tape was quite a feat.

On the following morning we were off early, and I again started the day on the forward slope with the party setting out the minefield fence. No sooner had we started work than there was an explosion back over the brow of the hill. This had happened so soon after our arrival that I sensed something might be wrong, so hastened back to where I had left the fencing party and was told that one of my sappers had set off a mine. The injured man was only about fifteen yards inside the minefield, and between us we carried him out, having located the lie of the local tripwires. We did what we could for him, but he died on the way to the medical post.

Evidently the poor chap had been sent for stores and had taken the shortest route, straight through the edge of the minefield, which was fully fenced and properly marked with its red triangles. A friend had shouted 'Stop', but the victim had answered cheerily, 'They are not armed', and had gone ahead. It was the more sad because it was such an unnecessary accident, only too typical of the many which were going to occur as the months went by.

In a highly sober mood we continued minelaying at a good speed, but to make up the numbers for the last few mines, we had to use some of our own British bouncing anti-personnel mines, of which we had been the ungrateful recipients. These had a poor reputation at the best of times and, sure enough, I managed to get into difficulties when arming the very last ones. I had the tripwires rather too taut, had pulled out one of the two safety pins with which the mines were fitted and could not budge the other. Nor could I get the first one back in. Apart from Sgt Marshall, I was the only United Nations soldier on the Chinese side of that hill, and suddenly felt exceptionally lonely. Fortunately, Marshall came along the minefield fence a few minutes later to report that he had finished his half of the arming and I told him that I was stuck. He promptly said he was sure he could put things right and, knowing how easy it would be for us both to be killed by trying to deal with one mine, he asked me to withdraw further back. He had the job finished in a matter of seconds and we had the doubtful satisfaction of knowing that we might have laid the last of that particular type of mine ever to be used in anger.

One evening Dan was told by the Adjutant that a South Korean soldier had been killed in one of the old minefields behind us and that everyone would be much obliged if he would please get him out. After a rather sleepless night, Dan set off next morning and described what happened:

From the track beside the minefield, the poor chap's friends pointed out to me in which direction the body lay. Although, luckily from my point of view, he was not very far into the field from the fence, only about twenty-five yards, the undergrowth confirmed my worst fears. The field had been laid with trip wires over unharvested rice the previous winter, then the summer growth had swamped the evidence and died off in the frost, to leave a tangled mat of what looked like long-dead grass. Even without the weed tangle, there was obviously no chance of identifying the location of individual mines from the information on the minefield record.

There was no point in hurrying, and I didn't. Having sent the Koreans down the track in one direction and my driver and jeep in the other, I crawled under the fence and into the field. Never have I concentrated so continuously, as every piece of very cold dead rice had to be combed with my fingers to find any trip wires. If the rules for laying minefields were obeyed, no mine or trip wire should have been nearer than five yards from the perimeter fence, but I was in no mind to trust those who had laid the field a year earlier.

I never was the best shape for elegant crawling, and it was a relief to stand up every few yards, stretch and attempt to see the casualty. On the second occasion I did, and luckily was not far off the shortest route to him. I pegged a tape beside me as I went, and had some safety pins with me in case I came upon a mine actually on my route, which I did not. I only found two trip wires, both slack, so it would have been safe to cut them, but I had a fear of jerking them in so doing, so laid a white handkerchief on top. I then had to stand up, take a step over the handkerchief, kneel, and start combing the foliage again with all too numb fingers before continuing again at the crawl.

It took me nearly two hours to reach the poor little Korean, who was so small that I could carry him under one arm. Back down the marking tape I walked, again stepping with great care and considerable fear of wobble over my hankies on the trip wires, and was back at the minefield fence and onto the track in no time.

It was not long afterwards that it was the turn of Jock Cormack's Troop to be in support of 3 RAR in the area of Pt 227. As a first requirement the battalion needed the clearing of mines and booby traps from an area forward of their defences and then to gap existing minefields to provide patrol routes. It was not possible to do this work by night and, apart from the considerable danger from the mines and unknown booby traps themselves, any movement by day was extremely risky as the whole area was directly overlooked by an enemy OP, 200-300 yards away. The work was successfully concluded and hugely impressed the Australians.

As minefields were laid, so the report forms came into Regimental HQ for the Intelligence Officer to mark on the master map and file for safe-keeping. It was up to him, too, to ensure that the standard of reporting was uniformly good, and it was only too easy, from the comfort of a warm office some miles back, to demand precision and classroom neatness in every report. It was only when Jock Cormack submitted a report with the heading, 'Laid in the presence of the enemy. Accuracy cannot be guaranteed' that the IO realized that allowances needed to be made. In fact, it was very seldom that such reports were not full and excellent. Every officer knew that he might well be asked to lift a similar field later, or to make a gap in one of our own minefields.

Spring weather was, by day, really hot and a side effect was the 'forest fire'. The three months of intense frost had killed off all the grass, rice and weeds, and the scrub oak and chestnuts, with their undergrowth of creepers and wild azaleas, were parched dry too. Before the sap rose, the fires started and very attractive an uninhabited hillside could be if it blazed at night. When there was a fire in a minefield beside the road, matters became less attractive. One offshoot of these fires was that more and more of the old minefields became of questionable danger to the enemy, but remained a perishing nuisance to ourselves.

On 6 April 1952, the Regiment suffered a sad accident which caused more casualties than any single enemy action. 3 Troop, 12 Field Squadron had been tasked with laying an anti-personnel minefield for one of the battalions. The mines had been taken to the unit rendezvous but due to a heavy enemy attack the operation was postponed for twenty four hours and the mines had been brought back. On the following evening, three boxes containing 150 Schu-mines (75lbs TNT) were being reloaded into a truck when they exploded, killing five Sappers and wounding two. A most searching inquiry revealed no lack of safety and no definite proof of sabotage. The Troop, with commendable courage, completed the minelaying operation two nights later.

On the night of 9 May 1952 Lieutenant Colin Carr was engaged in the hazardous task of clearing old minefields in front of the forward positions of the Welch Regiment. These minefields were particularly dangerous to enter since they were in full view of the enemy and had been churned up by shellfire, thereby making the mines difficult to locate. Colin's Troop was starting to lift part of an existing field when four of his men were wounded by incoming shells. The following day, Colin located and lifted all the remaining mines, and that night super- vised the laying of 300 new mines. By this time he had been working for almost thirty-six hours and the CO forbade him to do any more clearing himself before dark. It was then that a deeply-buried mine resulted in one sapper being killed and another wounded. Colin organized the evacuation of the casualties.

On the morning of 13 May, Colin stepped on a mine which had been displaced and buried by shellfire. As a result he lost one foot and had his other leg broken. Despite being in great pain, he shouted instructions to his radio operator and, while being carried to the Regimental Aid Post, gave an accurate account of how the accident had happened and provided the information necessary to complete the mine-clearing task. He was awarded an immediate MC.

While recuperating, Colin modified his old bicycle so that he could ride it with one leg and when he went swimming in the sea he removed his artificial leg, planted it upright in the sand and ordered his dog to stand guard to dissuade other canines from mistaking it for a tree stump.

Accidents in our own minefields continued all the year round. As most of the fields had been laid by Sappers we felt a responsibility for preventing casualties to our own side, but however much we tried we could suggest no easy answers. With a view to analysing what went wrong, we kept a tally of all accidents. About half of the casualties were due to warlike circumstances, such as a shell splinter cutting the minefield perimeter fence and a returning patrol walking in by mistake, and half due to plain stupidity. We had soldiers running into minefields, perhaps after a drink or three, and shouting to military police, 'Come and get me', sensitive souls who were determined to get behind a bush or bank before spending a penny, or more, and soldiers chasing deer. All set off mines.

By 1952 there were some 350 minefields within the divisional area, many of them marked insufficiently or even not at all. Many minefield records had been lost, were incorrectly made out, or had been mislaid. There were numerous minefield accidents and a large number of 'near misses' usually involving Sappers as we were the people everyone turned to when there was a problem. Thus, in September 1952, the Regiment established a Mine Training Area and ran one-day courses for All Arms on how to avoid casualties on mines, especially our own. This mine training proved its worth many times over though, sadly, there were still a number of casualties.

For our own part, we sent out parties whenever possible to check and, if necessary, repair perimeter fences. In the event of casualties, it was always felt that rescuing victims was an officer responsibility. It was not a task that anyone relished.

Because of the high incidence of minefield accidents, a routine became established known as the Bluebell Drill. Each Troop Commander had in his Jeep, items known as his Bluebell Kit, consisting of wire feelers, for brushing through undergrowth, safety pins and morphine syrettes as well as shell dressings and tourniquets. In emergencies instructions were to inject straight through the tunic into the deltoid muscle. This had nothing to do with one's day-to-day tasks but solely to facilitate urgent response to incidents. By force of circumstances, officers in their Jeeps were usually first on the scene and associated with rescue work.

A few months later Jeffery Lewins, a Troop Officer supporting the King's Liverpool Regiment, was tasked to lift a section of anti-tank minefield to provide a counter-attack route for our armour. There were already electrically controlled anti-personnel mines immediately in front of the position to allow patrols to pass through, and to deny passage of the enemy, especially when a patrol was withdrawing under pressure. These controlled mines, the concept of Major Jimmy Grice, commanding 12 Field Squadron, were based on two-way switches in housing made by Ted Sharp, at that time the Regimental Signals Officer.

In this particular case, Minefield Records showed that the anti-tank minefield had a standard pattern of three double rows: the rear rows were soon found, in accordance with the record, and Jeffery and his Recce Sgt went on to locate the two further forward rows, with the former taking the furthermost. While searching on his stomach – it was broad daylight in full view of the enemy, though it was hoped that with the early morning sun behind them they might not be seen – Jeffery heard an explosion behind him. It turned out to be the very nice recce Corporal Lipscomb, a South African, who had been killed by a so-called 'anti-tank' mine.

It was quickly concluded that chemical fuses for anti-tank mines could become sensitive to the point of turning into anti-personnel mines after two winters in the Korean ground. The CRE opined that this was a tricky problem and that we would not know how to deal with it until the mines were brought in for examination. Jeffery was detailed to collect all the mines, a daunting prospect, but fortunately his OC provided an 'interpretation', which was to tell him to go out and pull all the mines and blow them in situ. However, the matter turned out to be rather more difficult – although the mines in the rear row were undoubtedly there (and armed), the middle row was there but not armed and the front row nearest the enemy could not be found at all. Jeffery had a difficult couple of days in the fresh air, watched by the puzzled Chinese, before he could convince a suspicious CRE that he really had lifted all the mines that were there.

So what had happened to all the mines? Nobody enjoys laying live mines, even 'just' anti-tank mines. Perhaps the mine layers had not been monitored by requiring arming rings etc to be accounted for, and what about safety pins? Though forward troops carried a pocketful of pins for disarming mines, it did not necessarily mean that they had come from mines which they had just laid.

The forward minefields required constant inspection and repair. On one particular night one of the Troop Commanders in 12 Field Squadron, John Elderkin, was accompanied by Sapper Howell Davies who had become something of a specialist at inspecting and checking the state of minefield wiring. The Sapper, who was leading, suddenly realised that wiring had been cut away by enemy fire and that they were already in an anti-personnel minefield. The Sapper crawled very slowly forward, telling his Troop Commander to put his hands where he, the Sapper, had put his knees. He then led his Troop Commander out of the mine-field. Perhaps not surprisingly, they subsequently became firm friends and were still in touch fifty years later, the Sapper in question, Howell Davies, retiring as a sergeant.

On another occasion, a Troop Commander was carrying out a recce with OC 55 Field Squadron for a new MSR (Main Supply Route) when they came across minefield markers denoting a minefield stretching across the proposed alignment. They had the supposed minefield record with them and the Troop Commander had just stepped over the perimeter fence when he called out to his OC, 'Don't move, I'm standing on a tripwire!'

They both survived and went on to higher things (on earth and not in heaven).

Dealing with anti-personnel mines, whether laying them or lifting them, was the least popular pastime, particularly in bad weather. Often the trip-wires crossed other wires. If tripped or cut, these mines detonated. It was believed that these mines had been responsible for the deaths of three officers and a senior NCO. One dealt with them by lying face-down with one's face about a foot from the mine. One then had to insert a safety-pin through the holes in the sleeve and a corresponding hole in the striker. It would then be safe to cut the trip-wires and unscrew the fuse. If the pin would not go through, then one had a choice: one could very carefully push it in, or pull it out. This did not call for judgement but for luck, to be guided one hoped, by Providence. Sometimes one did this at temperatures of −25 degrees C. At the time, perhaps not unsurprisingly, sweat covered one from top to bottom.

For our own part we sent out parties whenever possible to check and, if necessary, repair perimeter fences. In the event of casualties, minefield rescuing was considered to be an officer's perk. This did not mean that others could not do it, but that officers felt it was beyond self-respect to ask others to undertake this duty. It was not a task that anyone relished and Oliver Keef earned everyone's gratitude when he undertook many more than his share of rescues or retrievals, always with no fuss. On two other quite separate occasions, Ted Sharp rescued a soldier from the Royal Tank Regiment and then two Korean Service Corps soldiers.

All three were alive when he got them out, but all of them died sub-sequently. He commented later how they had seemed fairly lightweight on his back, having lost most of their legs. There was very little blood and he recalled their eyes blinking as they passed over to what he hoped was a better place.

On one occasion a Troop Commander in 55 Field Squadron was contacted by a forward battalion to say that there had been an explosion in a minefield just behind their position and it was suspected that a soldier had entered it to recover a silk parachute from a flare. Would we investigate?

The Troop Commander collected the minefield record from RHQ and went with his Troop Officer to the site. Minefield records in those areas of paddy fields were difficult to prepare because there were no permanent features such as trees, walls or fences to act as datum points: angle iron pickets were driven in to form the datum point and the bearing marker, but such pickets were also used for the fencing at a later date.

Nobody from the companies could identify where exactly the explosion had occurred, so it was decided to enter the minefield to investigate. They found what was 'obviously' the datum point and the bearing picket, and the Troop Officer marched out into the minefield on the correct bearing, followed by the Troop Commander; they saw no sign of either the explosion or a body. As they stood there discussing which area to search next, the Troop Commander happened to look down and saw, between the feet of the other officer, the three prongs of an anti-personnel mine ... Why on earth two officers were standing close together in the middle of a minefield, contrary to everything one was taught, has never been disclosed, but the body of a soldier was eventually recovered without any further problems and the Troop Officer went on to become a Professor of Nuclear Physics at Cambridge University.

An infantry battalion, newly arrived in the theatre, were visited by a Sapper staff officer from Divisional Headquarters to find out if there was anything they would like the Sappers to do on their behalf. The Adjutant pointed out that the HQ was sited downwind from a very busy cross-roads, the dust made life very uncomfortable and would the Sappers please clear the adjoining minefield across the road so that they could move there. The Sapper officer took a deep breath, pointed out that the minefield in question was covered in deep undergrowth and he really didn't think it was worth hazarding sapper lives merely so that

131

the Adjutant could sit at his desk more comfortably. If that was his only request, he would leave him in peace with his dust-covered files. The Sapper officer was not known for showing restraint and it was thought that the Adjutant had got off remarkably lightly.

A colourful Sapper officer was posted to the Regiment as Second-in-Command from Hong Kong. He was a distinguished officer, with a DSO, who had travelled out from England on the *Empire Halladale*, the original 'Slow Boat to China', and been dropped off at Hong Kong the previous year where he had taken off his Lieutenant Colonel's badges of rank on the quayside and declared that he was now back to what he was doing in 1940, commanding a Field Park Squadron. In the intervening years, as he told us, he had held a lieutenant commander's rank in the Navy, as well as his Sapper one, as he had been tasked to sink the German battleship *Tirpitz* in a Norwegian fiord. For this, he had first recruited 200 Wrens and had then been involved in midget submarines. He never sank the *Tirpitz* but it made a good story and we never knew quite what to believe, though he did have the DSO. After the war he became involved with guided weapons and was the Army's greatest expert, or so he told us. He could certainly give an excellent lecture on the subject as everyone on the boat could testify.

After dinner one night he came up to one of the Troop Commanders, explained that he was disappointed to have missed so much of the war in Korea, with all its excitements, and wanted to know what it felt like to go through a minefield so would he take him through one now? The Troop Commander's reply is not repeatable.

Perhaps it is not so surprising that Sappers are called 'Mad, Married or Methodist'. History does not relate whether he was a Methodist, but he was certainly mad and he did have six children.

Back in the Line

The Division was due to return early in April 1953 to the same sector of the front which it had held previously, so Commanders and staffs had been keeping a keen watch on events that had been occurring in their absence. Where previously the Chinese had relied on a great weight of artillery and mortar fire before an attack, they had recently been putting in several silent night attacks with the object of avoiding the defenders' defensive fire. This may well have been because of the American defensive tactic of holding an outpost line, which lent itself to being 'taken out' in this manner. Commanders were certain that the Chinese could be expected to revert to their earlier methods of heavy bombardments once the Commonwealth Division returned to the line, and preparations were made to reinforce our positions with bunkers

132

and overhead cover. The first week in April was devoted to preparation for Operation COTSWOLD, the relief of the 2nd US Division in the line by the Commonwealth Division, and by the night of 5/6 April the relief had been completed and the Commonwealth Division was disposed on its old front, with 29 British Brigade on the left, 25 Canadian Brigade in the centre and 28 Commonwealth Brigade on the right. The Black Watch returned to their former positions on the Hook, with the American Marines on their left, relieved later by the Turkish Brigade.

28 Field Engineer Regiment quickly settled down again to the never-ending tasks of tunnelling, fieldworks, minefield checks and, as always, road maintenance. 12 Field Squadron, back on Hill 355, continued its work on the defence positions and were kept extremely busy – a catalogue of their activities, covering just one month, is in the Annex on p. 199. 55 Field Squadron, for their part, moved elsewhere with their own Brigade into a re-entrant with a marshy patch in the middle, the home of numerous resident frogs making a remarkable din – no doubt the mating season.

During our absence from the front line the Chinese artillery had been becoming more and more active, with the weekly average of just over 500 shells and mortar bombs in the beginning of 1952 increasing to three times that one year later. This was to increase even more dramatically after our return to the front line when the weekly average was over 4,000, with 20,000 rounds in the final week of May. There was a continual small drain of casualties due to the enemy using harassing fire to a greater extent than formerly. One effect of this greater volume of shelling was that infantry units became much more willing to dig and the Sappers found that ever larger numbers of prefabricated shelters were needed. Further problems were created by the Chinese using larger calibre weapons, aimed initially at our tanks but then increasingly at Observation Posts (OPs) and strongpoints, all of which had to be strengthened with extra overhead cover.

12 Field Squadron developed a very close and effective liaison with the infantry units in their Brigade. Captain David Brotherton recalled the wide variety of tasks they had to carry out, including the construction of defence works and Gunner OPs, patrolling, mine clearance, road and track building and maintenance including bridges and many culverts, running a quarry and, of course, water supply. Much of this was carried out during periods of heavy Chinese shelling and mortaring. His main memory was of the sheer hard work carried out by his sappers, all with great cheerfulness and good humour. Their reward was to know that all this work, and what they achieved, was greatly appreciated by the infantry commanders. The Commanding Officer of the Durham Light Infantry, Lieutenant Colonel Peter Jeffries, once told him that he was 'thrilled' by his sappers' work.

Mike Bruges was the Troop Officer and, to relieve the monotony of road making, he decided on one rest day to take his men on a bit of an expedition to investigate a Buddhist temple in an adjoining valley. An exhilarating climb up the adjoining ridge gave them a good view of a disappointingly small and ruined building in the valley below. The descent to the valley floor was tricky but they all regrouped by the stream at the bottom and were happily eating their sandwich lunch when the whistle and bang of mortar bombs set the cat among the pigeons and called for a bit of 'leadership'. Mike broke the party into three groups, instructed them to keep in touch with each other and to reassemble at a prominent rock feature on the ridge. They moved with commendable zeal and, fortunately for his military career, they all made it to the RV, where they were all sworn to silence on the whole episode when returning to camp. Mike had failed to check in advance and they had strayed into an American firing range. Oh Bruges!

Mike's luck soon ran out and, having come too close to a, definitely Chinese, mortar bomb in the Bowling Alley behind Hill 355, he was treated to two days' hospitality in the Indian Field Ambulance's Forward Dressing Station. Apart from its medical prowess, it was renowned for its hospitality and its midday curry was well known throughout the Division.

Doubtless still recovering from a surfeit of curry, Mike returned to his Troop and the subject of mines, a change from road maintenance. Basic training at Chatham had prepared subalterns for minefields laid out in a pre-determined pattern to conform to the Geneva Convention on conducting warfare, a convention seemingly unknown to the Chinese as they were inclined to enter our minefields and shift the mines, a practice which foxed us a bit. One cold and bleak night, David Brotherton took Mike with him to check one of our minefields, a mixture of anti-tank and anti-personnel mines. Crawling along with great care David's foot slipped and knocked over an anti-personnel mine within a few feet of Mike's face: he quickly grabbed it and to his horror found that the trip-wire had been cut but the mechanism was still intact. The firing device had clearly frozen up; replacing it carefully, he crept on behind David, hoping that on a warmer night a Chinaman might be the next person to pass by and be tempted to blow himself up.

Mine recognition was not always as good as it might have been. The Troop also had a New Zealand engineer section and, returning one night from a patrol, their Corporal proudly presented a Chinese mine he had found on the forward slope of Hill 355. His courage in snipping the two wires that were protruding from this relatively light device was much admired until it was realized that this was no ordinary mine but a Gunner sound-ranging device. The incident took a bit of explaining: *Quo farce et gloria ducunt.*

134

Infantry units were accompanied frequently on their patrols by Sappers, especially for the distasteful task of putting quicklime on the Chinese bodies which had been caught by artillery fire on the defensive wire. David recalled two individual memories, the first when he accompanied a party down into the valley in front of Hill 355 to help bring back the body of a company commander in the DLI who had been killed in an ambush while on a patrol. His second concerned the frequent and heavy shelling aimed at a dug-in Centurion tank on the extreme right of the Divisional line. The aftermath was always the need to destroy numerous unexploded Chinese shells, a task he enjoyed as when it was completed the tank commander used to reward him with a large tot of whisky. And so it went on to the very end: David even spent the first evening of the Armistice helping to rescue a wounded signalman who had strayed into a minefield.

At the 'sharp end' the Chinese became adept at using their mortars, particularly their 60mm mortars. With bombs only weighing 3½lb, they could be easily stockpiled and the mortars could be sited with only the muzzle or spout showing through a very small hole or placed on a reverse slope where they were virtually invulnerable. They did not need highly skilled men to fire them and though their penetrative power was not great, if the bombs landed in a trench or shelter entrance, their blast could do a lot of damage. The 60mm could be fired with remarkable accuracy and being sniped by one was not fun, even though the danger area from its burst was not large. Continued light harassing fire by day and night from only a few mortars was very nerve-racking for men in forward positions.

Though there was plenty of activity along the whole front, with patrolling to dominate no man's land the priority, most of the fighting took place in the 29 Brigade area, principally on the Hook and its adjoining hilltop positions, and involving all their battalions.

On returning to the front line in April 1953, the Black Watch found that much of their hard work before Christmas had come to naught and David Rose, their Commanding Officer, set to with a will to put things right. 1 Troop of 55 Field Squadron was deployed fully in support of the battalion, and rebuilding and strengthening the trench connecting all the section posts along the front of the position became their prime task. In their absence in reserve, it had become virtually untenable and formed a wide V. The trench, about 100 yards long, had to be deepened to a minimum of nine feet so that six-inch by four-inch frames could be installed, lined with timber and with several feet of overhead cover, including a burster course of rock. A compressor was brought up to the roadhead just below the Company HQ, but it was too far for the hose to be of much use in the forward trench. Digging by hand went on, day and night, with constant shell and mortar harassing fire by day and the ever present need to be alert to enemy activity at night. The sight of a pickhead, or a shovel of earth, above the parapet could be guaranteed to bring a response, usually a mortar bomb, but sometimes something heavier.

The Black Watch CO was well aware of the importance of holding the Hook. It really was the 'vital ground'. Apart from the lateral trench linking the various strongpoints, he demanded a further prefabricated Gunner OP which was started immediately and was completed by 19 April.

Immediately in front of the position was a re-entrant which provided the enemy with a protected approach to the Hook in dead ground. To counter this threat, what came to be known as the 'Green Finger' tunnel was started on 18 April below the adjoining ridge. It started with a twelve-foot vertical shaft, just behind the forward trench and was to run down the ridge for thirty yards, branching into two light machine gun positions on either side of the ridge to cover the dead ground. Work carried on continuously in eight-hour shifts, with close timbering

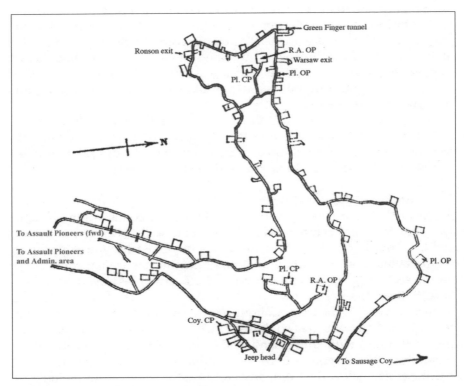

Map 3. The Hook Company Trench Layout

throughout. 1 Troop was able to maintain a fair rate of progress, though work had to be halted when enemy patrols were nearby. The soil being typical decomposed granite, the work soon reached the stage where the main tunnel split into the two fighting positions. The preliminary planning for this tunnel is depicted in Terence Cuneo's picture, entitled 'The Hook', which hangs in the Headquarter Mess at Chatham. It shows Lieutenant Alec Rattray, a Black Watch platoon commander, who had won a Military Cross a few months earlier, discussing the problem with the author in front of our forward position. Tragically, Alec was killed two or three weeks later.

Two Centurion tanks were positioned just behind the saddle connecting the Hook position and the company immediately to its east. The crews had little to do, other than to drive the few yards to the crest and snipe at enemy positions with their 20-pounder main armament. One of the tanks was also equipped with a turret-mounted searchlight for use at night, as can be seen to the left of Cuneo's painting. The light hampered its own ability to fire but its neighbour, being slightly off to a flank, could fire at any target that was illuminated. The tanks were not at all popular in daylight hours as they were apt to move forward to the crest and fire at some known or imaginary target and then reverse quickly back out of view, closing their hatch in case the enemy retaliated. This the enemy almost invariably did. The tanks had usually forgotten to tell the infantry or sappers in advance and anyone caught in the open found themselves on the receiving end of the retaliatory fire. One morning one of the tanks did its usual trick of opening fire without any warning to nearby working parties and then withdrew quickly but, on this occasion, the tank commander was outside his tank when the enemy opened fire in retaliation. A piece of shrapnel hit his leg, slicing into his Achilles tendon, very painfully. The incident was seen by two nearby Sappers who pulled the officer into the Company Command Post (CP) where he was treated before being taken to the Regimental Aid Post. Shameful though it may be to say, the Sapper reaction was to laugh at the officer's predicament and say a heartfelt, 'Serve you bloody well right, Sir. Now you know what it is like for us.' Happily, George Forty, the officer concerned, recovered and went on to become the very successful Director of the Royal Armoured Corps Museum at Bovington.

All this time, further strongpoints were being built in the forward platoon position and the Gunner OP was extended with a concrete lintel and better overhead cover. Building these strongpoints off the forward covered trench was a formidable task, especially with the enemy being so close, and is also graphically depicted in Cuneo's picture. By April/May 1953, when this scene is depicted, construction of the tunnel and the forward covered trench was well advanced. Shelling and mortaring were fairly continuous and almost all work was being carried out by night. Every vestige of cover had long since disappeared and the ground was littered with all the debris of war: tangled barbed wire, bent pickets, shattered timber, torn sandbags, scattered ammunition, enemy stick grenades and the odd dead Chinaman stuck in the wire or, in one case, bent up double in the bottom of the trench leading to the Gunner OP. Nobody wanted to bury the poor man and one had to put a foot in the middle of his back if one wanted to pass along the narrow trench. A camouflage net had to be placed in advance over the site for each bunker and a twelve and a half foot deep precisely square hole had then to be dug at night and the camouflage net replaced by dawn. The smaller prefabricated timbers could be carried up the communication trench, but the heavy twelve-by-twelve-inch roof timbers and the reinforced concrete lintels had to be carried or dragged over the top of the Hook on special sledges. The roofs required five feet of overhead cover, including a two-foot rock burster course. All this extremely hazardous work needed plenty of luck, and a dark night. After ten days or so, the infantry company would be relieved and move into reserve for a much needed bath and rest or on to a neighbouring, quieter position. The Sapper Troop remained, plucking up its courage each evening at dusk for the nightly tasks ahead. The comparative security of the Troop rest area three miles to the rear made the journey forward all the more nerve-racking.

The work did not always go entirely smoothly and on one occasion the Troop Commander was with the Company Commander in his Command Post on the reverse of the hill, discussing future requirements. The night had started quietly enough; the sapper working party had arrived an hour earlier and were busy with their work on the tunnel when suddenly an intense enemy bombardment opened, obviously heralding an attack. Our own patrols were hurriedly called in, defensive fire tasks added to the noise and every infantry position was manned. The forward platoons were well dug in and, though nervous, everyone was confident.

The intense fire soon resulted in the land lines to the forward platoons being cut and radio contact was intermittent. The Chinese gained a foothold and were soon on top of our position. It was vital that we should hold on and the Company Commander decided that the only way to clear the area would be by firing airburst shells over our own position. He turned to the Gunner FOO and asked him to locate every gun he could find and bring fire down on our own heads. The Gunner officer blanched and pointed out that such drastic action would surely result in casualties to our own troops. The infantry commander looked at him and said quietly 'Fire'. There was a pause while the FOO turned to his radio, gave his call-sign followed by 'Victor target, Victor target,

138

Victor target'. It was the call for every gun in the Corps within range to open fire. The result was devastating, the whole ground trembled and the noise was deafening, even inside the deep dugout that was Company HQ. The enemy were swept off the position, while our troops shook themselves before putting their heads up again. By some extraordinary good fortune we had suffered no casualties, though that could not be said for the enemy. The Sappers resumed their work, the whole episode having lasted not much more than an hour.

Shortly after this incident the Troop Commander was moving along a communication trench when he found himself in the midst of some very heavy shelling. He dived into the tunnel entrance being used for patrols moving off the Hook out towards Warsaw – a patrol moving out is shown in Cuneo's painting. On this occasion, though, a patrol was returning and had taken refuge, too, in the tunnel. There was little room to move until what was a very frightening barrage stopped and an infantry soldier was heard to say how pleased he was that a f . . . ing officer was blocking their exit. When the shelling stopped, the officer made his way to the Company CP where he told them how he had been shelled so heavily and that the Chinese must have brought up some new artillery. Everyone in the CP listened in silence and the Gunner officer looked decidedly embarrassed. The Troop Commander looked at him and burst out, 'You bastard! It was your own guns, wasn't it?' The Gunner sheepishly tried to explain that there were two batteries firing on a Defensive SOS task and he knew that one of the batteries was firing short, but he couldn't tell which battery it was so, as it was an SOS target, he let both carry on firing and hoped for the best. He rather shamefacedly added, 'I'm glad you are alright!'

With 28 Engineer Regiment well dispersed, especially the individual Troops, good radio communications were essential. 55 Squadron had a particularly efficient set-up, achieved by holding illegally at least double their equipment entitlement, and by having a very good Signals Sergeant! At times the Troop Commanders felt that officers were expected to be too readily available on the radio rather than directing the work they were on. This was exemplified by Major Bob Frosell, OC 55 Field Squadron, who demanded to speak to one of the Troop Commanders on the radio at about 10.00pm one night. The officer was brought to the radio and told by the OC that he was to return immediately to the Squadron Headquarters. He explained that he couldn't do this as the Troop was being quite heavily shelled at the time and he felt it was his duty to stay with his men and to keep on working as the job was so important. However, the OC brushed all this aside and demanded his presence immediately. As this was a direct order, he climbed into his Jeep and set off to Squadron HQ, several miles along a dirt track, in the dark and with no lights. On arrival, he asked what it was that was so important and was told by the OC that his Troop State that morning had been incorrect! He rather icily told the OC that the Troop State was prepared by his Troop Sergeant every morning, that he apologized if there was a mistake but that if the OC really needed to know, he could tell him what every single man was doing out of the sixty-four men in his Troop and if the OC had no further queries, he would like to return to his Troop who were having a difficult time, with constant enemy shelling. He drove off in an absolute fury, but determined not to be caught out again like that.

The OC, without doubt, ran a most efficient Squadron, but it was not altogether a happy one. With his funny accent – nobody knew whether it was genuine or not, but he claimed some form of Lithuanian ancestry – the soldiers liked him, especially as he played up to them and enjoyed making fun of their superiors. The officers saw him somewhat differently: he was a bully, he was bombastic and he was quite capable of bending the truth when it suited. His officers were determined that he would not find fault with them, hence their resolve to be the most efficient unit in the Regiment. One night, the OC returned from an O Group with the Brigade Commander who had informed them that he was planning a major raid on some enemy positions and that a gap was to be made in a certain minefield. 'I told that stupid Brigadier that I knew he would want to carry out this raid so we had already made the gap in the minefield. He was astounded that I had already thought of this and was most impressed. Now, get out and make the gap before dawn.' It was always astonishing how he got away with such brazen untruths, but the Squadron was determined to uphold the reputation of the Corps and could only admire the effrontery of the man. He was certainly a 'character' and was well known throughout the Division.

Chapter 13

Night Life in Korea

Three anecdotes illustrate conditions on the Hook at this time.

A Quiet Night
It was a dark night and strangely silent. Normally there was sporadic rifle or machine-gun fire with the occasional crump of a bursting shell, but tonight there was utter silence – so far. The sentries found it an eerie task, staring out into no man's land and listening for any sound from the enemy. Suddenly the searchlights came on from their positions two or three miles to the rear. They were aimed at a low angle, not against enemy aircraft, there were never any, but so that they could reflect off the low cloud and thus illuminate the enemy positions on the hills opposite. They were a mixed blessing though as they cast innumerable shadows which seemed to move as the light flickered. The sentries stirred uneasily. Ian Kaye, who served in the Black Watch, vividly portrayed what goes through every sentry's mind in a forward position, be he infantryman or sapper:

> *Have you known the lonely silence ...*
> *Not a bird or bug is stirring?*
> *Your 'Mucker' lies there snoring*
> *In his blankets at your side.*
> *The dew drops off the Bren gun ...*
> *You can hear the damp grass growing;*
> *And each squeak of your equipment*
> *Is thunder multiplied!*
>
> *Have you known the lonely silence ...*
> *At the witching-hour of midnight?*
> *You've patted each grenade ten times,*
> *And even whispered to your Sten ...*

Dozed off – then woke in panic
With fear of death upon you,
And every shape and shadow seems
Chock-full of 'little men'!

Have you known the lonely silence ...
In the hour before 'Stand-to'?
When every nerve is screaming
That there's enemy around ...
Then let your mess tins rattle,
Like a herd of berserk cattle ...
Or stood and coughed (with hair on end!)
And shuddered at the sound?
I have!

The sapper working party came forward with their stores along the narrow communication trenches to strengthen some forward positions. There was a Korean carrying party to assist them, bringing along great baulks of timber and concrete lintels. It was an extremely hazardous task as, due to their size, these had to be carried across open ground, above the trenches. The Korean Service Corps men didn't like coming so far forward (nor did any of us!); the enemy lines were only a few hundred yards away, their patrols even closer, but the Sappers looked after them well and encouraged them along. They showed great courage. Quietly and efficiently the Sappers got to work, making little noise and showing no lights. One of the problems of being in the open like this was the danger of being caught by flares and now and again they would have to freeze quite still as a parachute flare opened in the air somewhere along the front. On a dark night the flares seemed even brighter than usual and anyone exposed in the open felt very naked. It was no good flinging oneself to the ground as any sudden movement immediately attracted enemy attention and invited mortar attack. It was difficult, though, to persuade the carrying party to stand absolutely still until the light went out, but perhaps the presence of an officer with his drawn pistol, threatening to shoot the first person to move, helped, not that he ever would have actually used it. In the distance, over to the left where the American Marine Division was dug in, there was the faint drone of a 'Flare Ship' flying slowly round in circles, tossing out parachute flares to illuminate the battlefield. It was too far off to affect the working party, but nevertheless it was disturbing.

After about an hour an enemy propaganda broadcast started, with a girl speaking very good English but with an unmistakeable Chinese accent. She promised safe conduct and good treatment to any soldier who crossed over to their side. She pointed out how the ordinary private soldier was the dupe of American big business. She asked why we were fighting in Korea and why our Government would not agree to a ceasefire. Her voice came from a loudspeaker placed somewhere on the hills opposite and her messages were interspersed with music, often quite recent popular tunes. The soldiers enjoyed the broadcasts but I was not so pleased as the work was slowed down by men stopping to listen and it was important to get the job finished and the men off the hill before first light. As a propaganda mission, the broadcasts achieved absolutely nothing.

By two o'clock the job was completed and the men moved quietly back to the rear of the position and down the track to their waiting vehicles. There was no dallying here as the place was a favourite target for enemy harassing fire with their mortars and the men were all looking forward to getting back to camp, tucked into the side of a hill three miles away, where hot cocoa and bed were awaiting them.

I followed along after them but first of all checked in with the forward platoon commander to let him know that the job had been finished and the men were leaving. I stayed a few minutes for a gossip. The Command Post was dug well in to the hill with three feet of earth above it, safe from all but a direct hit from a very heavy shell. Just as he was leaving, a whispered message started coming through on the radio. The platoon commander listened intently. Enemy movement was heard in front of one of our standing patrols. He had to determine whether it was an enemy patrol or the start of an enemy attack. I withdrew quietly down the narrow trench as I knew I would only be in the way if anything started and I had still to see Keith, the Company Commander, before being able to go off to bed.

As I entered the Company Command Post I heard Keith turn to his Gunner officer and say, 'John has just told the standing patrol on his left to come in. It looks as if there is going to be an attack'.

The Gunner nodded and said, 'Shall I bring some fire down then? As you know, it's one of our Defensive Fire (SOS) targets and our guns are laid on that target, just in case'.

Keith told him to wait a few moments to let our patrol get in and then to give the position a good thump; it was only a hundred or so yards away on a narrow ridge connecting our positions with the enemy's. It was a favourite line of approach. The position had also achieved a certain notoriety within the battalion as the enemy had taken to sneaking out and leaving small packets of tea there, with a slogan saying, 'Why not have a good cup of char and forget this hellish war.' Pinned to each packet was a small porcelain 'peace dove'. This was all part of the Chinese propaganda to undermine our troops' morale, but it had quite the opposite effect and soldiers who had been there on a standing patrol took to wearing these peace doves in their balaclavas to show that they had been out on patrol at the real 'sharp end'.

Minutes later the Gunner brought his fire down. From inside the Command Post, dug into the reverse slope of the hill with several feet of earth on top, it was impossible to hear the shells landing but the two soldiers on duty in the Forward Observation Post said they had landed on target. These two men were connected to the Command Post by telephone line and they were there at night when their officer had to be beside the Company Commander – by day the officer went forward himself. These lines were laid along the sides of the communication trenches and were often the first casualties from enemy fire but on this occasion they remained intact.

No sooner had our shells landed than there was the unmistakeable crump of answering shells overhead. I was unable to leave due to all the shelling but after a further few minutes the firing died down. It looked as though it had just been a probing attack to test the defences, so I decided it was time to go home. It had been another quiet night.

The Patrol

In war both sides try to dominate no man's land. In Korea this was not so easy in the last year or so of the war when the line was largely static, each side was dug in on the tops of the hills and movement during the daylight hours was almost impossible on the bare forward slopes. To control the valley bottom meant getting one's patrols down there as soon as possible after last light, not so easy for the British when the opposing Chinese lines were cast into shadow before ours.

The battalion commander was concerned that there was activity immediately in front of our positions, probably caused by the enemy lying up there during the hours of daylight. Due to the convex nature of the hill it was not possible to see what was happening at the base of the hill in the valley bottom. Air photography was inconclusive as the Chinese were adept at concealment, so a reconnaissance patrol was the only alternative.

Briefing took place in late morning, when everyone had had some sleep after the previous night's activities, and it was decided that the patrol would be led by one of the platoon commanders from the reserve company who knew the general lie of the land. He would take a radio operator, one man to act as a scout and a sapper. As I was the affiliated Sapper Troop Commander, and feeling that I needed to know what lay in front of the forward company, I decided to go myself. The patrol spent the rest of the day in preparation, studying air photos, ensuring that none of our equipment rattled, cleaning weapons and liaising with the forward platoon, through whose position we would move out and also return. They would not be able to speak on the radio, other than by whispering, due to the proximity of the enemy, so the patrol commander arranged a simple series of signals using the radio's pressel switch only.

Late in the afternoon, a message came through that the battalion commander had vetoed my presence on the patrol as he had found out that I was senior to the patrol commander which would place him in an invidious position should the patrol run into trouble. At this short notice, and after a personal appeal to the Commanding Officer had been turned down, the best available sapper NCO in the Troop, an outstanding young Lance Corporal called Milne, was hurriedly briefed and set off to join the patrol which was getting prepared just behind the forward company. They set off as soon as it was dark enough. The weather was in their favour: no moon, overcast sky and a brisk wind making the clouds scud past and helping to conceal their movement. They made their way quietly along the narrow trenches and through the forward position and out into no man's land. They were on their own now.

Moving forward was not at all easy due to all the debris of battle and the coils of barbed wire and other obstacles which impeded progress. They crouched low to avoid anyone being silhouetted from below and it took the best part of an hour to reach the valley bottom. In the meanwhile, still feeling upset that I had been prevented from going on the patrol, I stayed in the forward company's Command Post. Suddenly the field telephone jangled. It was the forward platoon reporting an explosion in the valley bottom. Whether it was a grenade or an anti-personnel mine, it was impossible to tell. An almost interminable seeming fifteen minutes followed. There was nothing to do but wait. There was no firing to be heard so it didn't seem likely that the patrol had bumped into any enemy. It became increasingly likely that some-one had set off a mine. The suspense was unbearable.

All of a sudden the tension was broken by the radio coming to life. The patrol was on radio silence as it set out but now there was a whispered message to say that there was a casualty, severely wounded, and that they were returning. More silence. The Company Commander had to stay in his Command Post but I moved forward and joined the forward platoon commander ready to give any help that might be needed. It would not be easy to bring any casualty back, especially if he was unable to walk, as the hillside was extremely steep and there were so many obstructions. After a long wait the patrol commander whispered over the radio that Lance Corporal Milne had set off a mine, had been desperately wounded and had now died. It was a bitter blow, and it need not have been him if there had not been that last minute change of plan. It took a further two hours to get him back to our own lines, such was the nature of the ground. And what had been achieved? The patrol commander could only say that he had not made contact

145

with the enemy and it seemed that they were not lying up in the dead ground in front of our positions. This was not to say that they could not do this on any future occasion but for the foreseeable future they need not be too concerned.

Lance Corporal Milne's funeral took place the following afternoon on a lonely hillside behind our lines. The Padre from the nearby Armoured Regiment presided while every available Sapper in the troop attended, together with the Squadron Commander. It was raining but nobody seemed to mind. He had been an extremely popular man and everyone felt his loss deeply. Halfway through the simple service, a jeep drove up and Barry Kavanagh, a Company Commander in the Dukes whose company was attached to the battalion as an extra sub-unit, alighted with profuse apologies for being late but he had only just heard the dreadful news. Lance Corporal Milne had been attached to his company the previous week, had impressed everyone with his ability and invaluable advice, and he just felt he had to come along and pay tribute on behalf of everyone in his company. There cannot be many Lance Corporals to have earned such an accolade as this.

The Troop slowly dispersed, each man with his own thoughts. I followed alone, wondering how I was going to explain things to Lance Corporal Milne's parents. It had been a long twenty-four hours, but I still had a letter to write.

All Hell ...

A few days later the Chinese shelling began to increase and it looked as if an attack was looming. Several days of intense bombardment reached a crescendo and on 7 May the company braced itself for action.

1 Troop had just finished work on the Hook and I had called in on Alec Rattray, one of the two forward platoon commanders, to say that I was leaving when a faint message came over the radio from the standing patrol on 'Ronson' to indicate enemy forces approaching. Alec sat at a makeshift desk, constructed from empty NAAFI beer cases, with his platoon sergeant sitting beside him and the signaller in a corner, his earphones over his head, waiting for any messages from the patrols out in front. I thought I had better get out of his hair and went on to the Company Command Post (CP), arriving just as all hell was let loose with DF SOS barrages being fired, followed by the noise of enemy shelling and mortar fire. Communications with the two forward platoons soon broke down, with telephone wires being cut by shellfire and radios being blocked. Tony Lithgow, the Company Commander, sent his 2IC forward along the left-hand communication trench to assess the situation, but in the confusion he could not get anywhere where he could influence the battle and nothing further was heard from him.

After an anxious wait, with a dearth of information and silence in the CP, I realized that all eyes were on me, so I 'volunteered' to go forward again to find out what was happening. Scurrying along a deep communication trench on the right of the position, I had only gone about forty yards when I was bowled over by an explosion at my feet from a 60mm mortar. Picking myself up, and finding I was completely unhurt, I made my way back to Alec Rattray only to find him dead, along with his platoon sergeant and runner. They were still sitting just as I had left them only a few minutes before and a shell must have burst right in the entrance to their CP, killing them instantly with the blast.

There was nothing more I could do there so I moved towards the other forward platoon and met two Jocks coming towards me carrying their platoon commander, David Haugh. Apparently a 60mm mortar bomb had landed at his feet and he had taken the full blast in his stomach. David was a much loved young officer and the two Jocks were in tears but it was obvious that he had been mortally wounded and he died moments later as I was holding him.

With both forward platoon commanders and a sergeant killed in the first few minutes of the action, things did not look too good, but the enemy had not yet been able to get onto the position in any numbers. I managed to get the news back to Company HQ where Tony Lithgow had already called for reinforcements, and made my way to the Forward Observation Officer's (FOO's) daytime OP from where I tried to co-ordinate the artillery and mortar fire. Things eventually began to quieten down, though our own artillery and mortars were still firing. Reinforcements began to arrive and a little later, David Rose, the Commanding Officer came on the air, ordering a counter-attack to sweep the forward slope of any enemy. The Company Commander protested that it would be too dangerous to do this as it was almost daylight, but quite calmly and in a voice that brooked no argument, the CO said, 'Do as you are told'. There was a deadly silence on the radio as everyone digested what had been said. It was a supreme example of a Commanding Officer asserting his authority and it was no wonder that the whole battalion held him in such awe. The platoon carrying out this order was commanded by a young second lieutenant who had never been on the Hook before and as dawn came up he moved forward with his men and I showed him where to go. The forward slope was swept and a very relieved second lieutenant returned with his whole platoon intact.

My Jeep had been left just below the Company CP and on returning to it later that morning, I was greeted by my driver, Sapper McLaren, who commented that it had been 'quite a night'. When questioned about where he had been, he said that he had met up with 'a few friends' in the Company and had joined them in their slit trench and 'chucked a few hand grenades' at the advancing enemy! He was supposed to have been looking after the Jeep and I was rightly annoyed, but McLaren was always a law unto himself.

Chapter 14

The Cruellest Months

Derek Halley was a National Service soldier serving with the Black Watch in Korea who was caught up in this same battle on the Hook in 1953. He must have been standing within feet of me at one stage, unknown to me until his story came to light over fifty years later. This extract from his book, *A Conscript's Tale*, starts a little bit earlier and describes what it was like as a junior NCO. It is reproduced here in its unedited form:

> It was April but it wasn't raining violets. Korea's April showers brought ever more shells and shrapnel and communist claptrap. Winter was going gracelessly, with no intention of dying alone, taking its favourite hell-hole with it. The Hook, that most Korean of hills, had been born yet again to die yet again, the assault pioneers having worked their guts out to create new hootchies, new tunnels and new trenches, new targets not just for the Chinese but sometimes our own mortar platoon – too many of their shells had faulty tail-fins which fell off and brought the things crashing down around our ears. The showers which came our way rained violence, not violets. Al Johnson had died just as the Chinese had marched into our war and had taken his April with him, leaving us with T. S. Eliot's The Waste Land's Cruellest Month ...
>
> Even the ironies were cruel. Just before the slaughter began cranking up towards top gear, I was offered a job which would have taken me off patrol duty. Tony Lithgow assigned me to the small canteen, but I turned him down. Somehow it didn't suit me and I told him I didn't count too well and my talents, such as they were, would be better used elsewhere, so the job was snapped up by a young lance-jack called Craig. It was to cost him dear.
>
> The Chinks were shelling us with increasing ferocity and our overland telephone cables were continually being broken, so we

were despatched to the command post for more digging. The work was almost easy, securing the new cable in that softer, soggier ground, particularly for young Kioy, a Katcom (Korean Soldier attached to the Commonwealth) who until the war had seen nothing but the paddy-fields above Mokpo, some 200 miles to the south. He never saw them again. Stretching for one moment, he stood up beside me, all 5′ 8″ of him. I thought he had winced with pain, a twinge perhaps in that supple back of his, but it was a sound: a rush of whining air pitched so high not even a dog would have heard it in time, a noise so slight it might have been a mosquito landing on his ear. If only.

He took the full force of the shell. As he fell I pushed my chest into the last furrow he had ploughed in the bog, holding my head as low as the shallow water allowed while the rest of the new volley passed over us. When my eyes slammed shut they saw him standing there again, wincing again and exploding for a second time. When I flashed my eyes open to wipe the sight away it was only to have them slammed shut by that same sound. As I watched Kioy explode one more sickening time I heard the shell fizz into the rocks a few safe yards away. Then I heard a voice which even in full scream rang with echoes of James Square and King Street and home: Peter Cramb, yet another Crieffite serving time for no crime, had scrambled from the command post with a stretcher and needed another bearer. I dragged myself up and helped him get Kioy back there, but it was only to administer last aid. In silent, staring agony the lad watched as we lifted the remains of his stomach back into his gaping body, which barely flinched as I strapped my clumsy bandage to it. Peter struggled to get a broken cigarette going for him, but by the time the thing was producing smoke Kioy had no breath to draw it. His lungs had emptied with a tremulous sigh as his stare had frozen.

Even the sight of all that gore on my hands couldn't force my eyelids shut. I had seen enough replays. For a while I wondered if I would ever be able to shut them again. I knew so little about Kioy, the few words between us had hindered communication more than anything, but I had a sinking feeling he was going to be with me the rest of my life, however long that might be. After the last shell had fallen we regrouped and I heard that Craig had been another casualty. He was alive, but one of his legs had been shattered. I heard later it had been amputated.

The digging went on. In broad daylight we laid our cable a few hundred yards more, standing up to stretch only when the sun ducked. After a fortnight we were moved out, but only

150

nearer the enemy – not at the front of The Hook but the very front of it. The closest the UN forces had come to the Chinese, it was where the real casualties were, where Tokyo Rose came across louder and clearer than anywhere. She knew the moment we arrived: 'Welcome, A Company! I can tell you, you're in for a hell of a time boys ...' In return, her boys got letters and some of them blew back, in our faces. Signed by Mark W. Clark, Commander-in-Chief of United Nations Army, they promised any Chinese or North Korean soldier a safe exit from the violence if they wanted to hang up their helmets. It made for some very interesting reading over the hot chocolate.

Ronson Patrol was just about the most harrowing in Korea. People got killed on it in large numbers. There was a small trench, perhaps 40 or 50 yards from the main line, where the unlucky few sat every night listening for any movement ahead, ready to alert the platoon to imminent attack. On their way to the trench the patrol passed through a gap in our line which some patriotic wit had dubbed 'Marble Arch', alluding to the proud monument which had originated as a triumphal entry to Buckingham Palace, that great seat of empire. In Korea, the allusion raised eyebrows more than morale. We crawled through the thing on our bellies, in full battle order, past the Browning and on to a sandbagged trench, patrolling in threes: a wireless operator and two observers, one of whom clung to an indispensable new gismo called a Sniperscope. Mounted on a rifle and powered by a battery strapped to the man's back, it emitted a beam invisible to the enemy and revealing anything up to 100 yards ahead. In those murderous April showers it was a tiny ray of sunshine for us outdoor types, until it went under a cloud, along with its operator ...

It was around midnight when we heard movement ahead. The wireless operator reflexively contacted HQ and received the signal 'Hellzapoppin!' We had 30 seconds to cover the ground back to the front trenches before a barrage of British shells went down. It might sound easy, covering 50 yards in half a minute, but for men exhausted after long hours on watch, weighed down by battledress and equipment, over slimy rocks and ruts, in the dark, bent double – sometimes treble – it was a Herculean task. We made it just as 100 shells landed in front of the patrol post. Then the nasty job: after the all-clear we were sent back out to clean up and check for anyone left over or wounded. It was just about the most terrifying task we could land – particularly without the Sniperscope. I would name him if I considered him responsible for his actions, but after so much sterling service the

151

operator that night simply flipped and ran, taking the thing with him. There was no time to give chase and reclaim it, we had to move forward not sideways. Dick, never one to shirk a challenge, volunteered to make up the numbers (he was to remain in the service for many years and I hope he eventually writes his own story) and Roy Nicol followed him. The four of us set off into the night, back through Marble Arch, down the slope, past our small trench and out into no-man-or-beast's-land to where the shells had exploded. After sweeping the area and finding nothing we headed back to the tiny trench for more hours of torture, listening for the rustle of a Red Ant. Eventually, after returning on my knees through Marble Arch, I joined the lads for a rum to celebrate the first of six whole days free of Ronson Patrol. It still tasted like sump oil but on that happy morn it went down like hot chocolate.

And the shells kept coming down like ... shells. Every night during Stand To they would be showered upon us and we would fire back at anything that moved. There was a tree stump about 100 yards away and the more we stared the more convinced we were that the thing was a Red ant-hill. I often wonder if it's still there with all its bullet-holes. Our Brownings had fixed lines, set each day to fire straight into the trenches across the valley and every night they rattled away into Tokyo Rose's rubbish. Often she literally asked for it: 'Hey boys, why don't you give up now? Come on, let me know you want to go home. Fire once to tell me you want to give up. But if you want to go on for a little longer that's all right, just fire continuously.' She was no fool. The amount of ammo we spent despatching our replies ...

Our resolve never melted, but the hootchies were made of lesser stuff. With April's showers heavier every day they came to leak like sieves and the sandbags started moving. Most of the time we were too exhausted to do anything but pray for a new posting. I was due for a birthday and wanted to celebrate it somewhere else. Anywhere else, we all felt we were due it. Then the Chinese panicked: if they weren't quick, Corporal D. D. Halley was going to live beyond his teens and it called for desperate measures.

On the 16th, the eve of my 20th birthday, all hell broke loose: we could see an artillery duel going on in the distance, between the Commies and the Americans; Old Baldy, one of the hills close by, had been overrun by the Chinese who intended driving on to the next vantage point, much to the Eighth Army's disapproval. The shells rained for 48 hours as two companies of

152

the 17th Infantry held their position – it was the start of the epic battle for Pork Chop Hill which was to rage on into the summer with massive casualties on both sides. The Chinese bombarded Stonk Alley, our supply route which led up to the back ridge, many of the shells falling around our command post, and if the noise ever dropped it was only so that that other show could go on: 'Hi there Scotsmen! Are you settled in for the night? I thought I would entertain you while you kept your heads down.' The cow would then pour music over us, 'Loch Lomond' one of her favourites, which was usually followed by 'There's No Place Like Home': 'Don't go out on patrol tonight boys. We can shell you any time we like, with shells that blind the eyes . . .'

All the same, I had made it to my twenties. There was no cake, no skoosh, no parcel-passing or postman's knock, but I was alive and that was celebration enough. In a fairer country they would have called it quits, but this was Korea, the land of the marauding carve-up – and it was all just warming up.

May took up where April had left off, and by the 18th the Chinks were massing as never before. From deep dugouts in a semi-circle of hills around us like Betty Grable, Rome, Goose and Pheasant, 122mm guns launched a barrage at us. The patrol on Warsaw, next to us, was drawn in after reconnaissance planes noted movements in caves below. Then the standing patrol reported the places were filling up with Chinese infantry. The US Corps's 8-inch 'persuaders' were put on overtime, their shells designed to penetrate the ground before exploding, but even with the earth erupting all about them the ants just kept coming, oblivious to the shrapnel and splinters of rock. They advanced along Ronson Ridge, where the standing patrol were waiting, and with 60mm mortar flares and searchlights on them they were soon caught in the crossfire from A Coy on The Hook and B Coy on Pt 121 – but they swarmed on. The artillery sent fused high-explosives over the ridge and the Black Watch lobbed their mortars, but still the ants kept coming.

Having just survived one disaster with the Americans, the Turks over on our left were desperate to avoid another one with us and in the Command Post the Commanding Officer received a telephone call. In his best English the Turkish commander inquired if we had sustained many casualties? 'A few.' And we would be withdrawing? 'The Black Watch don't withdraw.' Phone down.

By then the ants were within 20 yards of our trenches and grappling with the Dannert wire. Private Cash fired 6,000 rounds into 50 of them through his Browning, only to earn himself a

153

verrah stern reproof later from RSM Scott: 'Wi' that many roonds ye should've taken oot the whole bloody Chinese Brigade!' (Private Cash he may have been, but those were public resources he had spent).

On they came, cutting their way into our ground, all ghoulish screams and empty eyes, each little ant doped up on the worthlessness of its own life and dazzled by the price put on mine. I watched a young private tackle the first arrival by scrambling onto its back and smashing its face with a rifle butt. It died instantly. The second one got the same, but as three more broke through he pulled back. Another private had his Bren snatched, so tore off his helmet and crashed the rim into the ant's head, splitting it open and leaving it to die under his boot.

It was a blur. Panoramic panic. Bugles blaring, rifles and Brens and Stens and burp-guns blasting, shells screaming, mortars thundering, ants screeting. The trip-flares soared over it all to display the awesome density of the ant hordes, which multiplied as they died – each ant that fell seemed to give spontaneous birth to twins, which emerged through the showers of bone and blood to take up the remorseless advance. Our own umbilical cord of communication had been cut and the ammunition was running perilously low. The Browning was so hot it was reddening and the trenches were collapsing under the weight of numberless shells as more and more of us resorted to bayonets, knives, shovels, fists, fingernails ...

Desperate for back-up, I made it to the command post. Dick had had the same idea, but it was just as pointless – the carnage had beaten us to it. The wireless operator sat beside his crocked equipment, tending his own wounds with the others, unable to assist. Lt Haugh and Sgt Wilson were both dead ...

The cruellest irony: Tug Wilson had once tugged me back to earth for posing as an old soldier when I was nothing more than a nyaff in a dirty nappy; he had marched me up and down the platform at Inverness Station and hauled me off to Fort George to give me the benefit of his boot, and there he lay lifeless at mine, his unseeing eyes staring at a real old soldier at last.

We were on our own. 1 Platoon A Coy had lost their officer and sergeant. It was think-on-your-feet time, every-man-for himself – old soldier time. We left the command post and headed for the Browning pit in the hope of finding more firepower. Our light-automatic Patchets were something to hold onto in the night, but even full their magazines held just 32 rounds, not too handy when Red ants were swarming into the house. The evil bastards were even upstairs, within ten feet of me ... I heard them clicking as I passed a darkened hootchie, little hidden Red ants, mumbling and clicking in the blackness. Red pin-pricks pierced it as I stood transfixed. When they flared at me I clenched my fingers and the Patchet flared back and spat its last rounds at them. Sparks of metal cascaded into them, put them out, extinguished them. With my trigger finger still locked I stood there, on my black watch ...

Dick urged me away, yelling about pits. We found ours soon enough, despairing at the sight of nothing but grenades, everything else long gone. After stuffing them anywhere they would go, loading pockets and arms and fists with them, we clambered to what was left of the trenches and started lobbing the things into the horde. The Black Watch did not withdraw. That was for the ants ... And suddenly the buglers were singing a sweeter tune through their mouth-pieces and the shells were melting into smoke-bombs. The spray of shrapnel became just a misty shroud, a soft fog enveloping us so densely it muzzled the screaming mouths and muffled the madness. After half an hour we were finally swathed in silence. It came as suddenly as the ants had, out of the red, and when the fog finally cleared the ants had gone. All of them. We were left with dead and dying communists, scattered around our tattered trenches and into the distance. I did not attempt a count – as I had told my commander, counting was not my thing – and as I surveyed the devastation I knew that even if I had been an Einstein I could not have cared less. That was the Gooks' problem. Those other conscripts, the local civilian porters, could count them as they cleared them away, in their time. They could even leave them where they lay, as far as I was concerned. Old soldiers only carried their own. The platoon had lost 2nd Lt Alec Rattray MC and Privates Irvine and McKell along with our officer and sergeant. Enough numbers. So many had been wounded, all of us having been struck by shrapnel or shards of stone. The lucky few had escaped with nothing in them: we were left to pick the lumps out of our clothes ...

Chapter 15

Routine

After all this excitement, the Company on the Hook was relieved and there was a noticeable lessening of enemy activity, though it was not to last long. 1 Troop remained and carried on strengthening the defensive positions and was based some three miles back from the Hook and four or five miles north of the River Imjin. It was just west of the bridge over the River Samichon and was tucked into the side of the hill to the north of the road where there was some protection from any long-range artillery fire. It was approached by a short track across some abandoned paddy and bays were dug into the hillside for the vehicles. *Hoochies* for the men were scattered wherever there was a sufficiently flat piece of ground and they were usually occupied in pairs.

Great ingenuity was shown in the provision of beds, with frames made from poles, metal tubes or any other material, and a network of telephone wire woven across. A dining/canteen tent and the inevitable volleyball pitch completed the picture. Volleyball provided the only form of recreational exercise readily available and was played widely throughout the Division, from the General downwards. Overseeing the move of one troop to a new location, a newly arrived Troop Officer told his men to stop what they were doing, footling around trying to level a bit of ground, and to get on with digging shelters for the vehicles and explosives. Seeing this, the Troop Sergeant drew the officer to one side and said 'Sir. If you don't put the volleyball pitch to the top of your priorities, Sir, you won't last five minutes with the Troop, Sir.' He got the message.

Another Troop was based on the lateral Main Supply Route behind the forward troops and there was constant movement along it so that repairs and maintenance were at a premium. One day the driver of a Centurion tank, not believing the bridge classification sign or the diversion sign to the ford through the river (or perhaps he couldn't read?), decided to drive straight over, with disastrous results. The Troop was detailed to replace the bridge with a Bailey, as a matter of urgency.

Unfortunately, it became a matter of 'more haste, less speed', the bridge was launched on a skew and soon there was a new Troop Commander. There, but for the Grace of God ...

Though there were nominally sixty-four men in a troop, there were numerous posts to be filled on a daily basis: drivers, radio operators, cooks, R&R, sick and wounded, men on waterpoint duty, and so on, leaving perhaps not much more than half the men available for duty in support of a forward battalion. Every Troop consisted of a mixture of National Service and Regulars, with a number of Reservists in the early days. There was little to distinguish the groups, though the Regulars tended to be rather older, and the Troops were like close-knit families. As such they felt casualties acutely, but were pretty philosophical, realizing that some were inevitable, and soon cheered up and got on with life. Each Troop had its share of 'characters', some living up to their soubriquets, and others perhaps better described as 'scoundrels' of one sort or another. Some were brave, some were foolhardy and others quietly got on with things. Through force of circumstances they formed a cohesive whole and the Sapper squadrons were held in high esteem by the other units in the Division.

One troop had a double tragedy when someone stole the tin holding the canteen money. A search next day failed to find any trace, though suspicion fell on one particular Sapper, who vehemently protested his innocence. Two nights later, he was mortally wounded and died in the Norwegian MASH. Further searches still failed to find the money, not that it would have done the perpetrator much good as the money was in BAFs (British Armed Forces currency), the scrip money used in Korea and which would have been worthless elsewhere.

Another Sapper who was also wounded was quick to recover and went off to the Rest Centre at Inchon, from where he was returned after being found in an 'out of bounds' area, dressed improperly as a Military Police NCO. After swearing he was going to behave in future, his Troop Commander pleaded with the Squadron Commander to be lenient. He repaid their belief in him by promptly stealing his Troop Officer's Jeep and driving off to Seoul. Twenty-eight days' Field Punishment followed this time. Unfortunately, for him, his wounds went septic and he was shipped back to the British Military Hospital at Kure, in Japan, from where he rather cheekily asked to see his Troop Commander when he was passing through Kure a few weeks later, again swearing to be on his best behaviour in future. Nearly fifteen years later he was picked up by the police as a deserter and housed in the guardroom of the Duke of Wellington's Regiment where he told anyone who would listen how he had supported them in Korea. Next morning, his cell was empty.

The vast majority of the men slept, played, ate and drank, and wrote letters in what little leisure time was available. Some liked to read, others played cards and some just sat round the canteen heater, smoking and telling stories. 'Dear Mum, please sell the pig and buy me out', with its chorus of 'Dear Son, pig dead, soldier on' was an old favourite, with a variety of endings. Though their Troop Commander might have been called a bastard, he was defended vigorously and praised when comparing him with others. The generals, though, were always complete idiots.

If one was fortunate, a newly-joined Troop Officer might have a couple of days after joining his Troop in which to be acclimatized and get to know the area. Settling down the first night could be fairly testing, though, particularly in the winter. One newly-arrived officer was accommodated on his first night in a round American 'Pup Tent'. The ground was frozen two feet deep so he raised his camp bed onto a couple of empty beer crates, got into his sleeping bag, zipped it up to his neck from the inside and fell into a deep sleep. In the early hours of the morning the bed came off the beer crates and he crashed, face down to the frozen ground with his body curved round the inside of the tent and unable to move. He survived. It was a rude awakening.

Troop Officers might have to collect explosives from the Ammunition Point, take men down to the Mobile Laundry and Bath Unit for a shower and a change of clothes, stop at the NAAFI Roadhouse just south of Teal Bridge, see Medevac in US helicopters taking place and hope they would not be a customer. The post and papers would have to be collected, only three days after being posted in the UK, and of course there were endless road recces, checking for damage. They might also have to collect stores from the railhead at Tokchong or POL from Uijongbu. Issuing of petrol every evening was very important, particularly in winter, as vehicles would get condensation in the fuel tanks unless they were topped right up at the end of the day.

Keeping an eye on the beer distribution was also an important task. About 10,000 cases of Asahi beer were shipped over from Japan twice a week, intended for forward troops (as well as other, perhaps less deserving, men farther back), but an awful lot seemed to go astray on the way. The sight of a stack of cases waiting overnight on a jetty at Pusan led to endless pilfering. In winter, the beer might come frozen with the bottles broken. If the neck of the bottle was intact with the cap then NAAFI gave a refund. This was too much of a temptation, especially to the Australians who would smash any undamaged bottles, poured the beer through a filter before drinking, and then claim back a full bottle from NAAFI.

Though there was little to do in the way of administration, it was always important to see to the welfare of the men. Mail was of vital importance and the Sapper Postal Service could not have been bettered. There never seemed to be enough time to write letters oneself and one

Troop Commander found, fifty years later, that his mother had kept all his letters from Korea. In one, he apologized for not having written for three weeks and explained that the only letters he had written had been to the next of kin of the seven men who had become casualties in the previous two weeks. As he was only averaging twenty-eight men on active work, losing seven was a severe blow. Fortunately this did not happen very frequently, but it did make him wonder why the training of Young Officers did not include some hints on how to communicate with next of kin. Similarly there was no advice on how to write citations for awards. Some units were past masters in putting people up for awards, but in the Sappers there was so often a comment that the person concerned 'was only doing his job'. Others didn't think so. As an example, a Sapper was put forward for an immediate Military Medal and when it was awarded, someone asked why he hadn't been put forward for the Distinguished Conduct Medal as it was such an extra-ordinary act of heroism. The Troop Commander concerned admitted that he had never written a citation before. What a pity he had never been taught how to write one.

After the initial deployment of 55 Squadron and the formation of the Commonwealth Division the following year, things became more stable and officers were rotated round the regiment to give them more experience. This was particularly so amongst the Troop Officers who were never allowed to remain long in post. Though the CRE was keen to give every young officer a 'smell of the powder', this did make it difficult for them to get to know their men. This meant that NCOs, and even sappers in the sections, knew when personal problems were cropping up, well before their Troop officers. One Troop Commander noticed that one of his two sergeants was always finding 'good reasons' to leave the Troop 'to go and collect rations', or 'to order more stores or equipment'. This was happening more and more frequently and seemed to coincide with increased shelling or mortaring, and the men were making their dislike, and even contempt, for the sergeant pretty clear, long before the officer had noticed anything wrong. The sergeant was removed quietly and posted elsewhere. Where a Sapper or junior NCO was popular though, the men would cover for him if they thought he was becoming too stressed.

Fear is a funny thing. There is a limit to how much strain an individual can stand and sometimes it is the last person one expects who cracks first. Fatigue is also a factor and in a busy period, this could lead to sleep deprivation and subsequent breakdown. There might be a gradual erosion of courage, or a sudden breakdown, not surprising when men had been exposed to a fearsome period of conflict. One of the Squadron Commanders, Spencer Hannay, wrote, many years later that he was always impressed 'how well the Sappers coped with the daily ordeal of leaving the relative safety of their camp, to climb up to work on company forward positions often subjected to continuous shell and mortar fire. I think they were under more stress than the resident infantrymen were.' That there were so few cases of what people now call 'battle fatigue' is a great tribute to the self-discipline and morale of all our Sappers. Nevertheless, after enduring constant shelling and mortar fire, particularly in the vicinity of the Hook, many of the Sappers and NCOs were beginning to react to enemy fire with increased levels of caution, but no one hesitated to go on duty.

With officers, fear manifested itself rather differently but was not to be confused with fatigue. Lack of sleep, combined with the stress of continuous action, had a debilitating effect and impaired one's judgement and ability to function properly, but was usually righted by a good rest. In the former, it was more a case of 'fear of fear', a fear of being seen to be afraid. It was much easier for officers to conquer their fear: they had to set an example and they had more responsibility and had much more to occupy their thoughts. Most didn't have time to be afraid, though one officer confessed, years later, how he had a sudden moment of absolute terror when he found himself alone in a communication trench with nobody within sight or sound. It was a hot, sunny day and he was on his way forward to see some of his men, with desultory mortar fire and shelling close by. Suddenly, in a moment of panic, he froze and wondered what he should do. With only a beret on his head, he felt extremely vulnerable but, catching sight of a discarded steel helmet, he grabbed hold of it and put it on his head. Suddenly he felt much better and then he thought he must look an awful prat with the helmet perched on top of his beret, so he took it off and hurled it away. The moment had passed and he carried on to his objective.

The corollary of fear is courage. Some have more than others. It takes courage to overcome one's fear. For one rather highly strung officer in the Regiment, it must have taken an enormous effort to overcome his fear but he never faltered and if anyone deserved a medal it was him. Another courageous officer was the legendary Peter Moore, the first Commanding Officer of the Regiment, who was always to be found in the thick of things and had three DSOs. He set the most wonderful example and not only to the men under him.

Spencer Hannay always seemed to know when he was needed and, just when things were hotting up, a Troop Commander would turn round and find him at his shoulder quietly asking how things were getting on and enquiring if there was anything he could do to help. He may not have known it but he gave the most tremendous boost to every man in that Troop. His predecessor never came near a Troop in a forward position, unless he was accompanying the Brigade Commander.

Morale amongst the men was never a problem and a wonderful team spirit existed in every troop and even in each section, but their exuberance had to be curbed at times, especially in relation to our American allies. The American custom of declaiming how good or famous they were, such as 'Second to None' would lead to the next door British unit painting a sign saying 'We are None'. Strangely, the Americans took exception to this, or perhaps our superiors thought it was not politically correct to tease our allies, though they never seemed to object to the song that reverberated nightly throughout the Division which referred to the disastrous withdrawal from the River Yalu on the intervention of the Chinese. Sung to the tune of US Country/Western airs, it always seemed to start with a variation of:

> *The pitter-patter of tiny feet,*
> *It's the 1st Cav Div in full retreat.*
> *They're movin' on – they're movin' on.*
> *You can bet your bottom dollar, they're movin' on.*
>
> *The Chinese are coming in one big mass,*
> *Don't want a bayonet up my ass.*
> *I'm movin' on, I'm movin' on.*
> *You can bet your bottom dollar, I'm movin' on.*

There were innumerable further verses, getting ruder and ruder as the beer flowed and they were not just confined to the Americans. Even the RSM was not exempt: 'going down the track, and we don't give a f . . . if he never comes back'! Luckily he didn't seem to mind and enjoyed it all.

Chapter 16

The Dukes' Battle

Soon it was the turn of the Dukes to face an assault. The planned relief of the Black Watch in the second week of May 1953, by the Duke of Wellington's Regiment, had to be postponed for twenty-four hours due to torrential rain and necessitated engineer effort being diverted onto flood prevention and road repair. This coincided with increased enemy activity and damaging shellfire, and Spencer Hannay, by now OC 55 Squadron, had the task of judging priorities between work on the defences and preventing the Hook road system collapsing. The Brigadier and the battalion commanders needed convincing but an acceptable solution was found.

While work on the Hook defences was going on, 2 Troop, under Captain Tom Watling, were put to work on the Hook roads. Their first task was to make a short loop to bypass a section of the main supply road which was under observation and shellfire – this was completed about a week later, but still required an extra sixty yards of screening. Work continued on the other Hook roads while Captain Ross Mason's 3 Troop spent the month in support of the remainder of the Brigade in the usual tasks of minefield maintenance, road repairs, waterpoints and assistance to the other battalions. They were also tasked with widening a gap in our own minefield near Yongdong to give better tank access to the Samichon valley. Second Lieutenant Jeffery Lewins and a party carried out this work in the early morning when our lines were still in shadow. The clearance was completed and the Troop started a check on all minefields in the Brigade area – this was expected to take some time as a number of unknown fields had already been discovered.

Just to add to the pressure, Teal Bridge over the Imjin, which was immediately behind the Hook and vital to its defence, was bombed. On this occasion, I had just come out of my *hoochie* and was stretching my arms when, at 5.30am on 20 May, I saw six aircraft dive-bombing the bridge which was just over the brow of the hill behind me. Surprised,

I thought that the Chinese had somehow got new aircraft and were flexing their muscles. Fortunately the bridge was not hit directly but when we listened to the radio later that morning we heard that six American aircraft had destroyed a large bridge in North Korea! It was hardly a coincidence and, surprise, surprise, we heard later that six American pilots had been flown back in disgrace to the USA later that day. 3 Troop, who were nearest, replaced some damaged decking and the bridge was opened to one-way traffic within three hours, while subsequent repairs to restore it to two-way traffic were carried out by American Corps Engineers.

Though much of the limelight was focused on 55 Field Squadron, and the Hook in particular, 12 Field Squadron was very involved in rather less glamorous, but nevertheless important, work in the other Brigade area. They were back on the infamous Hill 355 and continued their work on the defensive positions. A very close and effective liaison developed between the Sappers and the Infantry and the latter were frequently accompanied on their patrols by Sapper detachments.

When the Dukes took over the Hook, the Troop Commander of their supporting troop was asked by the CO to inspect all the bunkers on the reverse slope which were used for sleeping and rest. There were some thirty bunkers in all and after he had checked them, the CO asked if they were safe. All the Troop Commander could say was 'In peacetime, I would condemn every one as totally unsafe, but all we can do now is to put some props in the worst.' Luckily, none actually collapsed while being occupied ...

Every effort was made to conceal the relief from the Chinese. The Black Watch formed the patrols on the night of the handover and their operators continued to man the radio sets so that, if their frequency was being monitored, the change from Scottish brogue to Yorkshire vernacular could not be detected until it no longer mattered. In fact, four days of peace and quiet enabled the Dukes, assisted by 1 Troop's sappers, to work like beavers to improve the defences. Bunkers were strengthened, communication trenches were deepened and more barbed wire was strung out in front of the weapon pits. In their account of the subsequent battle, the Dukes described the sappers' work as vital and that their regiment was lucky to have them.

Work also proceeded on the Green Finger tunnel, but there were frequent interruptions from enemy activity. The tunnel had been started in great secrecy several weeks before, but one night enemy activity had been heard in the immediate vicinity and work had halted. When he heard this, David Rose, the Black Watch CO, had exploded and demanded that work should be carried on regardless, despite his earlier instruction that the work should be carried out in the greatest secrecy. This decision was to have disastrous consequences.

The Chinese had not been put off by the failure of their attack on the Black Watch on the night of 7/8 May. They brought up more heavy artillery and were determined to succeed next time, renewing their shelling with enthusiasm. The Dukes watched with growing unease as the Chinese caused more and more damage to the defences, their heavier guns penetrating the overhead cover of the bunkers with delayed action fuses and it was only too evident that a major attack was imminent. Shelling increased in intensity, 20,000 rounds landing on the position, half of them on the final day before the expected attack, and all of them on a company position only 300 yards by 150 yards. Even the Somme couldn't match that. Meanwhile the sappers worked frantically to maintain and strengthen the defences.

To the Duke of Wellington's Regiment, the Hook had a certain reputation, described by Private D. Miller, one of their soldiers:

A hill stands in Korea, they named it the Hook,
You won't find it on a map or in a Guide Book.
It stood dark against the sky, a place men went to die.
Men blanched at the mention of its name,
Prayed they'd never have to go there again.
Just half a mile of trenches and barbed wire.

No colour to be seen
Only shell holes where the grass had been.
No animals, no birds, no grass or trees,
No springs flowed down to the paddy fields below.
The hill looked like the landscape on the moon,
Craters covered the ground from shells falling all around.

After a week of this intense shelling, things reached a crescendo and the Chinese launched a sudden attack, just before 'Stand To', catching the forward troops before they were fully prepared, though they responded quickly and fought back ferociously. The enemy troops were well equipped, and brave. The leading men carried rocket launchers, and satchel charges for destroying bunkers; follow-up troops were often unarmed, ready to pick up rifles or Burp guns from those killed or wounded in front of them, but also carrying spare rockets, grenades and extra ammunition. The sapper working party for the tunnel had not arrived yet as they were waiting for darkness before breaking out into the open down the spur in front of them and installing the bunkers from which the LMGs could fire in enfilade on anyone approaching up the re-entrant. The tunnel was one of the first objectives of the Chinese onslaught as they knew exactly where it was and explosive satchel charges destroyed weeks of hard work, but fortunately there were no sapper casualties. It was a long night but by 3.00am the Chinese were eventually beaten back by the Dukes and an unprecedented volume of defensive fire, including a phenomenal number of airburst shells which caught the enemy in the open and caused enormous casualties, but not before the Dukes had suffered nearly 150 casualties themselves, including twenty-nine killed and sixteen taken prisoner. *Virtutis fortuna comes* (motto of the Duke of Wellington's Regiment) – Fortune had indeed favoured the Brave. Chinese casualties were estimated at 250 killed and 800 wounded.

With first light on 29 May a scene of utter devastation was revealed. Ten thousand Chinese shells had utterly destroyed trenches which, less than twenty-four hours before had been over eight-foot-deep and were now scarcely knee high; weapon pits had ceased to exist and bunkers were filled with rubble. Shredded sandbags and tangles of barbed wire littered the area. Then there were the dead and wounded. The Chinese had taken most of theirs with them, but many of the Dukes' casualties were still buried in bunkers or tunnels. The Hook was effectively un-occupied and the area resembled some shattered lunar landscape.

Brigadier Joe Kendrew, the Brigade Commander, came up to the Hook later that morning to see for himself what had happened. He had won three DSOs in the Second World War and so was no stranger to conflict but even he was shocked. Grave-faced and shaken, he said, 'My God, those Dukes! They were marvellous. In the whole of the last war I never knew anything like that bombardment. But they held the Hook ... I knew they would.'

When it had become clear that the battle was imminent, Spencer Hannay had assembled all three Troops in shelter behind the Hook. In addition to acting as an infantry reserve should the enemy break through, the Squadron would be ready to move quickly to repair defences. The OC took up station at the Dukes' CP and when it was learnt that the position was clear, he ordered 1 and 2 Troops onto the Hook under cover of artillery smoke, committing 3 Troop later after assessing the situation himself. It was evident that a lot of work would be needed if it was to be held against further attacks. The remnants of tunnels and bunkers had to be cleared, the whole trench system was in tatters and there were still dead and wounded on the position.

One of the people rescued was Lewis Kershaw, a forty-year-old Major who was commanding Support Company but who, in a conversation with the author the previous day, had bemoaned the fact that he was considered too old to command a company and was now little more than a Patrol Master coordinating the battalion's patrols. He had gone up to the Hook that evening and clocked in at the CP but he and 'Baron' Emett, the OC, did not get on together and when it came to the crunch the Baron meant to fight the battle with a minimum of interference, and Lewis was senior to him. 'You can't work here,' he snapped. 'You'd better find somewhere with one of the forward platoons.' Lewis Kershaw didn't argue and humped his radio set forward to 10 Platoon's headquarters dug-out. When the battle started, the forward sections were overwhelmed by screaming, yelling Chinese firing their automatic Burp guns and throwing grenades. Forced to evacuate his platoon CP, Second Lieutenant Ernest Kirk and Lewis Kershaw took refuge in one of the tunnels. This had two entrances and one was soon petrol-bombed and then destroyed by explosives, burying Kirk, while Kershaw held the other end which was also blocked after some fierce fighting. When the tunnel was opened by Sappers soon after dawn Lewis Kershaw was pulled out, unconscious, with one foot hanging off and a ghastly wound to his head which looked as if it had been made with the edge of an entrenching tool. He was placed on a stretcher and 1 Troop Sappers helped to carry him out. After a few minutes he regained consciousness, looked up, remarked how good it was to see a Sapper officer carrying him and after confirming when he had last had morphine, relapsed into unconsciousness. Miraculously he recovered, after having a foot amputated, and was awarded a DSO for his work that night. The badly burnt body of Ernest Kirk was pulled out later and I was very upset when the Company Commander failed to come out of his CP to identify the body of one of his own platoon commanders. Perhaps he was just too tired after the night's exertions, though not too tired to leave the Hook with the remnants of his Company without waiting for a relief.

As the company was trooping down the reverse slope, a 'Stars and Stripes' reporter was waiting at the foot of the hill. He addressed a question to a young, newly-commissioned officer straight from Sandhurst, 'Gee, Lootenant,' he said, 'it must have been hell up there last night.' The young officer gave it some thought and in measured tones replied, 'Yes! It was absolutely appalling. It rained the whole time.'

The infantry company having withdrawn, two troops of Sappers were left to hold the position until relieved by fresh troops shortly before last light. In the meantime the least damaged bunkers were repaired, but movement in the open was restricted severely and greeted by mortar fire. No Gunner OPs were serviceable to bring down counter battery fire, and even when the top of a steel helmet showed, the enemy brought down 60mm mortar bombs with incredible accuracy. Their nearest positions were less than a hundred yards away so perhaps this was hardly surprising, but it was particularly tiresome for Sappers working against time to restore some semblance of a defensive position before last light. One could hear the bombs being dropped down the barrel, but at least it gave one several seconds to dive into the nearest shell scrape or fold in the ground and physical casualties were remarkably light, though the effect was pretty unnerving.

Moving round what was left of the position, I heard cries of pain coming from somewhere out in front. On enquiring from nearby sappers, I found that a Korean soldier attached to the battalion had evidently been captured but being wounded and difficult to carry the Chinese must have dropped him. The subaltern in charge of the working party thought it was too dangerous to rescue the man in broad daylight, whereupon I am afraid I snapped, grabbed the nearest sapper and with a quick 'Come with me', and before the poor man had time to protest, leapt out of the communication trench we were in and dashed forward to pull in the wounded man. The enemy must have been taken by surprise as they did not open fire and the casualty was gently lowered back into our position. Just as I jumped in after him, Major Spencer Hannay, the Squadron Commander, turned up demanding to know what was going on. He turned on me, asking why I wasn't getting on with what I was supposed to be doing. A rather weak reply that I didn't really think I could leave a wounded man lying out in no man's land earned me one of the biggest rockets of my life. I have never forgotten his explosive comments, including phrases like 'risking soldiers' lives', 'wasting time', 'the importance of getting defences restored', on and on, rang in my ears. They were entirely justified: I shouldn't have let my emotions get the better of me and been so foolhardy. So no VC there!

The two sapper troops worked furiously to restore some semblance of order, not easy when every open trench or weapon pit had been reduced to a shallow scoop in the ground, littered with debris, tangled wire, torn bits of clothing and ammunition. As a defensive position it had almost ceased to exist but work went on ceaselessly. In the middle of the afternoon, while I was working with one of my sappers in the confined space of a half-demolished bunker, shovelling earth behind us and trying to prop up the roof, we suddenly came across an arm sticking out of the earth attached to a very dead body. This was too much for the poor sapper, already exhausted from lack of sleep and days of constant shelling, who collapsed on the ground with a strangled cry. Weeping and wailing, he could work no more and was hurriedly evacuated off the hill and taken to hospital. After a few days' rest, he rejoined the Troop, apparently none the worse, but restricted to less stressful work.

The Royal Fusiliers were moved over during the day from 28 Brigade and with last light looming, Major Henry Hill, one of their Company Commanders, turned up, followed shortly after by the rest of his Company, including an obscure cockney, one day to be known to the world as Michael Caine. Henry had never seen the position before and, as there was so little daylight remaining, I told him where to put his platoons and sections, brushing aside his protests and saying he could move everything round the next day if he wished but this was what he

167

had to do before dark. To give the Company Commander his due he accepted this sapper guidance and advice with good grace and did as he was told. Sufficient bunkers and weapon pits had been cleared to enable the infantry to hold the position should it be attacked again and, as soon as it was dark, some very tired sappers trailed back to their troop locations, and a hot meal.

The enemy must have been tired too as the night was quiet and, on 31 May, my Troop withdrew from the Hook and returned to road and camouflage maintenance, and to a rest. We also reverted to supporting the Black Watch who were now on the eastern end of the Brigade's area of responsibility. Lieutenant Dick Dowdall joined the Troop as the second officer and soon saw his first piece of action. He was in charge of camouflaging a section of road and, despite being warned not to go to a certain point, showed himself in the open. He became very excited when the enemy rewarded him with his first taste of shellfire, but was somewhat chastened when his Troop Commander pointed out that being shelled was entirely his own fault and that some of his men might well have been killed or wounded. He was quick to learn, though, and soon became an excellent Troop Officer, and a firm friend.

Tom Watling's 2 Troop continued to work on the east side of the Hook, with 3 Troop on the west. Five sappers had been wounded on 30 May, three were wounded by mortar fire the next day and one more the following one. Sapper Vaughan was also wounded but died of his wounds. The two Troops worked day and night shifts to repair the damage on the Hook. An armoured Dozer from 1st Royal Tank Regiment was used to make a track up to Pt 146 to the right of the Hook and this was extended a couple of days later to the Sausage, a feature between Pt 146 and the Hook.

At about this time the Squadron War Diary had a plaintive entry saying 'For the last few days we have suffered from being on the regimental radio net, giving a total of 72 stations. No one could get a word in edgeways. Today we thankfully returned to the Squadron net!' And the Squadron returned to normal working, in more ways than one.

Chapter 17

Rip Van Winkle

They send us in front with a fuse an' a mine
To blow up the gates that are rushed by the Line
'Sappers' Rudyard Kipling

In early June Brigade Headquarters was still concerned about the enemy's intentions. For six weeks the Chinese had been trying to dislodge the 1st Commonwealth Division from the Hook and air photographs showed that they were digging shallow tunnels close to our positions, particularly on the reverse slopes of Warsaw, a feature about 250 yards to the north where their troops could lie up unseen. The digging was similar in appearance to the tunnels dug at the end of the previous November prior to their battle with the Black Watch. One important difference with these new tunnels was that they were constructed right at the foot of three particular re-entrants which could not be observed by our artillery or by our tanks across the River Samichon on 'Yong Dong'. There were definite signs of increased enemy activity and the Brigade Commander had a feeling that the enemy must be crossing the valley bottom by night and lying up in these caves, probably as a prelude to another major assault. He decided that the time had come to destroy them.

On the evening of 2 June 1953, I was brought down to earth from our Coronation festivities by a phone call from Ian Bruce, our squadron 2IC, telling me to be in the Command Post at 10.00pm for an O Group. A warning was also given that I would be wise not to let the men celebrate too much in the canteen. I was intrigued and apprehensive as we had just been relieved from our somewhat hazardous weeks on the Hook and had been promised a quiet time elsewhere. At the O Group my Squadron Commander, Major Spencer Hannay, informed me that there was to be a raid on the Warsaw caves with the aim of destroying some fifteen tunnels in three re-entrants, to be known as 'Rip', 'Van' and 'Winkle'. A frontal attack was not considered practicable so the Brigadier had determined to attack the caves from their rear by making a long detour from the east through no man's land.

He decided that the only way to be certain though was for some-one to have a close look on the ground while the raiding party made preparations for a raid on the caves. The next night two reconnaissance parties went out, the first to find out a suitable route into the valley bottom through the wire in front of our positions and a second one consisting of an infantry officer and my Troop Recce sergeant, Sergeant Shirley MM, who crept out from positions on the flank and made their way along the valley bottom to get as close as they dared. There was quite a lot of activity in the area and they were very nearly captured, but they confirmed that there were indeed numerous tunnels and that the Chinese were definitely up to something. They had also found a suitable area by a stream-bed running along the valley bottom where our troops could lie up prior to any assault.

The Brigadier confirmed that a company-size raid should take place the following night, with the aim of destroying any enemy positions in the three re-entrants. An infantry company from The King's Regiment was to be supported by a demolition team of sappers and my Troop was detailed for the task. This provoked a storm of protest from my men, pointing out that they were supposed to be supporting the Black Watch and in typical soldiers' colourful language exclaimed, 'Why should we now go with a lot like the King's?' They were only placated when I told them that we had been selected specially for the job and they should be proud of this. I also told them to just get on with it and to stop moaning. The men grinned and got on with it. There was not much time to get ready so preliminary arrangements were made that night for the supply of satchel charges, extra automatic weapons and all the other items that would be required.

Having debriefed the recce party it was decided that the sapper element would consist of an officer and fourteen men. Each man would have to carry 20lb of explosive across some 4,000 yards of enemy territory so it was important that they should not be encumbered by too much extra equipment. Rifles were exchanged for Sten guns and grenades were issued to each man; the demolition charges consisted of 2lb blocks of TNT packed into haversacks, which could be carried conveniently on a man's back and which could be slung into any cave utilizing the haver-sack straps. At least one wouldn't know much about it if one was hit. Drills were practised, weapons tested, grenades primed and RVs fixed in the event of anyone becoming separated. I also gave instructions that should anyone be wounded on the way in to the attack the others must not stop to help, but leave the person to be picked up by the infantry. I had a feeling though that things might not go according to plan and, though I was confident that my own men were fully prepared, I was concerned that there was no proper rehearsal arranged with the

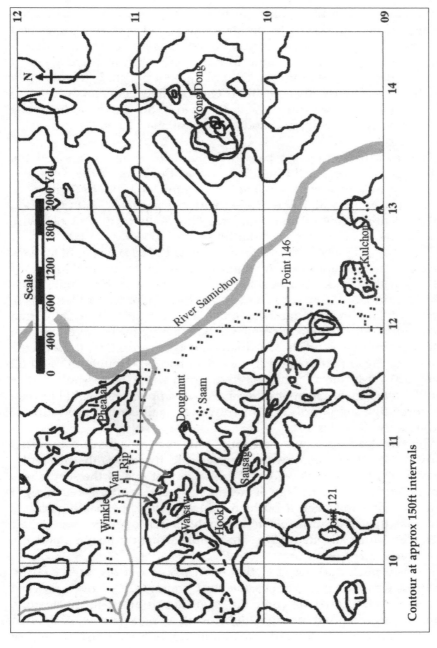

Map 4. The Hook, showing the location of the re-entrants Rip, Van and Winkle

Contour at approx 150ft intervals

171

infantry. For the first time, I wrote a letter home, to be posted if I did not return. Others did the same.

We met up with the infantry in the company locality at the ruined village of Kulchon shortly before dark and sorted ourselves out as best we could. In the rush, I had neglected to darken my face but the King's Company Sergeant Major came to the rescue and, to the enjoyment of my Troop, smeared my face with black boot polish. It was the only laughter I was to hear for some time. Our OC, Spencer Hannay, came to see us off and chatted quietly with the men in the darkness. Everyone was naturally pretty nervous and we were all glad when the time came to move off.

The track from Kulchon passed through three minefields and the plan was to move out through a gap near the bank of the Samichon river, and then turn west, passing through the long-deserted village of Sa'am. The entire valley was littered with old, scattered and uncharted nuisance minefields of both sides together with tangles of old wire fences. The area had been constantly shelled for long periods.

The Assault Pioneers moved forward ahead of us at last light to mark the route through our forward minefields with white tape and luminous discs and then took up a position guarding the exit. The main body, which included a Gunner FOO and a Mortar Fire Controller (MFC), moved off later in pitch darkness, making a lot of noise, especially from their radios, where nobody seemed to be ordering the operators to turn down the volume controls. One platoon was to move forward with the Company Headquarters and form a firm base at 'Doughnut', a knoll some 500 yards short of the objectives from where the assault parties could move forward to attack the caves. My sappers were split between the three fighting patrols and there was a small control group to co-ordinate the final assaults.

The two leading scouts had only gone forward about a hundred yards or so when enemy were reported and there was the noise of a grenade exploding, followed by a message that one of the scouts was wounded. There was no sign of any enemy reaction and it was thought that they had mistaken a bush 'moving' against the passing clouds and that they had probably failed to lie down after throwing their grenade – after all, the enemy always die instantly in films and the home side never gets hurt.

It was a pitch dark night as the moon would not rise until 2.00am. Progress was slow until Pat O'Kane, the Company 2IC, moved forward into the lead. The whole company then moved along fairly steadily, bunched together and in single file, moving along a narrow, ill-defined and overgrown path towards Sa'am. Suddenly a man just in front of Company HQ trod on an anti-personnel mine, blowing off his leg, killing three men and wounding another twelve, including the FOO,

Second Lieutenant Brian Parritt, who received three fragments in his leg. His small party was vital for controlling our artillery fire support but their radio set also was hit by a piece of shrapnel, though this was not discovered until the operator removed his flak jacket next day and found the fragment embedded just by his spine! Some thirty men must have passed over the same spot already without harm.

The Company Commander had failed to make a proper plan for casualty evacuation so there were any number of 'volunteers' eager to help take the wounded back to the safety of our lines. Despite the mine, and ignoring the possibility that it might not be the only one, the Company Commander decided to make his firm base where he was, in the middle of a minefield as it turned out. He was also very concerned, as well he might, about the enemy reaction, at one time exclaiming that we were being fired on by enemy machine guns. He only relaxed when it was pointed out to him that the fire was over our heads and coming from positions on the hill above us, which was in our own hands. Things did not augur well for the rest of the night.

The casualties and the men required to evacuate them severely depleted the assault parties and necessitated a quick change of plan. The Company Commander formed the three fighting patrols into one strong one, plus some extra sappers, with orders to attack only the nearest of the three groups of caves. The remainder of the sapper assault teams were left to help protect the company firm base. The enemy were by now thoroughly alerted and the prospect of success with so few men did not look too promising. By now it was 2.00am and what was now a single fighting patrol moved off as quickly as possible, skirting the ruined village and slipping into some bushes beside the stream running along the valley bottom. The control group, which included Pat O'Kane and me, brought up the rear, not having a lot to do at this time, except to crouch low at every halt to have yet another pee and wonder why we were there! (Pat kept asking what he had done wrong to be posted to this Regiment when he was really in the Parachute Regiment, but he had probably volunteered for Korea.) A small paddy-bund ran about thirty yards from the stream and provided a convenient place behind which our small control group could take up a defensive position while the assault party covered the final fifty yards or so. Sixteen men, of whom nine were sappers, made the final assault. The infantry were to lead, closely followed by my sappers. As they moved up the re-entrant the infantry were to deal with any enemy encountered, throwing grenades into any trenches or tunnels they passed and take up a position above the furthest tunnel until the sappers had placed their charges. They were then to withdraw, the sappers pulling their igniter switches as they accompanied them, and pass back through the control group who would cover the withdrawal to the firm base. Speed was essential.

173

The artillery fire to keep the enemy's heads down was intermittent as it had not been realized for a while that the Gunner FOO had been wounded in the first mine explosion. By the time the assault party was ready to move up the re-entrant the only way the artillery fire could be co-ordinated was via the somewhat inadequate radio set carried by the sappers. Sapper McLaren, normally my driver, had volunteered to be my radio operator and, knowing how vulnerable the '88 Sets' were, had stuffed a spare aerial down inside his shirt – without it, the raiding party could never have called for fire support. The tanks, out on a flank, were firing tracer on fixed lines and though they could not reach the caves they could at least serve as a useful indicator of the direction in which to move.

By the time the assault party was ready for the final dash, the moon was well up but there was considerable smoke due to the continuous shelling and mortaring and it was difficult to see. As soon as the guns stopped firing the assault went in. The first tunnel was grenaded and passed, but then opposition was encountered and some close-quarter fighting took place. One of my NCOs, Corporal Digby, killed at least one of the enemy with his Sten gun before being wounded himself. The Chinese were there in force and used Burp guns and stick grenades. Several men were wounded, though none seriously, and fell back to the control group where they were told to make their own way back to the firm base. Sapper Smyth knelt before the entrance to one of the tunnels to ready his explosives, placing his Sten gun on the ground next to him. At that point some Chinese soldiers ran past him; he saw one look at him but keep on running. Having prepared the charge, he saw the Chinese soldier running back towards him so he picked up his Sten gun and stopped him with a short burst. He then destroyed the tunnel and went on to help elsewhere. Opposition in the re-entrant increased and the assault party found they could make no further progress; two more wounded returned to the control group and told us that the attack was being beaten off, but not before the sappers had hurled all their demolition charges into the caves. The officer in charge of the assault party, Second Lieutenant Williams, was forced to order a withdrawal and he himself dragged one of my sappers, Sapper Harris, badly wounded with six bullets in his thigh from a Burp gun, to the bottom of the re-entrant where he found temporary safety in some bushes, covered by Sapper Smyth.

Meanwhile, the control group was waiting anxiously near the stream. We waited as long as possible to cover the withdrawal but were running out of time, and ammunition – the Bren gunner was down to his last magazine and I was trying to make myself ever smaller behind the paddy-bund beside him. Concerned about being cut off, we eventually had to leave and started to withdraw the way we had come, but the leading men found that we had already left it too late and we were cut off. With Chinese all around us we decided to cross the stream, moving north as far as we dared towards the main enemy positions and then east again. The stream was nearly waist deep and we had difficulty in getting some of the wounded across. On the far side of the stream our small party regrouped before moving on.

A few minutes later Sapper Smyth, who had stayed behind with the wounded man, rejoined us and asked for help as they had been unable to move Harris any further. Smyth had left his Sten gun with Second Lieutenant Williams and set off for help, completely unarmed. Unfortunately the control party now consisted of only nine men, of whom five were wounded, so nobody could be spared. I gave Smyth my own Sten gun as I still had a revolver and, without a second's hesitation he returned to the re-entrant where he had left Harris. We heard nothing more from them and I feared the worst but they eventually turned up next morning having managed to bring back the wounded man through our own lines, both of them being given immediate awards for their courage, Second Lieutenant Williams, on his last night in Korea, being awarded the Military Cross and Smyth the Military Medal.

The control group party got back to the firm base and found that the Assault Pioneer Platoon had moved forward to help. Preparations were being made for casualties to be evacuated and everyone to withdraw. Aware that we were probably still sitting in the middle of a minefield, Sapper McLaren quietly detached himself, took out his prodder and started to look round for any mines in the area It was now about 4.30am and beginning to get light but then another mine exploded, wounding five more men and slowing things down even further. Smoke was put down by the Gunners to cover our withdrawal and as the company neared our lines Centurion tanks moved forward in case the enemy should be following up behind.

I was left to bring up the rear, carrying half a dozen rifles discarded by men wounded in the raid. It had been a very long night, but my sappers at least had acquitted themselves well, though five had been wounded including Sapper Beck who died later from his wounds. Never had a mug of tea, liberally laced with rum, been more welcome and we were all thankful to get back to our own beds. I retrieved the letter I had written the night before, tore it into tiny shreds and decided I was allergic to night operations. They were much too exciting.

The company raid had been little short of a disaster, due to lack of planning, and out of some 130 men nearly one third had become casualties. It is virtually impossible to find scattered mines on a dark night and in ground that has been heavily shelled, where electronic mine detectors were useless and prodding was too slow, added to which was the difficulty of knowing when and where to start searching. That every casualty was brought back is a tribute to the determination of the British soldier not to leave his comrades, but those injured on the approach march should have been carried by men from a reserve platoon and not by men from the assault parties, thus jeopardizing the whole operation. Nevertheless the night was not entirely wasted as the Chinese evacuated their caves, thereby removing one threat to our positions. The King's casualties were three killed and twenty-three wounded, while my Troop lost one killed and four wounded – out of fourteen of us.

Chapter 18

A Fragile Peace

Last Days

Immediate repairs to the Hook defences in the first few days after the Dukes' battle had been little more than just 'make do and mend'. More long-term repairs were needed and by 10 June the Hook and the adjoining company positions had all been repaired, with the exception of the Green Finger tunnel, which was finished some time later. The tunnel entrance and the firing positions had been destroyed by demolition charges but the tunnel itself was still useable. Nevertheless, work continued to improve it over the next few weeks and it was completed finally on 18 July. The Section tunnels and the sleeping tunnels where many of the Dukes' survivors had taken refuge were likewise undamaged, except at the entrances which had all been blown in.

Meanwhile, a detailed report was produced by OC 55 Squadron and in the light of this it was decided to undertake extensive tunnelling to provide underground shelter for a complete company. The complex was to consist of three tunnels totalling some 500 feet of galleries, driven from the reverse side, under the highest part of the hill. This work was to complement the repairs already started on the forward slopes in the immediate aftermath of the battle. Work was started by 2 Troop under Tom Watling on 13 June by winching a 315cpm trailer compressor up to the jeep-head and placing it in a specially constructed bunker. The compressor was only marginally better than the one tried out earlier, due to the distance the hoses were from the furthest tunnels. In any case, the compressor could not be used at night as it was too noisy. Recourse had to be made to drilling and shot-firing but nevertheless progress averaged five feet a day. The tunnels were fully timbered for the first fifteen feet and thereafter frames were put in at five-foot spacing. Work continued without break until 12 Squadron took over the Hook on 10 July. By 25 July work on all the tunnels was nearing completion and lighting was being fitted.

Chinese forces had launched attacks on the Commonwealth Division throughout July. On the night of 23/24 July, the divisional artillery fired 13,000 rounds in support of the American Marines immediately to the left of the Division and some of our units were also involved. Over 4,000 mortar bombs fell on our own positions, mostly on the Hook, on the same night and the attacks were repeated the following night.

Hostilities ceased at 10.00pm on 27 July. It was three years and one month after hostilities began, two years and eleven months from the time the first Commonwealth troops had landed at Pusan, and two years all but a day after the formation of the 1st Commonwealth Division. It was also just over two years since 'Cease Fire' talks started.

Cease Fire Talks

It may seem extraordinary that it was back on 23 June 1951 that M. Malik, the Soviet Representative at the United Nations, had suggested in a broadcast that ceasefire talks might profitably be held in Korea. The talks began after a couple of weeks but only concluded over two years later, and then it was only to be an Armistice.

Disagreement was evident at once, starting with the question of fixing a Demarcation Line. The Communists suggested the 38th Parallel while the United Nations insisted on a line approximating to the existing front line, a view which eventually prevailed even though in general it was some miles to the north of the parallel. The next sticking point was to agree concrete proposals for a ceasefire, including the composition and functions of a supervising authority to carry out the terms of any agreement reached.

Perhaps the most contentious problem concerned the question of exchanging prisoners of war. The issue was complicated by the disparity in numbers between the two sides, the United Nations holding some 132,000, of which 47,000 were unwilling to return, against the 12,000 held by the Communists, virtually all of whom wanted to be released. On 8 June 1953, agreement was finally reached, with the Government of India being invited to provide a Custodian Force for prisoners. The agreement nearly unravelled when the President of South Korea, Syngman Rhee, unilaterally released nearly 27,000 North Korean prisoners who were refusing repatriation. The United Nations Command disclaimed all responsibility for this and the terms of the Armistice were agreed eventually.

Armistice

There was no great feeling of euphoria, and certainly no big celebration, on the signing of the Armistice. It was more a sense of relief that it was all over at last. It was however only an armistice and troops were prepared to resume hostilities should the Armistice Agreement break down or be violated. There was no more shelling or mortaring and the silence seemed rather uncanny at first. Lights were seen again at night. In the Duke of Wellington's Regiment sector, word came over the radio from Battalion Headquarters that other ranks might venture into no man's land, but no officers were to do so. A rather strange order and soon disregarded, particularly by 12 Field Squadron who were now working on the Hook where they were building more tunnels and blasting rock to make space for more bunkers. They were particularly relieved at being able to take off the body armour and steel helmets which their OC, Major Logan Scott-Bowden (Scottie), always insisted should be worn.

Within a few hours little clusters of Chinese appeared in front of the wire, bearing bottles of rice spirit and little glass rings inscribed with the word 'peace'. Second Lieutenant Sam Sowton, one of the Troop Officers, remembered going out in front of the Hook and fraternizing with the 'enemy'. Some of the Chinese officers were very friendly and were very articulate in English. Terry Cleary, a subaltern in the Field Park Squadron, came forward and also went onto the Hook, subsequently finding his photograph in 'Picture Post'. It was interesting, too, to walk forward to see what our own defences looked like from the enemy viewpoint. The terrain in front of the Hook in particular gave the Chinese the advantage of being able to creep up close under the convex hillside to within eighty or ninety yards of our own positions. Nevertheless, it was a surprise to find that an officer and a small party had been able to live in a cave immediately under one of the forward trenches.

Prisoners of War
One of the first benefits from the Armistice was the return of our prisoners of war from their camps in North Korea. One of them described his longings:

> *If, when I return to you*
> *Free from this strange land,*
> *You find that I have changed, sweetheart,*
> *I hope you will understand.*
>
> *Many months of loneliness,*
> *A life I can't describe,*
> *I know has made some changes*
> *That I can never hide.*
>
> *I hope, my darling,*
> *The changes that you see,*
> *I hope they are constructive*
> *And make a better me.*

For I have learned the value
Of a buddy and a friend
And just how much, my darling,
We all in God depend.

I have seen men suffer
And never know relief
All because they wouldn't turn
Against their own belief.

And I have seen the opposite,
And this I can't forget.
A man that turned traitor
For just one cigarette.

All this, my darling,
Every word is true.
I only hope I can forget
When I return to you.

It is hard to imagine what it must have been like to be a prisoner of war of the North Korean/Chinese Forces. The first prisoners, captured early in the war had been marched north for ten or more hours a day, few of the wounded received medical treatment and water was often withheld in the height of the hot weather. More prisoners were taken after the Chinese army entered the war and at the soldiers' level they were treated more humanely by the Chinese than by the North Korean People's Army. Nevertheless, their prisoner of war columns were marched north unrelentingly but not brutally.

The Commandant of No. 1 Prisoner of War Camp on the Yalu gave a warning that:

> After capture, prisoners must be friends and no longer adopt a hostile attitude; they must learn repentance and the meaning of peace. They are lucky to be alive after fighting for the capitalists and they should be grateful that they are prisoners of the Chinese and have the chance to study until they go home ...

Punishment was at the discretion of the captor and used as a means to coerce 'reactionaries', which included those attempting to escape. At a North Korean interrogation centre known among prisoners as 'Pak's Palace', torture was common: one officer, Captain 'Spud' Gibbon, had bamboo slivers thrust under his fingernails to elicit information and others were subjected to the 'water treatment'. Solitary confinement was common in all the camps. One of those to suffer more than his share of solitary confinement was Sam Davies, the inspirational padre of the Glosters who had been captured after their heroic battle in April 1951. After the war was over he wrote of his experiences in a book entitled *In Spite of Dungeons*, a reference to the hymn the other prisoners used to sing to bolster his morale when he was incarcerated. However, the opening of peace talks in the second half of 1951 led to an improvement in the organization and handling of prisoners as the Chinese realized that prisoners would have to be exchanged at some point. Nevertheless, the Chinese considered that disobedience of any sort was morally wrong, obedience was good, co-operation was better and subscription to the system was best of all.

The main part of each day was occupied in 'education' such as political indoctrination, and instruction in the aims and activities of American imperialism, with occasional reference to British subservience to it. It was into this environment that Lance Corporal Brown and Sappers McGowan, White and Wilkinson came after they were captured on the Hook during an onslaught by the Chinese in November 1952. All four were in 3 Troop of 55 Squadron, commanded by Captain Alan O'Hagan.

During the peace talks the Sapper Postal Service provided a subaltern to take his turn at the thrice-weekly exchange of POW mail at Panmunjon. The exchange was made in a large tent furnished only with a folding table in the centre; the UN and Communist representatives would enter from opposite sides, synchronize their arrival at the table, salute and exchange mail against a signed receipt, salute again and leave without a word. If the peace talks were going well a slight informality might be accepted and an occasional 'Good morning' was possible; on bad days the Communist representative would drop the mail on the ground and indicate that it would go no further.

Following the Armistice, all prisoners who wished to be repatriated were to be handed over within sixty days. After their nine months in captivity, Alan O'Hagan greeted the first two when they reached the Peace Village at Panmunjon in August and the remaining two the following month. With all the rehabilitation procedures in train and a limited time in which to talk, he did not dwell too much on their time in captivity but they appeared to be in good health and did not seem to have experienced undue hardship or indoctrination. Lance Corporal Brown was even able to laugh about an incident, shortly before he was captured, when he had dropped the large flask of coffee habitually carried in Alan's Jeep as welcome refreshment for his men and smashed it to pieces, earning his Troop Commander's mock displeasure. Needless to say, they felt enormous relief to be free and the knowledge that they would soon be on their way home.

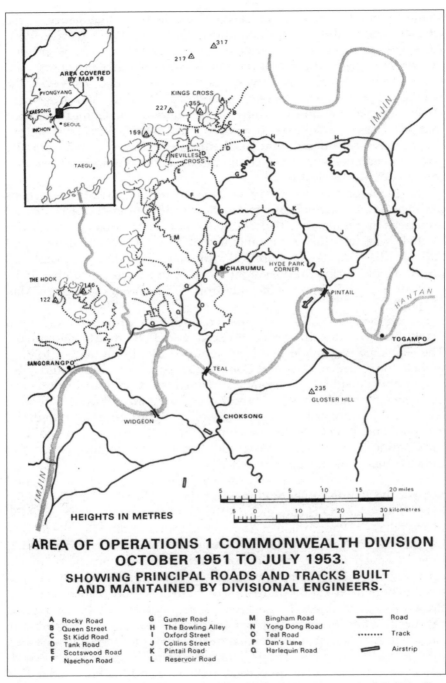

AREA COVERED BY MAP 16

PYONGYANG

KAESONG

INCHON SEOUL

TAEGU

KINGS CROSS

NEVILLES CROSS

CHARUMUL

HYDE PARK CORNER

THE HOOK

PINTAIL

HANTAN

SANGORANGPO

TOGAMPO

TEAL

235
GLOSTER HILL

WIDGEON

CHOKSONG

IMJIN

IMJIN

HEIGHTS IN METRES

5 0 5 10 15 20 miles

5 0 10 20 30 kilometres

AREA OF OPERATIONS 1 COMMONWEALTH DIVISION OCTOBER 1951 TO JULY 1953.
SHOWING PRINCIPAL ROADS AND TRACKS BUILT AND MAINTAINED BY DIVISIONAL ENGINEERS.

A Rocky Road	G Gunner Road	M Bingham Road	——— Road
B Queen Street	H The Bowling Alley	N Yong Dong Road	
C St Kidd Road	I Oxford Street	O Teal Road	········ Track
D Tank Road	J Collins Street	P Dan's Lane	
E Scotswood Road	K Pintail Road	Q Harlequin Road	Airstrip
F Naechon Road	L Reservoir Road		

Map 5. Area of Operation 1st Commonwealth Division, October 1951 to July 1953 showing principal roads and tracks built and maintained by Divisional Engineers

Chapter 19

The Immediate Aftermath

As mutually agreed, both sides were to withdraw two kilometres from the line of demarcation within seventy-two hours. Operation SWANLAKE, the withdrawal from the Demilitarized Zone to post-Armistice positions, began on the 28th and was completed by 31 July. The Commonwealth Division treated this as a tactical operation and withdrew a few miles to the area north and south of the River Imjin that had been held by the Division at the time it was formed two years before.

In the event that the Armistice Agreement break down or be violated in some way, the Division remained prepared to resume hostilities at short notice. Training for offensive and defensive operations, with particular emphasis on patrolling, was given high priority, though working hours were reduced and one day a week was devoted to relaxation. The construction of defensive works remained a priority, as did improved accommodation, before the onset of the Korean winter when such work would perforce be slowed significantly.

For Sappers, work in the former forward area was resumed quickly, but now in reverse. Under the terms of the Armistice Agreement, unarmed parties were permitted to enter the Demilitarized Zone for various defined purposes for a period of forty-five days after the Zone had been cleared. Field defences were dismantled, serviceable stores were recovered and battalion areas were cleared. One of the more distasteful tasks was to help locate bodies in the Demilitarized Zone and to see that they were buried properly. In the case of United Nations personnel, bodies were taken to the UN Cemetery just outside Pusan on a hill overlooking the sea.

THE FIELD OF CROSSES
by Dennis Woods

The years have passed in plenty,
Since the time that I was there;
Along with countless others,
The burden for to share.

Now I often think of those who stayed,
Detained against their will,
'Neath a field of painted crosses,
On the side of a sun-baked hill.

What price the golden glory,
In the winning of the fight?
With you not here to share it,
But gone for ever from our sight.

But you are not forgotten
And this I remember, too,
But for the grace of God above,
I'd have shared that field with you.

Shortly after the Armistice it was decided that the tunnel complexes on Hill 355, Yong Dong and the Hook should be destroyed. Special arrangements had to be made to re-enter the Demilitarized Zone and 12 Field Squadron was given the task. The Hook had been fought over more fiercely than any other position and its foremost platoon position was less than a hundred yards from the nearest Chinese so it gave particular pleasure to be ordered to obliterate it from the face of the earth. The OC, Scottie Scott-Bowden, decided that the task must be conducted as a proper operation, completed in a day rather than a bit-by-bit engineering task. With the war over, at least temporarily, with the Armistice there was no shortage of artillery ammunition so the explosive provided was cordite, supplied in cylindrical containers, together with a limited amount of guncotton and plastic explosive, plus detonators and primers for initiation. The squadron would deploy to the area, prepare the demolitions and, once he was satisfied that all was ready, Scott-Bowden would order the firing of each demolition in turn by radio from a central position.

The column drove out of camp early on the appointed morning. A short distance down the road radio communications failed. Scottie stopped the column, called the officers together, delivered the sort of rocket of which only he was capable and ordered the postponement of the operation for twenty-four hours. The following day the radios worked perfectly. Lesson learnt. The squadron drove up to the area, for so long the scene of bitter fighting and now deserted except for the debris of war. The tunnels were still in remarkably good shape and only needed a few hours of work to prepare them for their obliteration. This was achieved exactly as demanded, three mighty explosions going up in a great *feu de joie* on orders over the squadron radio net, changing the profile of the hills for ever. Scottie recalled vividly the indescribable charnel house stench that was released when the Hook was destroyed. It was a fitting and unforgettable end to a long nightmare.

An Uneasy Period

No sooner was the war over than the Troop Commanders were brought to heel. They may have felt isolated in their individual locations but they relished their independence. They now moved back to their squadron areas where better and more efficient use could be made of their manpower. The whole regiment, including B Echelon and the Light Aid Detachment (LAD), moved to the general area of 64 Field Park Squadron. For Ian Bruce, the 2IC of 55 Squadron, the move was just to yet another scrub-covered hill, except that this one was close to a Korean graveyard. It was not only memorable for being where the Squadron stayed the longest, but also because the autumn was enlivened by the chomping of millions of caterpillars. Later on some attractive butterflies appeared and one enterprising Sapper netted, mounted and then sold them to a dealer in the UK.

Reinforcements continued to arrive in the Division via the Japanese base as there were numerous sappers who had completed their tour in Korea, creating vacancies that needed to be filled. There was a rule that no one should serve more than one winter in Korea. One of these reinforcements was Second Lieutenant Gerald Napier, who arrived in Scottie Scott-Bowden's 12 Field Squadron about two weeks after the Armistice, via the Battle School in Japan. He was posted as troop officer to Captain David Brotherton in 3 Troop, the other Troop Commanders being Captains Stan Lewis in 1 Troop and Bill Macdonald in 2 Troop. Their first priority was the preparation of the new defensive line south of the River Imjin, roughly along the alignment of the former Kansas Line that had been the divisional reserve position during the later phases of the war. Gerald was disconcerted when he was asked whether the lintels of the bunkers he was constructing would stand up to a direct hit from medium artillery and realized that was something he hadn't been taught at Chatham. He felt he was on stronger ground, though, when he was constructing jeep tracks for the battalion he was supporting as that was definitely something he knew all about. He confidently got stuck into preparing his culverts and carefully pegging out his side-hill cuts according to his précis and the pamphlet from his YO Course at Chatham, but sadly Scottie thought his progress was pathetic. In his usual colourful language he pointed out that the aim was to get some sort of track through as quickly as possible, however rough, lest the enemy attack the next day, and not to mess about with beautiful profiles. Gerald was not the first, or the last, subaltern to find himself on the receiving end of a lashing from Scottie – after all, he ate subalterns for breakfast.

Gerald was also in charge of emplacing in their chambers the pre-prepared demolition charges for Pintail Bridge over the Imjin and for commanding the firing party, should hostilities resume. A rather less operational but immediate responsibility in the same area was running the Pintail Waterpoint, not a great challenge until the winter set in when 'winterizing' by enclosing the whole structure in tentage and running petrol heaters became essential. Some 120,000 gallons of purified water were needed for the divisional area every day, but it was important to ensure that chlorine-free water was delivered to Divisional Head-quarters – the General did not like the normal product near his whisky.

Captain Bill Moncur arrived in Korea a few weeks after Gerald Napier and found several changes taking place in the Division, the most important being the arrival of Major General Horatio Murray taking over from Major General Mike West as the Divisional Commander. Colonel Arthur Morris DSO MC GM took over from Colonel Paddy Hill as CRE, and Lieutenant Colonel Hugh Millar succeeded Lieutenant Colonel Arthur Field as CO 28 Field Engineer Regiment. Further down the ladder, Bill had arrived in Pusan from the Divisional Battle School, via the ex-Hong Kong ferry *Wo Sang* (and the Captain's table) from Japan, to find a scene of squalor typical of a port supporting a major war. There was filth everywhere and hundreds of orphans, some no more than toddlers, scraping an existence along the tracks and under the platforms, seeking offerings from generous and compassioned soldiers.

Escaping from the Transit Camp as soon as possible, he arrived in Seoul via the overnight American military train to find a similar scene of squalor. From there he cadged a lift in the back of a truck, bouncing amongst the mail bags until, cold, wet and disorientated, he staggered into Divisional HQ in the dark where he found he was to take over from the author as the Engineer Intelligence Staff Officer. It was raining and, with mud clinging to his boots, he slung his kit over his shoulders and set off to find a place of refuge. Slithering through the mud he was directed to a *hoochie* where he was greeted with a certain lack of enthusiasm as the arrival of another body, a soaking one at that, could only spell terrible inconvenience for the two incumbents. Parking his kit behind the door, he had still to report to the CRE, the formidable Colonel Arthur Morris who greeted him with 'Good, give me a report in the morning on the road up from Seoul'.

Arthur Morris, or 'Uncle Arthur' as he was known (behind his back), was a no-nonsense, hands-on officer who didn't suffer fools gladly, if at all. He had only been in Korea for a few weeks but had already made his mark as a hard-drinking, hard-living officer. He was also a born leader as well as a driver who brooked no opposition. It was imperative to establish a new defensive line, the Kansas Line, as soon as possible in case hostilities were renewed, and large amounts of timber were required for bunkers, accommodation and other defence tasks. Clearly beyond the capacity of the Divisional Engineers, he had sent for Captain John Elderkin, the Intelligence Officer in 28 Engineer Regiment, and told him to get hold of a sawmill. Just like that. John miraculously found a Korean sawmill and put it to work. After a couple of weeks he asked the CRE about paying for it, only to be told to run away and not bother him with such detail. Two more weeks elapsed and he had the same response, but after six weeks he was getting desperate for what had now become a large sum of money and, plucking up courage, he confronted Uncle Arthur who grinned and said, 'That's more like it. Now it's much too much to ask me to pay for hiring a sawmill without permission, so I'll go and tell the General how much we owe and the Army will just have to pay.'

Arthur Morris certainly got a move on and was frustrated by slow progress in 64 Field Park Squadron in the manufacture of the components and structures needed for Line Kansas and sent for me one day and told me to go and sort things out. I said that he had better tell the OC first and off I went to be greeted on arrival by a grim-faced Major Tom Morgan who said, 'I hear you've come to sort out my Squadron for me'. I was far junior to Tom but pointed out that if nothing was done we would both get the sack and that I merely wanted to help him out on the basis that two heads were better than one. Tom was a very nice man, and extremely competent too, and we were soon able to improve things with extra help from other sources.

Bill Moncur carried on the good work after I left, but found it the beginning of an uncertain period in his life and assessed his circumstances as being at best precarious. He was a thoroughly resilient officer though and was more than capable of standing up to Uncle Arthur or, for that matter, anyone else. His first duty was to be fully aware, at all hours of the day, of the activities of the Divisional Engineers and this was particularly important at dawn as the Divisional Commander held a full staff meeting ('prayers') at 7.00am every day and the CRE required to be briefed well before then. This meant getting to know everyone of any possible use throughout the Division and elsewhere. The supply of timber was still of great concern and Bill 'happened to note' that the American Marine Corps had a large timber supply dump. Nothing daunted, nothing gained, he contrived to meet their Chief Engineer and came out of his office at the Marine Corps HQ with a requisition note which authorized him to draw 'as much timber as he can remove this day'. On being contacted, Arthur Morris enlisted the help of the Divisional Staff and mobilized every truck in the Division and, working well into the night, they procured enough soft timber for the building programme to last the rest of the year.

The Regiment and the Field Park were working round the clock, racing to complete the Kansas Line before the onset of the deep-freeze winter when earth could only be turned over using explosives, but it became clear that, in addition to the defensive works and associated roadworks needed for the new defence line, a formidable task in itself, sufficient effort would not be available to undertake the accommodation requirement of the Division. There was no 'Works' organization as such and it soon became clear that the solution lay within the Divisional Engineers themselves. Bill Moncur suggested that Korean personnel should be employed under a suitable contractor. The CRE latched on to the idea and with his usual alacrity promptly told him to 'get on with it'.

All civilians were banned for fifteen miles behind the front line so he had to go some way south to have any hope of recruiting anyone suitable. After considerable negotiation and a large slice of luck, Bill managed to recruit a suitable Korean, Lee Pil Sin, who reckoned he could recruit the necessary skilled craftsmen, but they were a long way away and a financial inducement would be needed to entice them to come with him. Then there was the problem of transport, victualling, tools and so on, not to mention security. He returned to HQRE, cleared things with the CRE and obtained a cash withdrawal from the Divisional Paymaster, which consisted of a bulging sandbag of Korean Hwan.

Within two days the first artisans arrived, clutching their hand tools and anxious to prove their worth. Lee Pil Sin had even managed to find a chargehand and the group set up their camp near the Divisional airstrip. Their first task was the building of a much needed briefing room for Divisional Headquarters, the completion of which was celebrated by the General having a drinks party for all the Commanding Officers in the Division. This set the scene for what was to become a massive building programme to provide adequate facilities for the 25,000 troops manning the extended Divisional frontage along the Kansas Line, effectively along the River Imjin, with 1st US Marine Corps on our left and 7th US Cavalry on the right flank.

The Divisional Commander's 'morning prayers' soon began to include not only the work on the defences but also the hutting programme and associated welfare facilities. Defence work was the top priority but, as the pressure reduced somewhat, the whole regiment became involved in numerous projects to improve the accommodation and wellbeing of the Division. There was even a mineral water factory. Not the least of the requirements though was the provision of deep trench latrines. Large numbers were needed and they were manufactured by 64 Field Park Squadron in two standard sizes, four-seater and eight-seater, which would fit respectively inside 80lb and 160lb tents for the winter. Sides could be rolled up daily in fine weather to let in fresh air, as well as the gaze of passers-by. Only a very old and inadequate military pamphlet was available to provide dimensions, but it was useful as a guide to essential dimensions and heights and steered the manufacturers clear of some pitfalls.

The main accommodation available was the American Quonset hut and nearly 360 were erected in the next couple of months, which included provision for Messes as well as NAAFIs. The programme also included two 'Roadway Inns' on the Main Supply Routes (MSRs) and two officers' clubs on the banks of the Imjin, well above any possible flood level. Gerald Napier was responsible for the construction of one of them, the Junior Officers' Club, which included a bar, tennis courts and various other facilities. Though the work was not highly technical, it was thought that a clerk of works would be an asset. None existed in the Squadron, but one of the Army Catering Corps (ACC) cooks volunteered to help. It turned out that before his National Service he had been a highly-trained building technician, but the Army had no vacancy for his talents and he had been drafted in to the ACC where there was a shortage of cooks. While he had accepted this with a good grace, on the grounds that it might stand him in good stead in his future married life, he was delighted to step into the breach to help with any project work that came the Squadron's way. He was still paid as a cook though.

Production of printed matter in any quantity was outside the scope of the Division's resources but Bill Moncur heard that the Americans had their own printing organization so, when Colonel Arthur Morris decided that he would like a news-sheet which could be sent home by the troops, he set off to see what he could do. He discovered an astonishing unit called the 1st Loudspeaker and Leaflet Battalion, based alongside the HQ Eighth US Army airstrip in Seoul. The printing presses and paper holdings were held in acres of tents which would have done justice to a main Fleet Street newspaper, and he made friends with the key decision maker, a second lieutenant newsprint specialist who could produce millions of leaflets for airdrop propaganda purposes. He asked how many papers we wanted to print and Bill replied 'about two thousand'. His countenance changed as if Bill was trying to be facetious but, realizing he wasn't joking, said he couldn't switch off a printing machine under 3,000 as they just didn't operate in such small quantities. However, he was very keen to visit the front line and Bill was happy to oblige and to take him round, the lure of an offer to visit the Commonwealth Division prevailed and the technical difficulties were overcome and the first edition of the 'Kansas Tract' was produced. The second edition included photographs and Edition 3, the last before departure, was run off in colour.

On the operational side, the threat of war was never far away throughout the rest of 1953 and early 1954. The Division continued to train to that end and contingency plans to cope with a Chinese attack were made in case the truce should break down and were practised monthly. They culminated in a Divisional Exercise, SHAKE-UP, during the last week in November. Priority during the period September to December continued to be given to the construction of defences and all battalions spent four days a week on this work. The winter of 1953–54 was fairly mild, at least in comparison with previous Korean winters, and Sapper work continued unabated. It was also possible to give attention to the new camp sites and great efforts were made to make them as comfortable as possible. By March 1954 the situation had settled down enough for a Divisional bridge camp to be established and continuation military training took place.

News of the Divisional run-down plan was received in August; the Divisional Headquarters closed in November, 55 Field Squadron was the only Sapper unit to be left by March and the Division was to be reduced to an infantry brigade group by April 1955. The squadron stayed on for a further year before leaving Korea for good in May 1956.

Appreciation

D. W. Hall, a soldier in The Black Watch, wrote these lines in appreciation of 'The Royal Engineer':

> *To all you men assembled here,*
> *My toast tonight is to the engineer,*
> *Here's a man we know little about*
> *For the sapper doesn't boast or shout.*
>
> *The slave of the infantry, this silent one,*
> *Who carries a shovel as well as a gun,*
> *During the war he'll work and fight,*
> *He's the silent worker of the night.*
>
> *There's mines to lift, a field to breach*
> *Before the enemy we can reach.*
> *He lifts each one with calm and care,*
> *Suddenly an explosion rents the air.*
>
> *Some wounded moan, some lives are lost,*
> *The ones that're left say, 'that's the cost',*
> *And carry on with double care,*
> *But can be sure each says a prayer.*
>
> *A road to lay, this is the test*
> *But this is a team that will do its best.*
> *The road complete, supplies roll past,*
> *The sapper thinks of rest at last.*

Ready to answer that urgent call,
Ready to fight or ready to fall.
They'll destroy or they will build
Though oft it means they will be killed.

He's not a hero, nor yet very brave,
Though his work might mean the grave.
So I'll leave the sapper at his post
And to him I'll give this toast.

'Let the infantry all be praised
But the man to whom my glass is raised,
And may he ever have good cheer
The ever silent Royal Engineer'.

It may not be very good poetry, but the sentiment is there and it is always nice to be appreciated.

Was it all worth it? Looking back over half a century later, vindication for what the West achieved in that barren peninsula is to be found in the two Koreas today: one a thriving democracy and economic tiger, the other, one of the most wretched tyrannies on earth. At the time of the Armistice, Seoul was a shattered city and now it is a teeming metropolis with high-rise buildings, a dozen deluxe hotels, hundreds of smaller hotels and restaurants and one of the world's most impressive subway systems. What is more, the South Koreans are constantly at pains to express their gratitude and appreciation for our help in repelling the North Korean invaders and their Chinese allies.

Yes, unlike so many conflicts, the Korean War *was* worth fighting and the Corps of Royal Engineers, the Sappers, can be rightly proud of the part they played.

Chapter 20

Dejà Vu

Korea Re-visited

I remember, I remember
The house where I was born,
The little window where the sun
Came peeping in at morn.

From 'Past and Present', by T. Hood

Some thirty years after the Armistice was signed I visited Korea again. We landed at Kimpo airfield, outside Seoul, having flown in with Cathay Pacific to find all the modern extravaganza of an international airfield, with direct flights to all corners of the globe. How different from the last time, travelling in an uncomfortable transport plane, lugging my sleeping bag and few personal belongings, en route to join 1st Commonwealth Division Engineers. A swift drive over the brand new Olympic Highway, alongside the Han river, glistening in the bright but chilly autumn light, took us into one of the major capital cities of the world, a city of 11 million souls, its eighteen bridges replacing the single road bridge of its shattered predecessor.

A luxurious room in the Hyatt Regency Hotel was in marked contrast to my first night, north of Uijongbu, the former Forward Supply Depot for the Division, where I had perched my camp bed precariously on some empty wooden Asahi beer crates to get me off the ground, deep frozen for several feet in the midst of a bitter winter. Having zipped myself into my thick sleeping bag, I woke several hours later in utter confusion, wondering where on earth I could be – upside down, hands pinned beneath me, body twisted round the outer edge of the conical American 'Pup' tent. An inauspicious and inelegant entry to war.

Next morning, we drove through the teeming streets of Seoul, past Uijongbu, turning left towards Gloster Valley, scene of their famous stand in April 1951, and on over the River Imjin. Up till now we had been on a tarmac road, a change from the potholed, dusty gravel of a previous generation, but now we were turning left onto a dirt road over what used to be called Dan's Causeway, left again towards the crossing over the River Samichon, a tributary of the Imjin. The memories flooded back as we entered what was still classified as a war zone. I remembered how this had been the main lateral road behind the front in the final days of the war, how a Centurion tank had ignored a bridge classification and diversion sign and, instead of driving through the dried-up stream bed, had chanced his arm, only to find that the bridge had been correctly classified . . .

Half a mile farther on was the bridge over the Samichon and, looking over the parapet, I remembered how we used to relish the hot showers and clean clothes of the Mobile Laundry and Bath Unit on the river bank below. Just upstream from it we had operated a waterpoint run by a couple of sappers from my Troop. Then, 200 yards farther along the road, I glanced to my right and to my astonishment there was one of my old Troop locations, tucked into a shallow re-entrant across the intervening abandoned paddy field. There was still an old shelter where we had kept stores and I could see the vehicle bays which we had cut in to the hillside as protection against shelling. It was so unchanged that the memories came flooding back.

I remembered Sapper McLaren, my driver, who came as my radio operator one night behind the Chinese lines and provided our only means of communication when we needed fire support; he then quietly picked up mines when we found ourselves in an unmarked minefield in the dark. I remembered Sapper Smyth, the bravest of the brave, who got an 'Immediate' Military Medal that same night. Then there was Sergeant Shirley, my Reconnaissance Sergeant, who already had a Military Medal as an infantryman, who picked me up when I was stunned by a piece of shrapnel on the Hook. There were the bad guys too: the Sapper who stole the Jeep belonging to Dick Dowdall, my Troop Officer, and took it off to the bright lights of Inchon, and the Sapper who stole all the Troop Canteen money, but didn't live to spend it. And lots of others, good and bad, but mainly excellent.

We headed on along a dirt track towards the Hook and up to the edge of the Demilitarized Zone, two kilometres back from the Demarcation Line which had been set up after the Armistice, where we met the local Korean Brigade Commander, put on flak jackets and transferred into Korean Jeeps. The Koreans were wonderfully helpful and had arranged special permission for us to go forward to Point 146, where they had an Observation Post, just a few hundred yards to the right of the Hook, the Hook itself being inaccessible. This post overlooked the valley between the UN and North Korean lines and it seemed strange to be standing there in the open, with the Hook over to our left, and facing Pheasant in front of us. It was all so totally unchanged, as if time had stood still, the valley floor still covered in dried paddy, the ruins of Sa'am where we had run into a minefield during Rip, Van, Winkle, the company raid that had taken place all those years ago. On our way back, we discovered that the South Korean Army had deployed the whole of their divisional artillery – just in case. We later saw some of it returning to their normal locations. The whole area was still very much on a war footing, with defensive fortifications everywhere.

Moving out of the forward area, our escorts left us to our own devices. It was a glorious, crisp sunny day and we ate our sandwiches on one of the Glosters' old positions, south of the Imjin. We then got back in our vehicles and I succeeded in finding the old Divisional Headquarters, now a tiny Korean hamlet, with the long abandoned divisional airstrip nearby, on the south bank of the Imjin. I was particularly pleased, though, to find a road still in use that I had built all those years before, with the old minefield I had gapped still there. It was like going into some 'time machine', and I had to shake myself to realize where I was.

My memories are not unique. Others will have similar memories, and for many of us those memories came flooding back at the Dedication Service held at Chatham on 24 April 1988.

Epilogue

The Last Post

The Royal Engineers Memorial to those who lost their lives in the Korean War was unveiled and dedicated in the Garrison Church at Chatham. It was a most moving occasion, the highlight being the address given by The Reverend S. J. Davies MBE QHC, who had been the padre to the Gloucestershire Regiment at the River Imjin Battle in April 1951. Sam Davies was captured at the battle and was the only chaplain to survive the prison camps of North Korea. His words struck many a chord and included these:

> These members of the Corps of Royal Engineers who made the Supreme Sacrifice during the Korean War, and whose memory we salute this morning, were involved in what was probably the most difficult, exhausting and demanding conditions Sappers have ever had to contend with and overcome. The ingenuity of your great Corps was exercised to the utmost because of the sheer extremes of climate in Korea: because of the very primitive roads – in fact mostly tracks – which simply could not sustain highly mechanized modern armies, and because of the rivers, such as the Imjin, which could rise in the summer rains some forty feet in just over twenty-four hours and become a raging torrent sweeping away bridges, ferries and pontoons. And yet, in the depths of the fearful Korean winter rivers could freeze to a depth of two or even three feet.
>
> What immense challenges the Royal Engineers faced! Bridge-building, air-strips, tunnelling, road building which in winter required blasting of the concrete-hard ground before bulldozers could work, and in the thaw coping with hard road surfaces which simply 'boiled-up' and sank beneath the sub-soil. Thousands upon thousands of tons of stone had to be quarried for the roads by the Royal Engineers.

Sappers out laying mines on winter nights in front of forward positions could only carry out intricate detection work for a very limited time indeed, simply because their fingers would freeze to a dangerous numbness. I have only touched on a few of the problems which were faced. Add to this the fact that from time to time, as at the battle of the River Imjin, in those late April days of 1951, and on the Hook in May 1953, Sappers fought valiantly as infantry, as well as having to repair and strengthen the defence works under terrific Chinese bombardment, and you begin to get an idea of the life of the Royal Engineers in Korea, which I saw at first hand as Chaplain to the Gloucestershire Regiment, and of their achievements, which called forth the admiration of the whole Commonwealth Division and of our American, South Korean and United Nations allies. What a Korean War roll-call of honour it is: 55 Field Squadron first in the field (with 29 Brigade in 1950), 12 Field Squadron, 64 Field Park Squadron (would it be possible to count the vast quantities of sandbags, barbed wire and all manner of defence stores they unloaded daily at railhead for the defence units, and the repair jobs to Engineer equipment far in excess of normal duty), 145 Works Section and Bomb Disposal, and the essential Postal Services – all combined in HQ Royal Engineers 1st Commonwealth Division.

These men saw the huge and redoubtable Chinese forces at close quarters and the fearful casualties inflicted upon them by superior firepower; they saw the tragic, terrible plight of the Korean refugees fleeing south, they saw at times their brother Sappers killed or maimed and wounded; they saw the full horror of modern war between great powers in an underdeveloped country.

'What can separate us from the love of Christ?, said our Second Lesson from the New Testament this morning – *Can tribulation or hardship, persecution, hunger, nakedness or peril and the sword? As it is written – For thy sake we are killed all the day long.* How painfully descriptive these words from the Bible must seem of the conditions these dead Sappers, of all ranks, witnessed in Korea thirty-seven years ago.

But St Paul continues – *we are more than conquerors through Him that loved us, for nothing in death nor in life can separate us from the love of God revealed in Christ Jesus our Lord.* And that is the meaning and the message of all those crosses, line upon line, line upon line in the beautifully maintained United Nations war cemetery at Pusan, eleven thousand miles and more away, where our fallen lie buried. These officers, non-commissioned officers and sappers who were killed on active service in Korea between 1950 and 1953 are part of that host of a thousand British dead, and thousands more from the British Commonwealth.

Our Christian Faith is that the evils, the wickedness, the follies, the wars, the horrors of our world *Do Not Have The Last Word.* Our Saviour endured the cruel torments of the Cross on Calvary, and died in agony while the soldiers mocked Him, but *Love* won the Eternal Victory, which is our Victory too, over all the powers of darkness and evil and catastrophe. Christ rose in triumph from the dead that we might share His victory in and beyond the battles of this mortal life, the unceasing conflict between good and evil, in which we are all involved.

As the old Remembrance Day hymn says:

> *Still stands His Cross from that dread hour to this,*
> *Like some bright star above the dark abyss;*
> *Still through the veil, the Victim's pitying eyes*
> *Look down to bless our lesser Calvaries.*

We are commemorating here this morning our fallen in battle in the knowledge that they are alive in Life Eternal, in one of those many mansions in the Father's House.

What is the unique significance of the deaths of these men? It is that they died in the *First War* ever fought in the name of the United Nations against mighty powers who made an aggressive bid for total control of the whole Korean Peninsula. Would the United Nations accept the challenge or would it act 'merely with pathetic words of protest and not with deeds of decisive purpose'? The world watched and waited.

Suppose we had *not* acted, and the whole of Korea had fallen under a monolithic Communist dictatorship? Who can say what fateful results would have occurred for the balance of power; for the Pacific and the free world; for the freedom of Christian worship and teaching in South Korea and for Peace. The United Nations would have been totally discredited, and incalculable results would have threatened us.

The stirring for constitutional, democratic change in South Korea today would not have been possible if these men had not fought and died in the Korean War, nor would the continued free existence of the Christian Church in South Korea – for in North Korea still, all religious organization and teaching is absolutely forbidden.

These Sappers we honour today were men like us of many imperfections, 'of the earth, earthy'. They would not want us to idealize them. They did not want to die in that remote, far away land. What prayers they said, what faith they had is known

Only to God. But they died in defence of freedom, against ruthless aggression. They said 'No' to the tyrant's greed. The merit of their sacrifice will remain with humanity, and God the Judge of us all, will 'fulfil in them the good purpose of his perfect will'.

May they rest in peace and share in Christ's risen glory!

Greater love has no man than this, that a man lay down his life for his friends.

THE LAST POST – REVEILLE

We will remember them.

NEVER – EVER – FORGOTTEN

Absent Friends

Would that you could wander still
Through grassy fields, by wooded hill
When morning bird-song fills the air
And yet another spring is here.

If only you could feel sun
Upon your face when winter's done,
And smell sweet scented flowers fair
When yet another summer's here.

But Fate decided otherwise
And you, beneath Korean skies,
A gallant band of comrades lie,
Your duty done, your merit high.

No changing seasons can erase
That once familiar name, that face
Which comes and lingers in each thought
Of those with whom we lived and fought.

David Lidstone (1920–2004)
Private, The Gloucestershire Regiment
Korea, 1950–51

Annex

Tasks Undertaken

by 12 FIELD SQUADRON
8 April–11 May 1953

Notes:

a. These tasks are in no particular order, other than the receipt of the demand for them. Not all were completed by the end of the period.
b. JAMESTOWN, WYOMING, KANSAS are code names for defence lines
c. Colours are part of the road code name system.

1. Repair and re-erect 150 yards of road screens on MAROON 3.
2. Continue check of all KANSAS reserve position minefields. (Over 110 miles of fences and 78 minefields.)
3. Lift a small 'pirate' minefield.
4. Recce and repair fences of WYOMING reserve position minefields in Brigade area
5. Repair thaw damage and reinstate 600 yards of track up Searchlight Hill.
6. Repair thaw damage 120 yards back entrance to Main Division HQ.
7. Remove and salvage 400 yards demonstration wiring in Main Division HQ area.
8. Assist left forward battalion by lifting mines in area for new platoon position.
9. Dig and install standard prefabricated Gunner Observation Post on Hill 210.
10. Repair and maintain over ten miles of secondary roads in Brigade area, including making good after thaw, surfacing, ditching, culverting in preparation for rainy season. <u>Note:</u> Considerable lengths of those roads are in forward areas where work can only be done at night. (Continuous task.)

11. Recce and re-plotting all JAMESTOWN minefield fences in Brigade area onto 1:50,000 photos (99 minefields involved, almost all in forward areas where only last-light or first-light recce is possible).
12. Design and construct new shell-proof Battalion Command Post for right forward battalion.
13. Build new Command Post for left forward company of right forward battalion (double prefabricated shelter).
14. Recce suspected 'pirate' minefield in reserve battalion area.
15. Prepare and execute drainage scheme for Divisional Headquarters airstrip.
16. Resurface Divisional Headquarters airstrip 800 yards by 20 yards. 1 inch DG (Disintegrated Granite), 3½ inches river-bed gravel, 1½ inches DG.
17. Repair and maintain Aerial Tramway on Hill 355.
18. Build 2-stall shower (H&C) for Main Divisional Headquarters A Mess.
19. Doze and drain 250 yards track in forward battalion A Echelon area.
20. Doze 150 yards tank track up hill in right forward battalion reserve company area.
21. Quarry stone on INDIGO II and issue to all comers (Continuous task.)
22. Operate and maintain 40,000 gallons per day Water Point (Continuous task.)
23. Continue construction GREEN V1 – 2,000 yard new one-way 3-ton hill road in Divisional reserve area.
24. Repair and renew 250 yards road screen on Searchlight Hill.
25. Install double prefabricated shelter in centre company left forward battalion.
26. Breach patrol gap through two trip minefields.
27. Build 140ft × 3ft × 3ft rock retaining wall bound in Square Mesh Track as part of flood prevention scheme.
28. Level standing area for RNZASC Company.
29. Strengthen and brace Regimental Aid Post of left forward battalion.
30. 'Drag' all roads in Brigade area (Continuous task.)
31. Levelling site for 3rd Royal Australian Regiment (3 RAR) 'A' Echelon.
32. Dig Trash Pit for left forward battalion.
33. Level and prepare Brigade parade ground.
34. Survey alignment of GREEN VI onto 1:25,000 map.
35. Clear 1,000yds × 1,000yds suspected booby trap area in KANSAS positions.
36. Breach patrol gap through a trip minefield.
37. Re-open an old patrol gap.

38. Advise and assist in construction of a splinter-proof cookhouse for right forward company of left forward battalion.
39 Minor maintenance on Divisional Headquarters airstrip (Continuous task.)
40. Make tank crossing place over steep ridge left forward battalion.
41. Lift portion of minefield to enable digging in of new forward platoon position for centre company left forward battalion.
42. Strengthening a Headquarter bunker on Hill 210.
43. Improve jeep track up Hill 355 (Very steep track on rock).
44. Dig Brigade Trash Pit.
45. Build verandah for Main Division A Mess and replace all Window-light by wire screens.
46. Special check of one minefield's boundaries.
47. Check suspected 'pirate' minefield in WYOMING area.
48. Erect six Medium Machine Gun prefabricated bunkers on point 210.
49. Make suitable route for tank to cross defences on Point 159.
50. Remake entrance to Command Post of left forward battalion.
51. Doze series of tracks to tank firing positions in WYOMING hills.
52. Gap two forward minefields.
53. Destroy Napalm minefield on point 355.
54. Operate river gravel pit with excavator for road resurfacing by KSC Battalion (Continuous task.)
55. Plan and construct semi-permanent Water Point.
56. Doze and supervise revetment, drainage and road construction of new ammunition point.
57. Check condition and safety of all living shelters in right forward battalion area.
58. Check and reinstate for the flood season two cableways over River Imjin.
59. Hold stores and practise blocking of all minefield gaps in Operation WITHDRAW.

There were never enough Sappers!

Ubique.

Bibliography

History of the Corps of Royal Engineers, Vol X, 1948–1960 (Institution of Royal Engineers, Chatham, 1986)

Barclay, Brigadier C. N., *The First Commonwealth Division. The Story of British Commonwealth Land Forces in Korea, 1950–1953* (Gale and Polden, Aldershot, 1954)

Barker, A. J., *Fortune Favours the Brave. The Battle of the Hook, Korea 1953* (Leo Cooper, London, 1974)

Carter, Former 22525002 Sapper, *Sappering in Korea* (privately published, 2008)

Cunningham-Boothe, Ashley and Farrar, Peter (eds), *British Forces in Korean War* (British Korean Veterans Association, 1988)

Farrar-Hockley, Anthony, *The British Part in the Korean War: Vol I – A Distant Obligation* (HMSO, London, 1990)

——, *The British Part in the Korean War: Vol II – An Honourable Discharge* (HMSO, London, 1995)

Fisher, Peter and Lohan, Patrick, *Korean War – In Memoriam* (Ministry of Defence, London, 2006)

Halley, Derek, *Iron Claw: A Conscript's Tale* (Finavon Print and Design, Dundee, 1988)

Hastings, Max, *The Korean War* (Michael Joseph, London, 1987)

Holroyd, Reuben (ed), *Poetry of the Korean War* (British Korean Veterans Association, 2003)

Linklater, Eric, *A Year of Space: A Chapter in Autobiography* (Macmillan, London, 1953)

Miller, John jr, Carroll, Major Owen J., (US Army) and Tackley, Margaret E., *Korea 1950–1953* (US Government Printing Office, Washington DC, 1956)

O'Ballance, Edgar, *Korea 1950–1953* (Faber & Faber, London, 1969)

Raschen, Dan, *Send Port and Pyjamas* (Regency Press, London, 1987)

Rose, David, and Rose, General Sir Michael (preface), *Off the Record. The Life and Letters of a Black Watch Officer* (Spellmount, Staplehurst, 1996)

Salmon, Andrew, *To The Last Round. The Epic British Stand on the Imjin River, Korea, 1951* (Aurum Press, London, 2009)

Thomas, Major R. C. W., OBE, *The War in Korea* (Gale and Polden, Aldershot, 1954)

Tippen, Lieutenant Colonel John, *Below the Jetstream* (Plane Tree, Llanidloes, 2002)

Younger, Tony, *Blowing Our Bridges: A Memoir from Dunkirk to Korea via Normandy* (Leo Cooper Ltd, Barnsley, 2004)

Index

Library Link Issues (For Staff Use Only)

1	2	3	4	5	6	7	8	9
			4884			7178		